HYBRID ANXIETIES

Expanding Frontiers:
Interdisciplinary Approaches to
Studies of Women, Gender, and Sexuality

Series Editors:
Karen J. Leong
Andrea Smith

HYBRID ANXIETIES

Queering the French-Algerian War and
Its Postcolonial Legacies   C. L. QUINAN

University of Nebraska Press   Lincoln

© 2020 by the Board of Regents of
the University of Nebraska

Acknowledgments for the use of copyrighted material appear on pages xii, which constitutes an extension of the copyright page.

All rights reserved ∞

Library of Congress
Cataloging-in-Publication Data
Names: Quinan, C. L., author.
Title: Hybrid anxieties: queering the French-Algerian War and its postcolonial legacies / C. L. Quinan.
Description: Lincoln: University of Nebraska Press, [2020] | Series: Expanding frontiers: interdisciplinary approaches to studies of women, gender, and sexuality | Includes bibliographical references and index.
Identifiers: LCCN 2020010778
ISBN 9781496206817 (hardback)
ISBN 9781496224262 (paperback)
ISBN 9781496223593 (epub)
ISBN 9781496223609 (mobi)
ISBN 9781496223616 (pdf)
Subjects: LCSH: Queer theory. | Group identity. | Postcolonialism—Algeria. | Postcolonialism in literature. | Postcolonialism in motion pictures. | Algeria—History—Revolution, 1954-1962—Influence.
Classification: LCC HQ76.25 .Q56 2020 | DDC 306.76—dc23
LC record available at
https://lccn.loc.gov/2020010778

Set in Lyon Text by Laura Buis.
Designed by L. Auten.

CONTENTS

List of Illustrations   vii

Acknowledgments   ix

Introduction: Framing Queer Postcolonial Interventions after the War   1

PART 1: MASCULINITY AND MEMORY

1. Haunted Masculinity and the Wounds of War: Alain Resnais's *Muriel* and Laurent Mauvignier's *The Wound*   39

2. "You'll Never Give Me a Bad Conscience!": Masculinity and Postcolonial Guilt in *Caché*   71

PART 2: QUEERING POSTCOLONIAL LEGACIES

3. Eros and Eden: Pierre Guyotat and Queer Pleasures   97

4. Queer Palimpsests and October 17, 1961: Memory Politics in Leïla Sebbar's *The Seine Was Red*   127

5. Queering Identity, Embracing In-Betweenness: Disidentification and Re-membering in Nina Bouraoui's *Tomboy*   151

Conclusion: Queer Postcolonial Entanglements   179

Notes   189

Bibliography   229

Index   247

ILLUSTRATIONS

1. *Muriel*: Bernard as seen through a kaleidoscope 55
2. *Muriel*: Projector scene 56
3. *Muriel*: Bernard in front of the projector screen 58
4. *Caché*: Georges, Anne, and the bicyclist 82
5. *Caché*: Domestic and international crises in *Caché* 87
6. *The Seine Was Red*: Algeria and World War II as palimpsests 141
7. Protest by La Manif Pour Tous 184

ACKNOWLEDGMENTS

This book only exists thanks to the support, collaboration, and friendship of a network of colleagues, friends, and institutions. First and foremost, I would like to thank the entire team at the University of Nebraska Press, in particular Alicia Christensen, who believed in this project from the very beginning, and Emily Wendell. The commitment UNP has shown has made this entire process as stress-free as it could possibly be. I also extend a deep thanks to the reviewers of this manuscript. Their feedback was not only tremendously insightful but also kind, supportive, and encouraging. They set the bar for how generous the academic review process can be.

I am continuously grateful to my Utrecht community and to the Department of Media and Culture Studies, in particular my indefatigable colleagues in the Graduate Gender Programme: Rosemarie Buikema, Kathrin Thiele, Eva Midden, Domitilla Olivieri, Sandra Ponzanesi, Berteke Waaldijk, Layal Ftouni, Koen Leurs, Milica Trakilović, Jamila Mascat, Magda Górska, Julieta Chaparro-Buitrago, Katrine Smiet, Vasso Belia, Gianmaria Colpani, and Trude Oorschot. I also thank many other colleagues with whom I have had the pleasure of working in Utrecht, including Aggeliki Sifaki, Iris van der Tuin, Mariëlle Smith, and Birgit Kaiser. My friendship and working relationship with Marjolein van den Brink are always a breath of fresh air. Among those already named, a special shout-out goes to Kathrin, Eva, and Domi for being not only amazing colleagues but also great friends.

This project began to take shape during my time at the University of California, Berkeley, first as a graduate student and then as a lecturer. This book could not have been written without the support of my dissertation advisor, Michael Lucey, who has set an excellent example for rigorous and inspiring scholarship. I owe so much gratitude to my other dissertation committee members—Ann Smock, Barbara Spackman, and Charis Thompson—for their insights, support, and direction. Even all these years later, our conversations continue to inspire and motivate me to be a compassionate supervisor to my own students. Beyond my committee, I thank all those professors who have motivated me to be a better teacher and researcher, most especially Seda Chavdarian. In my very first year of graduate school, Trinh Minh-ha inspired me beyond words, and she has continued to inspire me ever since.

Throughout my many years of grad school, innumerable friends and colleagues profoundly shaped my thinking, including Robin Mitchell, Anastasia Kayiatos, Lowry Martin, Tara Daly, Araceli Hernandez-Laroche, and Laurel Westbrook. While I was at UC Berkeley, the Department of Gender and Women's Studies always felt like my true home. For that, I am especially grateful to Charis Thompson and Mel Chen—they are the kinds of scholars I aspire to be. I am also grateful to Juana María Rodríguez, Minoo Moallem, Barrie Thorne, Paola Bacchetta, Leslie Salzinger, and Evelyn Nakano Glenn. While I was teaching as a lecturer in GWS post-PhD, Barbara Barnes and Jac Asher became true comrades and great colleagues.

A network of scholars has inspired me, and I also wish to thank all of those colleagues who have shared their precious time and advice with me. Over the years, these conversations have helped form the ideas that would eventually appear in this book. Susan Stryker has been an amazing example in her generosity of time, spirit, and energy. I am especially thankful to have more recently gotten to know colleagues Davina Cooper, Verena Molitor, and Tatiana Zimenkova. I also want to thank my AtGender colleagues, in particular Giovanna Vingelli who picked up the slack when I was busy with the final writing stages of this book.

My research is fundamentally shaped by my teaching, and any form of an acknowledgments section would be lacking without an expression of my deep gratitude to all of the students with whom I have felt lucky to have shared a classroom throughout my many years of teaching, including students at UC Berkeley, San Francisco State University, University College Utrecht, and Utrecht University. Even if teaching always means less time for writing, I can unequivocally say that this book would not exist without that aspect of my life. In this respect, I am also especially appreciative to Juliette Sanchez-Lambert for reminding me—just when I needed it—why this work is important.

I am immensely grateful for all financial support that I have received for all stages of this research, from conception to completion, including various grants from the University of California, Berkeley, Utrecht University, and the Australian Department of Education and Training. Over the years, I have also deeply benefited from assistance I have received from student interns and research assistants, whether for this project or others. Mina Hunt, Aurora Perego, Nina Bresser, Cecilia Cienfuegos Martínez, and Dana Theewis have all tremendously supported my research, and I thank them for their amazing work and constant patience.

Late into this project, I was fortunate to have had the opportunity to spend several months based at the University of Melbourne. Although my time in Australia was largely devoted to a parallel project, the time and space this fellowship afforded me were instrumental in the completion of this manuscript. In this respect, my deep and heartfelt thanks goes to Ana Dragojlovic, whose support made this research visit happen. Ana has become the perfect combination of a supportive and rigorous interlocuter and a kind and generous friend.

My life has been thoroughly enriched by conversations, meals, and personal support from a strong community of dear friends in the Bay Area and elsewhere. Any list will necessarily be incomplete, but the deep love, support, and kindness of Ellen VandenBerg Johnson, Jennifer Daubenmier, Sarah Schoellkopf, Johnny George, Stephanie Tramel Green, and Sharon Page-Medrich mean more to me than they will ever know. Life and work have been all the more precious and meaningful because of these friendships, which, for better or worse, now stretch across wide oceans. I am also grateful for the friendship of Jenn Garlin, Manilee Bagheritari, Michael Meere, and Alicia DiPietro. Sophie Chapple and Nina Bresser, editors extraordinaire, not only were instrumental in reading my drafts and keeping me on track but also are great friends who make everything a bit happier. Thanks also go to Dickson Schneider, one of the most talented and compassionate teachers I have ever met.

Words cannot express how grateful I am to my parents, Joe and Ginny Quinan, who instilled in me from a very early age the value of higher education. The encouragement and support that they have provided to me are so incredibly meaningful, and I hope that, little by little, I can reciprocate the infinite care that they have shown me for all these decades. I also want to thank the rest of my family for always being there for me—in particular, Elizabeth, George, Brian, CC, Michael, and Gramma Doris. Joe Perry and Patricia Quinan, while no longer here, are always with me.

Finally, I thank Simone Jobig, without whom, I can say without hesitation, this book would not exist. She has shaped this project in more ways than I can count—and not just because she read all of my drafts and painstakingly left thoughtful comments. She also believed in me when I doubted myself, she cheered me on when I thought I would never make it through, and she made the most delicious food when cooking was the last thing I could think of. Every day, I am grateful to have her by my side to share this life and all its adventures.

Versions of chapters 1 and 2 were previously published in *Interventions: International Journal of Postcolonial Studies* 19, no. 1 (2017) and *Postcolonial Transitions in Europe*, edited by Sandra Ponzanesi and Gianmaria Colpani (Rowman & Littlefield, 2016), and I thank the respective publishers for allowing me to reprint them here.

HYBRID ANXIETIES

Introduction

Framing Queer Postcolonial Interventions after the War

> Queer, in its deconstructive sense, designates a kind of Derridean différance, occupying an interstitial space between binary oppositions . . . an uncanny, undead haunting of the other within but not of the category of the human. It is the inscription of a negativity that nevertheless may be said to have force, to act or be active in a positive sense. . . . Queer is what is and is not there, what disaggregates the coherence of the norm from the very beginning and is ignored in the force to make sense out of the unintelligibilities of grammar and syntax.
>
> —Carla Freccero, *Queer/Early/Modern*

Less than three years before he was assassinated, the overlooked gay French Algerian poet Jean Sénac (1926–73) composed the following lines, which foreground the themes of aesthetics, erotics, and revolution, themes that, for him, were inseparable:

> When I will have removed my poet
> My fag my beard my bastard
> My Algerian my sleep
> My sun (skimpy underpants) my
> Chitchat my sea,
> Undressed like a pope on God's threshold
> Naked
> Like an emperor for the coronation,

(Worker in the shower)
—my vagrant—,
You will see me.

. . . .

You will love me.[1]

In this poem, originally published in the collection *Dérisions et vertige: Trouvures* and written during the tumultuous decade following Algeria's independence from France—a period in which he grew increasingly disillusioned with the contemporary state of Algeria—Sénac names and then disposes of the labels that came to define him throughout his truncated life: poet, fag, beard, bastard, Algerian, vagrant. It is through the dismantling of such categorical thinking that an authenticity emerges, allowing him to proclaim: "You will see me. . . . You will love me."

Born in Algeria to a French mother and a father whose identity he never knew, Sénac viewed the ambiguity surrounding his ethnicity as inescapably caught up with his queer sexuality. More generally, sexual freedom had, for him, been closely tied to the Algerian struggle for independence from France. Despite—or perhaps precisely due to—his "impure" national and sexual identity, Sénac, who became a symbol of pluriracial, plurireligious, pluriethnic Algeria, understood this historical moment as offering possibilities for new modes of engagement between communities and new ways of embodying gendered and sexual subjectivities. Nonetheless, Sénac was, perhaps unsurprisingly, regarded by many as exemplifying otherness. Although he consistently identified with the oppressed and displayed an empathy and solidarity with Algerians, in particular the Arabo-Berber population, who he felt were oppressed by an imperial French mentality and colonial paradigm, he was at the margins, sexually, nationally, racially, ethnically, and linguistically. While this had troubled him earlier in life, he eventually embraced his "in-betweenness" by reappropriating the Algerian term *gaouri*, a slanderous word for a foreigner or infidel. In laying claim to this label, he asserted his marginality in a manner that subverted monolithic notions of identity and embraced queer desires. This allowed him to speak for those without a voice and foregrounded the ways in which the individual and the collective were intertwined in his fashioning of national, sexual, and gender identities.[2]

While Sénac's poetry was politically motivated, it was also aesthetically driven. For him, reimagining form and style was an act of resistance, and his work highlights the role this reimagination played in a radical rethinking of genre in the period following the French-Algerian War (1954–62).[3] Notably fractured, fragmentary, and corporeal, his poetic style—which he termed the "corpoem" (*corpoème*), a neologism that combined the French *corps* (body) with *poème* (poem)—resisted not only nationalism and xenophobia but also homophobia. In a 1971 interview, he stated: "If in my wartime poems I confronted the oppressor, in these *corpoems* I face down alienation by admitting my homosexuality for the first time, in a way that is neither ostentatious no [*sic*] smug. This is essential; it is simply one component of my being that, like my socialist convictions, deserves respect."[4] Sénac's poetry became increasingly explicit about both his queer desires and his desire for a new Algerian nation. Yet these rousing and provocative stances came to characterize his poetic activism and eventually sealed his fate—he was assassinated in 1973. Why and by whom remain unknown, but his outspoken critique of both French colonialism and postindependence Algerian political forces combined with his homosexuality remain likely motives.

Although his literary contributions merit significantly more attention than they have thus far received, there has been a renewed interest in Sénac regarding both his (unsolved) murder and his commentaries on identity and hybridity.[5] Sénac's ethnic outsiderness and sexual nonconformity have, for example, been emphasized in scholarly work, but they are typically treated separately. For me, however, they are deeply interconnected. Embracing the *gaouri* epithet was a form of advocacy for identities and subjectivities that defied labels and a way for Sénac to articulate his own in-between or hybrid status. This embracing also signified a questioning of contemporary obsessions with "purity" at the precise moment when one nation became two. As France was losing its most valued imperial possession and Algeria was establishing itself as a new nation, debates over who or what was sufficiently "French" or "Algerian" laid bare the complexities and imbrications of race, ethnicity, and nationality. In this respect, it is not (only) Sénac's sexuality that I read as queer. His enactment of a contradictory and deviant sociality—linked to what I regard as a deep discomfort with and resistance to normative categories—I identify as the queerest aspect of all.

I open with the figure of Jean Sénac precisely because his story highlights the hybrid anxieties that have haunted France and Algeria since the long war of decolonization and that also permeate this entire book. Roland Barthes credits Charles de Gaulle with one common (albeit unnuanced) understanding of French identity at this moment: "regular, normal, national."[6] While de Gaulle's words downplay and oversimplify the exclusionary mechanisms that a category like Frenchness held (and continues to hold), particularly in the post-decolonization period, examples of sexual, national, and racial ambiguity, like the example of Sénac, speak to the complexity—and possible futility—of identity.

In the face of calls for assimilation and violence toward national, ethnic, gender, and sexual identities that did not concur with white, French, secular, heterosexual, cisgender norms, the work of poets, writers, filmmakers, and artists has offered other models by which to recognize the fractured and fragmentary impacts of the French-Algerian War and to subsequently cultivate different models for inhabiting bodies and subjectivities. In *Hybrid Anxieties: Queering the French-Algerian War and Its Postcolonial Legacies*, I look to a selection of this work in order to analyze the ways in which norms were explored and exploded in memories and testimonies of the war. This project brings together the entangled and composite aspects of identities with the underlying uncertainty that flooded the postwar moment and its extended aftermath—something that has equally been reflected in the consistent questioning and queering of literary and cinematic genres. Innovations in literature and film were directly impacted by the long and difficult process of (de)colonization and the fall of empire—not to mention the widespread use of torture and mass loss of life—as the war provoked a rethinking of politics, poetics, and aesthetics. This postwar fracturing had both salutary and injurious effects not only on bodies and psyches but also on artistic forms. Stylistic shatterings mirrored the splintering of identity and corporeality. *Hybrid Anxieties* traces this dual effect throughout a number of literary and cinematic works and political and cultural debates that, like Sénac's poetry, embrace the fragmentation of identity and reimagine subjectivity. To paraphrase Carla Freccero's epigraph, I identify the interstitial spaces between binary oppositions as those that disaggregate or trouble the coherence of—to again draw upon de Gaulle's words—the normal, the regular, the national. By looking to examples that interrogate hegemonic categories, I seek to *queer* this perception of nationality—but also of gender, sexuality, and race—as self-evident and closed. For me, this approach also maps to my method of close reading—a strategy Elizabeth Freeman names as "the queerest commitment" to the text—which is attuned to the unintelligibility, incoherence, and contradictions in both grammar and syntax that Freccero names.[7]

Much like Edward Said demonstrated in *Culture and Imperialism*, this book underscores how, as independence struggles result in new states and boundaries, "nomads and vagrants" are inevitably also produced.[8] Creating concrete or abstract taxonomies—be they national boundaries, sexual orientations, or gender identities—inevitably leads to a proliferation of those who exceed these designated domains and categories. The norm only gains its status as "normal" by virtue of that which falls outside this category.[9] As theories of performativity have taught us, subversion can occur through the destabilization of such norms. In this sense, many of the characters invoked throughout this book enact what Mireille Rosello would call "new subject-positions, a new language, and a new type of engagement" in which "an unknown protocol replaces the [normative] script" often dictated by stereotypes.[10]

Situated at the crossroads of queer theory and postcolonial studies, this book asks how the French-Algerian War and its legacies have precipitated a dynamic in which a contestation of hegemonic masculinity—as explored in part 1—has occurred alongside a production of queer modes of identity, embodiment, and engagement that subvert norms—as analyzed in part 2. While the first part of the book (chapters 1 and 2) reveals the deep and long-lasting traumatic violence and exposes the psychic and corporeal fragility felt by many postwar subjects, the second part offers examples wherein queer modes of agency take center stage to contest and subvert norms surrounding sex and sexuality (chapter 3), memory (chapter 4), and gender and nationality (chapter 5). It is this queering that opens up new spaces for thinking about the redemptive and productive possibilities of negotiating life in a postcolonial context. In this sense, my understanding and deployment of "postcolonial" is comparable to that proposed by John McLeod, who reads postcolonial as "connected to successful modes of resistance and transformation."[11] At the same time, I resist idealizing any notion of "success," for failure, as a growing body of queer scholarship has astutely argued, can also offer creative and counterintuitive forms of resistance and relationality.[12]

In line with queer theory, I understand gender and sexuality as neither essential nor stable aspects of identity but rather as performative, constantly in flux, and structured by normalizing regimes that regulate and control the possibilities of what "identities" can be inhabited or claimed. A Foucauldian framework dictates that power is exercised not only from above but also from below and in all directions, meaning that a nexus of infinite strategies for resistance exists, and I look to these interconnected and contradictory sites in which power manifests itself. Literary and cinematic works have enacted this changing landscape in their repudiation of the fixed categories tied to the extended post-decolonization period. Decolonization opened up not only novel possibilities but also new liabilities and risks, and the postcolonial subjects introduced in this book are constantly engaged in processes of becoming whereby social, cultural, and psychological moments of disruption can prove productive and may result in newfound forms of being and action.

This book also participates in a larger scholarly conversation about postcolonial memory. Colonial repercussions and memories continue to impact upon and shape genders and sexualities as they intervene in the present moment, often in discursively and physically violent events. Focusing on reconfigurations of gender and sexuality as spurred on by memories of the war reveals the sutures between the corporeal and the psychic—that is, how they are bound together in these vectors of identity and analysis. While the field of memory studies is flourishing and there is growing research into the complexities of remembering the French-Algerian War, a general lack of work on the gender- and sexuality-related aspects of memory in this context remains.[13] *Hybrid Anxieties* thus attempts to fill a gap in current scholarship on the theoretical stakes of applying a queer lens to this postcolonial context.

My corpus includes novels by Leïla Sebbar, Pierre Guyotat, Laurent Mauvignier, and Nina Bouraoui and films by Alain Resnais, Michael Haneke, and Merzak Allouache. This cross section of metropolitan and Francophone literature and film allows me to reveal how the queer—the less "pure"—can enable more creative ways of remembering the war and negotiating its psychic and corporeal effects. While nonnormativity—including forms of gender and sexuality that question Western norms—is positioned as a site of interrogation, it is important to state that not all of the works I have assembled explicitly engage with sexuality (although many do). Despite the fact that "queer" has evolved to function as an occasional synonym for "gay" and "lesbian," my use of queer and queering is often incommensurate with such categories. For me, queer is less about a way of "being" and more about a form of "doing" that unsettles power relations.[14] Queer is polysemic and fluid and references complex personhood, social marginality, and transgression. As an antidisciplinary mode of inquiry, queer theory encapsulates contradictions and paradoxes. Multiple meanings can be inhabited and transformed from within, even if they are seemingly incoherent or incomprehensible. It is a "continuing moment, movement, motive—recurrent, eddying, *troublant*," as described by Eve Kosofsky Sedgwick.[15] In this respect, I also attempt to dereferentialize queer, extracting it from a singular focus on sexuality. In the touchstone text "What's Queer about Queer Studies Now?" David Eng, Jack Halberstam, and José Esteban Muñoz similarly state that queer theory must not primarily concern itself with sexuality, but should be invested in analyzing additional axes of identity that also operate according to overarching logics that limit possibilities outside dichotomies. "At such a historical juncture," they write, "it is crucial to insist yet again on the capacity of queer studies to mobilize a broad social critique of race, gender, class, nationality and religion, as well as sexuality."[16]

This does not, however, mean uncritically embracing queer; rather, it signifies that one must remain critical and look as well to its cracks and pitfalls. In this respect, I am also attuned to critiques of queer theory, in particular the accusation that it is a white, Anglo-American elitist tradition emerging from academic institutions.[17] Even as I appreciate Sedgwick's aforementioned take on queer as fluid, I resist unreflexively romanticizing the mobility, fungibility, and indefinability of queer. After all, polymorphism and destabilization of identity categories pose their own problems, especially if they obfuscate the assemblage-like character of queer and allow it to stand for gay, and for "gay to stay white," to paraphrase historian Allan Bérubé.[18] Queer theory also risks falling into the trap of fossilizing or reifying itself. I respond by taking queer theory in new directions and contexts that push it further, outside its comfort zone, and, in line with Jarrod Hayes, I advocate for a queering of both queer and postcolonial theory to resist a fixing of either theoretical approach in time or place.[19] This is also precisely what Michael Warner means when he writes of queer theory that "whatever else it may be, it is not autochthonous. It cannot even be in diaspora, having no locale from which to wander."[20] Even if it may have no "home," when the word "queer" travels, its meaning evolves, and its inflections and nuances change. It is for precisely these reasons that I see the potential of applying queer to contexts that might not at first appear to demand it—where it might be unexpected—including the postcolonial legacies of the French-Algerian War.

True to its elusion of definition, I adopt "queer" in its multiple forms: as the messy, nonnormative, and subversive; as the socially perverse; as a disruption of a conventional logic of norms; and as a reordering of social relations. The texts analyzed in *Hybrid Anxieties* do, however, share some key characteristics that map to queerness: characters diverge from expected paths; traditional kinship structures and modes of belonging are undone; normative temporal logics are questioned; and different ways of being and doing are cultivated. What they enact is a blurring of genre and a destabilizing of categorical thinking at an extended moment during which identity categories no longer held. All of the texts I examine grapple with what it means to (not) belong or identify, and the term "queer" interrogates the performative and political underpinnings of gender and sexuality in light of the postcolonial phenomena examined in this book. In this respect, like Donna

McCormack, I understand queer postcoloniality as a methodological approach—not as a formula through which texts can be read but rather as the desire to open texts up to readings that do not assume any disaggregation of postcolonialism from queerness.[21] My queer reading also employs José Esteban Muñoz's conceptualization of disidentification in order to identify the "shadows and fissures in the text" where queer and racialized presences "can be liberated from the protective custody of the white literary imagination."[22] The queer approach I adopt reads between the lines in order to uncover how a contestation of dominant masculinity has occurred alongside the production of other, queerer modes of being. In other words, I read queer both as a form of radical critique and as a deconstructive practice focused on the challenging of normative knowledges, identities, behaviors, and spaces, as well as the creation of new modes of social and cultural engagement. The strength of queer theory rests in the acts of cutting, pasting, deleting, reordering, and reinterpreting that incessantly reimagine its contextual meaning. Its plasticity allows it to fit into different molds, both historical and geopolitical, and its applicability extends far beyond any narrow Western theoretical landscape. In short, I see queer theory as undertaking the daunting task of changing thinking and reshaping relationality.

The French-Algerian War: A Conflict over Identity

In his study of the role of intellectuals in the French-Algerian War, James Le Sueur sums up one aspect of the identity politics that lay at the heart of the conflict: the uneasy process of decolonization instigated a fundamental reconceptualization of French and Algerian national identity in a world without European empires and colonies.[23] Indeed, this war was a unique conflict. France was not willing to give up this highly valuable territory, unlike the neighboring countries of Morocco and Tunisia, which both achieved independence relatively peacefully in 1956. Once ruled by the Ottoman Empire, the region had been occupied by France for over a century before the Algerian Revolution took shape in the mid-1950s. Dating back to its 1830 invasion of the region that eventually became known as Algeria, France had always maintained a highly possessive relationship with this North African territory, much more so than it had with any of its other colonial possessions in North Africa and elsewhere.[24] This was in part due to the fact that Algeria was established as a settler colony, with the French government encouraging farmers to relocate where they were assured of vast agricultural lands and abundant natural resources. By the 1950s, the settler community (termed *pieds-noirs*) totaled more than one million, many of whom had been born in Algeria and had never set foot in France proper.

This complicated intertwinement between France and Algeria was compounded by the fact that there was no legal distinction between the metropole and Algeria, as the French government had annexed the region in 1834 and then declared it to be a part of France rather than a colony in 1848. It was composed of three *départements*, each functioning just like Paris, Loire-Atlantique, or Haut-Rhin in the Hexagon. Legally, this meant that Algerians became subject to the same legislation and should have enjoyed the same "privileges" as citizens of any other region of metropolitan France. However, this worked only in theory, and the truth was that those of Algerian origin living in Algeria were treated as second-class citizens compared to the *pieds-noirs*.[25] While Algerian Muslims were French nationals, this nationality gave them very few political rights.

Algeria was often considered the crown jewel of the Mediterranean, and its settler-colonial past meant that France zealously guarded the territory in the face of increasingly vehement calls for decolonization and Algerian independence. While the war is commonly considered to have begun on November 1, 1954, there had already been moments of intense strain and upswells of violence over the previous decades (most notably during the 1945 Sétif massacre, in which tens of thousands of Algerians were killed by French military forces). Reacting to rampant racism, as well as France's obstinate refusal to cede control of the region, in 1954 Algerian nationalists began an intense campaign for independence. On October 31, 1954, the National Liberation Front (Front de libération nationale, FLN), the Algerian socialist party and face of the struggle for independence, coordinated twenty strikes against French military posts and police stations in Algeria. These attacks signified a call to the Algerian public to join the fight for liberation. Although the FLN could initially arm only about eight hundred soldiers, they proved to be adept at guerrilla warfare and held their own against the much stronger French military. By the war's end, the total number of Algerian fighters would extend into the hundreds of thousands.

While the hexagonal French public was still largely oblivious to what was happening in Algeria (not least because they were partially distracted by the rapid post–World War II modernization that was occurring throughout Europe), increasing numbers of French soldiers were being sent across the Mediterranean Sea to quell a growing revolution. At the same time, Algerian immigrants were arriving on the shores of France to work in its factories. Violence in both locations was, however, escalating to new levels. Contempt and hatred, driven by the divisions between races, classes, and religions, intensified and were becoming more pronounced as France mounted a fierce military campaign to hold on to its dissenting province. A brutal eight-year war ensued, with as many as 1.5 million Algerians killed and 2 million relocated to detention camps. On the French side, approximately 25,000 French soldiers were killed and 65,000 wounded, according to the French military.[26] In order to maintain control in the face of growing unrest, as well as increasing dissent and calls for independence, the French military began to use questionable interrogation techniques. Revelations and condemnations of torture also led to the emergence of a much larger debate about imperial power and national identity.[27] Yet speaking out against torture did not necessarily translate into support for Algerian independence, which is encapsulated by French journalist and torture survivor Henri Alleg's rhetorical question: "Should we condemn only torture and France's involvement in the war, or more generally, the colonial system?"[28] While the French Republic was constructed on the universalist principles of *liberté*, *égalité*, and *fraternité*, many French citizens began to grapple with some of the paradoxical questions at the core of the imperialism/universalism debate: How can a nation be both colonialist and universalist? How can a state preach liberty, equality, and fraternity while occupying foreign lands?

It was in part due to the military's use of torture that the war began to bitterly polarize the French population. While many called for an end to this "dirty war," others ardently insisted on maintaining this valuable region that was so emblematic of the French Empire. This public divide, combined with governmental missteps, eventually resulted in the fall of the Fourth Republic. From the war's start in 1954, France saw seven prime ministers come and go before World War II hero Charles de Gaulle was called on to lead the Fifth Republic in 1958. This presaged a host of future imbrications between World War II and the French-Algerian War, some of which feature in subsequent chapters of this book. The next four years would see escalating violence and an intensifying conflict between the anticolonial camp and the proponents of l'Algérie française, including the Far Right Secret Armed Organization (Organisation armée secrète, OAS), whose motto was "L'Algérie est française et le restera" (Algeria is French and will remain that way). Knowing that Algerian independence was a foregone conclusion, de Gaulle began secret talks in 1961 with the FLN that eventually culminated in the Evian Accords and a call for a formal cease-fire. In June 1962 the French electorate voted 91 percent in favor of the accords, and on July 1, 1962, the Algerian electorate voted almost unanimously in favor of independence. Two days later, on July 3, 1962, Algeria became an independent country.

While this marked a significant shift for both regions—Algeria's newfound independence and France's loss of colonial empire—it is worth keeping in mind Edward Said's prescient words that "imperialism did not end, did not suddenly become 'past,' once decolonization had set in motion the dismantling of the classical empires."[29] Similarly, 1962 should not be simply regarded as a concluding moment when these nations became entirely separate.[30] Nonetheless, it does mark a disjuncture, particularly with regard to identity and subjectivity. In Algeria, this came in the form of expulsions of the *pied-noir* population and a long, difficult struggle to build a nation comprised of various ethnic groups and political forces, while in France it manifested itself as an increasingly restricted definition of what and who counted as "French." The implications of this changing identity landscape were not limited to nationality and also helped construct ideas about gender broadly and masculinity in particular.[31]

Although Algeria has now been formally independent for several decades, traumatic memories of this eight-year war remain lodged in the minds and bodies of citizens of both nations. This was exacerbated by the French refusal to recognize the war as such, referring to it instead—somewhat euphemistically—as "the events in Algeria" and thus effectively blocking any earlier possibility of collective healing. However, since the French National Assembly voted in 1999 to permit the use of the term "Algerian War" (guerre d'Algérie), a veil of secrecy has slowly begun to lift.[32] The consequent relaxing of colonial archives has also meant that stories of torture and war crimes have begun to emerge. The French-Algerian War is thus, now more strongly than ever, occupying the public consciousness. This recent reopening of old war wounds has also yielded a new set of historical and ethical quagmires in which competing narratives battle for a place in the collective memory. Crucially, this phenomenon is not confined to France and Algeria. There is now a global focus on the war, with even the United States, following the 9/11 attacks, looking to the conflict in an attempt to avoid repetition. Neil MacMaster makes a cogent connection between the French-Algerian conflict and the American invasion of Afghanistan and Iraq:

> The systematic occultation of both law and historical precedent [in the "War on Terror"] has been based on the dangerous argument that the attacks of September 11 constituted a world-shattering event of such an unprecedented kind that it demanded the slate be wiped clean: only new and exceptional measures could meet the threat of terrorism. . . . However, there was little that was, in the strict sense of the word, exceptional in the events of September 11, and almost every feature of the US response to the crisis had been prefigured in French counter-insurgency strategy during the Algerian war, a body of doctrine that had had a major influence on US "low intensity" warfare during the four decades after 1961.[33]

In this sense, one cannot ignore the political and cultural climate in which *Hybrid Anxieties* is written. The global rise of populism in response to migration and racial and religious differences is inescapable, as is the increased violence toward those who do not fit gender and sexual norms, to say nothing of the ascension of "posttruth" politics and the 2016 election of Donald J. Trump.[34] Furthermore, over the last decade the Far Right has been continuing to grow throughout the United States and Europe, bleeding into the mainstream political landscape. And despite the fact that in Europe such conservative political parties tend to position themselves as hostile to EU principles, they have paradoxically banded together and coordinated on a European scale in order to bolster anti-immigration, racist, and xenophobic policies in their respective national contexts.

Resonances with the French-Algerian War also appear right up to the present day. Far Right nationalist Marine Le Pen was, for example, the runner-up in France's 2017 elections, receiving more than ten million votes (totaling more than one-third of the electorate). It is here worth noting that Le Pen's party, the National Front (Front national, FN)—founded by her father, Jean-Marie Le Pen, who served in the military and was accused of engaging in torture during the French-Algerian War—was partially born out of dismay over the loss of French Algeria. Also worthy of mention is that Le Pen rebranded the party in 2018 by renaming it the National Rally (Rassemblement national, RN) in an effort to appeal to more voters ahead of the European parliamentary elections. In France today, a legacy of racism and fierce nationalism manifests itself in multiple forms—including (but certainly not limited to) escalating tensions around religious freedom and employment discrimination—presenting the country with the uncomfortable truth that it is no longer able to avoid a critical self-assessment of its handling of its colonial past and postcolonial present. Most recently, the January 2015 attacks on *Charlie Hebdo*, the terrorist acts of November 2015, and even the burkini debates in the summer of 2016 (not to mention slightly more distant events, such as the 2005 riots in response to police violence and hardline immigration stances) expose a growing nexus of inequality centered around race, gender, religion, and nationality.

It is in this context that an abundance of literary and cinematic works dealing with the French-Algerian War has emerged in recent years as writers and filmmakers grapple with its traces. The historical specificities combined with a number of unique aspects (including the pervasive nature of its violence in the form of torture, terrorism, and guerrilla warfare) have undoubtedly molded literary and cinematic productions about the war. While some works center on the lives (both past and present) of French conscripts who served in Algeria, others provide alternatives to the official historical record by telling the forgotten and erased stories of Algerian civilians and militants. All, however, take us up to the present day and effectively uncover the memory challenges the war has left both for those directly involved and for later generations. In this respect, *Hybrid Anxieties* asserts that literature, film, and art play a significant role in negotiating the colonial past and takes a specific interest in the ways in which subversions of these forms and genres mirror contemporary anxieties related to gender, sexuality, and nationality. By intervening in the contemporary memory landscape, the literary and cinematic texts I analyze bear witness to this imbrication of content and form.

Hybridity, Desire, and Anxiety

The genre-defying text *Tomboy* (*Garçon manqué*), written by French Algerian writer Nina Bouraoui and with which I engage at length in chapter 5, highlights the multiple, hybrid experiences of growing up in the wake of the French-Algerian War, which the narrator expresses as follows: "I go from Yasmina to Nina. From Nina to Ahmed. From Ahmed to Brio. . . . I don't know who I am. One and multiple. Lying and truthful. Strong and weak. Girl and boy."[35] Later, Bouraoui succinctly summarizes the existential crisis that lies at the root of these myriad identities: "Every morning I scrutinize myself. I have four problems. Am I French or Algerian? Am I a girl or a boy?"[36] Categories and labels—specifically those relating to gender and nationality—repeatedly fail to capture the multiple, sometimes contradictory identities and hybrid experiences of many postwar bodies.

The concept of hybridity indexes the urge to complicate identity that this book interrogates, a connection that Robert Young draws out in his assertion that "fixity of identity is only sought in situations of instability and disruption, of conflict and change."[37] Many different models by which to approach the mixing of races and ethnicities have proliferated in postcolonial studies, with Homi Bhabha famously arguing that, as an in-between space, hybridity is "a contesting, antagonistic agency."[38] Bhabha also specifically links the term to colonial anxieties: "Hybridity represents that ambivalent 'turn' of the discriminated subject into the terrifying, exorbitant object of paranoid classification—a disturbing questioning of the images and presences of authority."[39] While hybridity has at times been posited in an exclusionary sense (e.g., neither white nor black, neither woman nor man) that is "haunted by all that it is not," to use Sara Ahmed's words, it can also be conceptualized as a meeting or proximity of two distinct groups or categories.[40] In the latter sense, hybridity implicitly suggests that other modes of social engagement may be created through a disidentification with normative categories, offering a "third space" that enables other positions that are critical of essentialism to emerge.[41] Hybridity also references the rich body of work on the concept of *métissage* in the Francophone context, a concept that Françoise Lionnet has described as a process of "forms and identities that is the result of cross-cultural encounters, and that forms the basis for their self-portrayals and their representations of cultural diversity."[42] In accounting for how subjects constitute themselves across gaps and fissures, hybridity further complements queer analysis in its attunement to physical, symbolic, and textual boundaries, including gender and racial taxonomies.

Looking to the nineteenth century, hybridity can be traced back to questions of fertility and miscegenation, including ideas about who can or should reproduce—and who should not. While Young argues that this fundamental linkage to sex and procreation (and subsequent interdictions placed thereon) means that it "must always be a resolutely heterosexual category," I instead argue that hybridity is always already queer.[43] Indeed, I see critical connections with queerness, which itself is often equated with antireproduction and the termination of family lines. Taking a cue from Freccero, who argues that hybridity, *métissage*, *mestizaje*, and spectrality—all concepts that serve as theoretical anchors in this book as well—"find themselves in certain ways allied with *queer* as terms that do the work of *différance* in relation to the identitarian inflections they carry," I aim to change the terms around the debate of what counts as (re)production, including disrupting straight and heteronormative forms of representation as normative reproduction.[44]

As well, hybridity and queerness have semantic similarities and in meaning share a quality of in-betweenness and a notion of crossing and traversing. Although there is considerable debate over the origin of the word "queer," Bruno Perreau identifies its linguistic roots in the Indo-European root *-twerkw*, which signifies "across."[45] Meanwhile, the adjective "hybrid" is defined by the *Oxford English Dictionary* as "derived from heterogeneous or incongruous sources; having a mixed character; composed of two diverse elements; mongrel."[46] These elements of literal or metaphoric mixing and crossing common to both hybrid and queer not only are a recurrent theme in the texts I analyze but also provide a means by which to describe the form of the texts themselves: crossing many, but never quite fitting any single traditional category or genre. Muñoz further highlights the interrelation between queerness, hybridity, and fragmentation, writing that hybridity "captures, collects, and brings into play various theories of fragmentation in relation to minority identity practices. Identity markers such as queer . . . or *mestizo* . . . are terms that defy notions of uniform identity or origins. Hybrid catches the fragmentary subject formation of people whose identities traverse different race, sexuality, and gender identifications."[47] Indeed, these words could easily be applied to the lives of many of the characters I invoke in this book, many of whom traverse borders—material, psychic, corporeal, or symbolic—yet always emerge as something different, hybrid, mixed.

As an ideology, colonialism works according to the colonizer's deep-seated belief in an innate superiority. It also functions according to a logic of categorization that rests on assumptions about gender, ethnicity, religion, and nationality. In the French context, these dual rationales manifested themselves through the "civilizing mission" (*mission civilisatrice*) and through a fixation on naming and classification. Methodologically speaking, hybridity works against these impulses in order to denaturalize categories and destabilize binary thinking. While this approach is particularly formative for the way in which I undertake literary analysis in this book, I suggest that this can be nuanced by thinking about hybridity as an approach complementary to queer that lends itself to the subtleties of metaphorical and material borders. Hybridity implicitly references the uses and abuses of assimilation—a prime tactic used by French colonial forces, as well as by subsequent governments—but also looks to the oppressive and empowering impacts of merging, mingling, fusing, blending, and diversifying. In this sense, the overlaps between hybridity and queerness allow us to witness the shared interests of queer and postcolonial theory.

Yet in the post-decolonization period, this notion of hybridity has also provoked new desires and new anxieties. These anxieties about hybridity and difference arise in part from this mixing and blurring of categories related to gender, sexuality, race, ethnicity, and nationality. While an excess of anxiety is medically diagnosed as a pathological state and clinical disorder, anxiety has become such common parlance that it is simultaneously quotidian. Defined as "worry over the future or about something with an uncertain outcome; uneasy concern about a person, situation, etc.; a troubled state of mind arising from such worry or concern," anxiety arises from the not-yet-here, the anticipation of uncertainty about what is yet to come.[48] Another way of understanding anxiety, however, emerges via its second definition: "strong desire or concern *for* something to happen or *to* do something; an instance of this."[49] This coupling of desire and unease is compelling, and the idea suffuses this book. Critical disability studies scholar Margrit Shildrick writes of anxiety's complicated position as follows: "In order to more fully appreciate how the psychic register plays out in the material world of differential embodiment, it is important to note that anxiety is never merely negative but is generated as much by fascination as by threat. The fraught relations of pleasure and danger are always complicated by the ambiguous nature of desire itself."[50] Anxieties are, according to Shildrick, "never merely negative" and always already reference desire on a deeper level. If desire and unease are two sides of the same coin, anxiety arises both *out of* normativity (we feel uneasy because something or someone departs from the norm) and *outside* it (desire necessarily exceeds the norm).[51] Queer, then, is both a deconstruction of the first impulse and a celebration of the latter. Anxiety as such inhabits both.

In its anticipatory mode, the concept of hybrid anxieties also informs and appeals to the temporal dimension of this project. In contrast to fear, which can be figured as transitive and as having an object ("fear of"), anxiety is intransitive and, through its preoccupation with the future, is instead in suspense and lacking an object. Time and temporality thus serve as a central motif. Whether in the form of uncertainty toward the future or an obsessive reliving of the past, my analysis is cognizant of these anxiety-laden aspects of time, but it is also attuned to the notion that memory has the unique capacity to reverse the flow of time and to queer both temporality and anxiety. As well, I read the meeting of France and Algeria (both convivial and violent) and all its attendant fears, concerns, hopes, and desires as fundamentally anxiety-inducing. Some of the questions that guide and inflect my readings include: What kind of subject could emerge in the wake of hybridity and its attendant anxieties? To what extent are the pleasures, desires, and anxieties around fractured and fragmented bodies an integral part of gendered subjectivity? Could hybridity—as a theme, concept, and method—break open, subvert, or queer identity and subjectivity? Might tensions between desire and anxiety allow for new and different ways of embodying gender, sexuality, race, and nationality?

Gender, Sexuality, and Decolonization: Rethinking Masculinity

In 1954, just after the start of the French-Algerian War, Sénac declared: "Let the Man in me come into being, for the sake of my Algerian Homeland."[52] This was his call for a new vocabulary and language, a new consciousness, and a new relationality built on love and solidarity—in short, a new man. A few years later, Frantz Fanon, in his seminal text *The Wretched of the Earth* (*Les damnés de la terre*), similarly gestures toward the stakes this historical moment had for masculinity by succinctly stating: "Decolonization is quite simply the replacing of a certain 'species' of men by another 'species' of men."[53] He further cemented this link in his definitive proclamation: "Decolonization is the veritable creation of new men."[54] Ayo Coly persuasively argues how this can in fact be characterized as queer: "Reading Fanon today, against the backdrop of queer theory, his injunction to violence, his programme of 'complete disorder' and 'creation of new men,' was a call for a queering of the self, an unthinking of received categories and scripts of identities."[55] Moreover, with its investment in nonnormative futurities and its focus on unbecoming, Fanon's brand of decolonization was, in many senses, queer.

The language of "decolonization" that both Fanon and Sénac reference also had clear political implications. As Todd Shepard documents, the term "decolonization" (*décolonisation*) was first coined by journalist Henri Fonfrède in his 1836 tract "Decolonization of Algiers," in which he critiqued the French occupation of Algeria. However, the word disappeared from usage for decades, and in its reemergence it had taken on a new valence—"decolonization" became an avoidance strategy, an invention that, as Shepard shows, "allowed the French to *avoid* facing the challenges that Algerian nationalism and the Algerian Revolution posed to classic conceptions of French values and history, at least temporarily."[56] A gradual process of forgetting was central in identity formation because by imagining the decolonization of Algeria as a socially and historically progressive step forward, the French could "forget that Algeria had been part of France since the 1830s and ... escape many of the larger implications of that shared past."[57] Through this forgetting, there emerged novel understandings of Frenchness, and as Fanon's and Sénac's words also suggest, decolonization itself crystallized a number of issues related to gender.

In France, the regulation of sexuality takes on particular significance that is, according to Vinay Swamy, due to "the way in which public and private spheres have been defined and interpreted under the umbrella of the universalist republican ideology" that dictated that all people were equal.[58] Joan Scott has expertly documented the gendered dimensions of this paradox of French republicanism and how the universal, rights-bearing individual was simultaneously coded as male.[59] In the context of the French-Algerian War, the seemingly "neutral" and "unmarked" body of the French, heterosexual, Christian, white, male body was, however, called into question. It hence becomes ever more important, as historian Elisa Camiscioli also suggests, first to account for the ways in which gender intervenes in the invention of racial hierarchies and second to recognize the positions of those marked bodies—those bodies that do not quite fit—"in an order of desire, signification, and power."[60] Indeed, colonial subjects and gender and sexual minorities have been systematically omitted from this notion of an inclusive universalism.

Homosexuality, for example, became a divisive political issue when in 1960, just as the French-Algerian War was nearing its end, Law 60-754 was passed.[61] The first time it was codified in French legislation, homosexuality was characterized as a "social plague" akin to alcoholism, prostitution, and tuberculosis.[62] Curiously, this criminalization of homosexuality coincided with a period in which the French nation was beginning to see that Algerian independence—and the loss of its last remaining North African colonial conquests—seemed to be a most certain outcome. This parallel, between the French-Algerian War coming to an end and nonnormative sexuality being criminalized, was by no means coincidental; indeed, one of the ways in which the French nation has been consolidated is, as Perreau demonstrates in *Queer Theory: The French Response*, through the fear of homosexuality, against which the "ideal citizen" is defined.[63] Even though North Africa had long served as a "queer space" in the French imagination, with writers like André Gide detailing their sexual promiscuity with North African boys and men, there were now critical questions about what this meant for the future of the republic.[64] The 1960 law emerged just as France "promised to extend the quality of 'completely French' to some ten million North African Muslims whose sexual behavior is not always identical to that which our Judeo-Christian tradition imposes," effectively limiting the definition of what identities and what sorts of practices would be promoted by the state.[65]

It was in this moment that anxieties over sexual, racial, and national differences congealed. In *The Invention of Decolonization*, Shepard identifies widespread use of homophobic comments in political debates of the 1950s and early 1960s: "All sides sought to tar those they criticized with the names and the signs of male same-sex perversion. They did so to identify their opponents as abnormally French. If one could show that homosexual lusts motivated political adversaries, they would be understood as unworthy to speak as rational subjects, as citizens."[66] The Far Right was thus able to seize on the opportunity to "remasculinize" the French people, using images of violence (some rather tenuous or exaggerated) and assertions about masculinity when processing France's defeat. In his follow-up study titled *Sex, France, and Arab Men*, Shepard nuances this point by arguing that relinquishing Algeria was, for many, a sign of weakness that would "open the doors to uncontrolled 'oriental' perversion," effectively setting the terms for acceptable forms of masculinity.[67] This example illustrates what Judith Butler refers to as the "constitutive outside," an abstract space that is inhabited by "abject identities" or those who do not fit into normative gender (or sexual) categories.[68] According to Butler, this category must be continually identified, named, and othered in order to reify the validity of normative gender configurations. The "threatening specter" of failed gender and sexuality serves to constantly reinforce norms. Yet this homophobic discourse also lays bare the rampant anxieties about masculinity and queerness and, more broadly, anything else that stood in opposition to the hegemonic matrix of white, French, heterosexual masculinity—that is, all that did not quite fit normative categories not only of sexuality but also, as subsequent chapters acknowledge, of gender, race, ethnicity, and nationality. While Shepard turns attention to how such narratives attempted to mobilize French people to oppose "Algerianization," I am interested in how this "crisis" (whether actual or not) opened up possibilities for thinking gender, sexuality, and hybridity differently. In this sense, a guiding principle of this analysis could be summarized using Sara Ahmed's conceptualization of queer as referring not only to "nonnormative sexualities but to moments in which norms fail to be reproduced."[69]

The epistemological foundations (or antifoundations, if you will) of queer theory rest not only on the questioning of essentialism and identity formation but also on the precise dismantling of the unit *par excellence* of identity: the modern liberal subject. As Michel Foucault explicated, this subject is constituted through discourse, which also functions as a form of social control. As he detailed in volume 1 of *The History of Sexuality*, beginning in the nineteenth century there was a shift in focus from "acts" to "identities," with the apparatus of sexuality becoming a key element of this process of subjectification. In this sense, desires and practices are socially constructed, but with the emergence of myriad sexual classifications also comes pathologization. While the field of gay and lesbian studies grew out of this historiographical trend, queer theory precisely disidentified with this approach, which took the "modern homosexual subject" as its epistemological basis. In other words, queer theory dismissed the notion that the subject could ever be reduced to a core ontological unit. There is no prediscursive self: the subject is an artifact of discourse (in its broadest sense) and of normalizing regimes.

Queer theory is certainly not the first or only epistemological tool to grapple with multiplicity and fluidity. (The idea of identity and subjectivity as shifting and constituted in discourse had, for instance, already been well articulated by some branches of feminist theory and poststructuralism.) I argue that queer theory's momentum instead stems from its deconstructionist impulse ("the deconstructive critical practice of queering," as Jarrod Hayes calls it), which enacts a break with other theoretical strands that persist in foregrounding the sexual subject *as a subject*.[70] In contrast to such approaches, queer theory's promise or possibility lies in its poststructuralist "refusal to name a subject," in its embracing of an anti-identitarian standpoint, and in its commitment to the dissolution of the modern liberal subject as we know it (something explored more fully in chapter 3).[71] For this reason, it offers a particularly effective approach by which to better understand "identity" at a particularly contentious moment in history that profoundly precipitated anxieties surrounding hybridity. The French-Algerian War was, on a global scale, a watershed moment. Activists and intellectuals held out real hope that this war would usher in a new future free from the strictures of imperial powers. Like queer, the Algerian revolution has often been figured in precisely such terms that imbue it with a sense of radical and reimagined futurity—a horizon of possibilities.

Queer Postcolonial Hauntings

In *The Empire Writes Back*, Bill Ashcroft, Gareth Griffiths, and Helen Tiffin refer to postcolonial writing as "uncentered, pluralistic, and multifarious." In their elaboration, we might hear resonances in the way I have thus far deployed the term "queer": "Subjective agency has emerged in postcolonial writing from its beginnings through a resistance to singular and fixed notions of identity and culture imposed under colonialism."[72] Indeed, despite detectable overlaps, postcolonial studies and queer studies—as fields of study—are often treated as separate and distinct. I would, however, argue that similar investments and questions occupy them both. In this sense, *Hybrid Anxieties* aims to bring into closer dialogue these two fields of study not only as bodies of knowledge but also as critical perspectives from and through which to analyze contemporary phenomena. Both queer and postcolonial perspectives are positioned as active, interconnected, and critical processes that are able to disrupt systems and structures that do not adequately address the lives of those who surpass the limits and categories implied by terms such as "French," "Algerian," "man," and "woman," among a myriad of others.

Aside from a small number of book-length studies, there remains little research that explicitly unites postcolonial and queer approaches.[73] This book addresses this divide, taking an intersectional approach that reads (queer) genders and sexualities as inextricable from other vectors of analysis, including coloniality, nationality, race, ethnicity, religion, class, and migration status. While colonialism was partially sustained through racial and gender categorization and hierarchization, reading postcolonial and queer in tandem offers an entry point from which to analyze the contestation of colonial epistemologies founded on the categorization of peoples and practices.[74] Looking to a possible cross-pollination between queer studies and postcolonial studies also offers an opportunity to reinvigorate postcolonial studies, which has often offered only a passing glance to nonnormative enactments of gender and sex or has merely treated them as metaphors or allegories of the destructive effects of colonialism.

Reading the French-Algerian War and its aftermath through a queer lens does, however, present a conundrum. In the French context, just as this particular war and its long-term sequelae have been kept at a distance, so too has there been a resistance to acknowledging queer theory.[75] More generally, there has been an intense backlash toward the academic field of gender studies, as evidenced by the Non à la théorie du genre (No to gender theory) movement, which has constructed a fantasy world in which "gender ideology" will overturn civilization and corrupt children.[76] This is, however, rather ironic, as queer theory could itself be understood as emerging from a uniquely French approach to poststructuralism, as alluded to by Freccero in the epigraph. She follows up on this idea by arguing that the poststructuralist turn in

French theory "not only facilitates the rise of queer theory as a literary cultural practice in the United States, but also lends an 'always already' quality to the activity of queering. French theory has, in other words, made possible the demonstration of how tropological dimensions of language subvert the very heteronormativity of Western logocentrism and thus, for example, how desire and identification may be unfixed from their sexually differentiated and opposed poles. Indeed, queer may be said to emerge spectrally in deconstructive critique."[77] Yet while deconstruction has been embraced in the French academy, queer theory has been received with skepticism. As a tool, method, and lens, deconstructive impulses have also been profoundly influential in shaping both postcolonial and queer theory—a dyad that is, I venture to say, also haunted by Algeria. I am reminded here of Robert Young's pronouncement that similarly draws a parallel between Algeria and poststructuralism: "If so-called 'so-called poststructuralism' is the product of a single historical moment, then that moment is probably not [the student and worker movement of] May 1968 but rather the Algerian War of Independence—no doubt itself both a symptom and a product."[78]

My analysis also hinges on a triangle between deconstruction, queer theory, and Algeria, which I see as profoundly entangled. It is in this spirit that *Hybrid Anxieties* is shaped by a postcolonial and queer rejection of fixed identity categories and is anchored in deconstructive approaches that attempt to unmask the fiction of universalism, to see binaries as enacting epistemic violence, and to overturn dichotomous thinking. Deconstructive gestures, as anthropologist Ramy Aly points out, question and intrude upon the integrity of ideas considered normative and "common sense."[79] It is from these dynamics that they derive their force and their ability to subvert preconceptions regarding subjectivity and identity. In *Becoming Arab in London*, Aly elaborates: "The favouring of fixity over mobility, of 'roots over routes,' relies upon conventional modes of subjectivity that constrain the possibilities of subjecthood within rigid and exclusionary boundaries."[80] My book builds on this idea in order to look to deconstructive moments in post-decolonization France and Algeria and to interrogate how they counter the centrality of fixity and rootedness.[81] In this way, I work to excavate other modes of subjectivity, embodiment, and social engagement that open up once we look to identities that blur otherwise rigid boundaries.

The shadow that Algeria cast over deconstruction and queer theory is further encapsulated in Jacques Derrida's concept of hauntology, which he first articulated in *Specters of Marx* as a tool for grappling with how subjectivity is shaped by traces of the past in the present. Hauntology, which Derrida describes as the "*non-contemporaneity with itself of the living present*," evokes the question of time, simultaneously referring both to what is no longer *and* to what has not (yet) happened.[82] Mark Fisher gets at this double-move characteristic of hauntology: not only is it "the proper temporal mode for a history made up of gaps, erased names and sudden abductions," but it also signals a "refusal to give up on the desire for the future."[83] This is also a queer project, as Hayes describes in his assertion that "situating hauntology within the development of Derridean deconstruction can help us to further theorize the relation between deconstruction and queering as a critical move."[84] Indeed, in its interplay of presence and absence, queer always already hints at a Derridean hauntology. Once more returning to this chapter's epigraph, Freccero further underscores the spectral facets of queer: this "uncanny, undead haunting of the other within" is indeed "what is and is not there."[85]

Queering Temporality

Placing queer theory in conversation with postcoloniality allows us to contend with the dark histories that continue to reverberate today, for as Kadji Amin posits, both queer and postcolonial studies direct attention to "identities and communities built out of the emotional detritus of history."[86] In addressing transgression and haunting, as well as political potentiality for a different horizon of possibilities, queer and postcolonial theory contest traditional lines of futurity and counter narratives of progress and development. Bhabha, for example, writes that postcolonial time "questions the teleological traditions of past and present, and the polarized historicist sensibility of the archaic and the modern."[87] Meanwhile, building on Didier Eribon's work, Denis M. Provencher articulates the multitemporality of queer in its occupying of "alternative temporalities . . . moving back and forth across multiple sites."[88] Nonsequential forms of time are part and parcel of queer's and postcolonial's common characteristics and investment in rethinking unitary time (itself an effect of imperialism and globalization). Equally, queer and postcolonial share the idea that memory may provoke transgression, thereby offering potential for profound change.

Studies of memory, both personal and collective, have grown immensely during recent decades, with scholarly work that addresses the Holocaust and trauma being especially influential in the emergence of this field. Michael Rothberg's "multidirectional memory"—a notion that emerges from his work on remembering the Holocaust in the wake of decolonization—is profoundly helpful in thinking through the ways in which memories of Algeria overlap with World War II (as well as other historical moments). Characterized by "ongoing negotiation, cross-referencing, and borrowing; as productive and not privative," Rothberg's work also frames how memories need not occlude one another: "An overly rigid focus on memory competition distracts from other ways of thinking about the relation between histories and their memorial legacies. Ultimately, memory is not a zero-sum game."[89] In this sense, one could argue that most—if not all—texts about the French-Algerian War inevitably invoke (implicitly or explicitly) World War II and the Holocaust. While these conflicts are undeniably related, as will become clear throughout the course of this book, events in Algeria shifted the terms (and the roles) of perpetrator and victim upon which France had built its sense of national identity in the wake of Nazi occupation and wartime destruction.[90] The Algerian conflict held up a mirror that distorted the trauma and projected violence onto an Other.

France has remembered and forgotten—or, to use Richard Derderian's terms, "willfully forgotten"—its colonial past (and postcolonial present) in particular ways, and this collective memory and amnesia structures how writers tell the story of the war.[91] Benjamin Stora writes: "For the French, a 'war without a name'; for the Algerians, a 'revolution without a face': one of the hardest conflicts of decolonization in this century has never truly been 'assumed' by either side."[92] While Stora was one of the first to advance the argument that the French were too traumatized to speak about the French-Algerian War and that the war was virtually forgotten, recent scholarship has documented how forgetting only happened later. According to Catherine Brun and Todd Shepard, for instance, the war's violence was in fact widely discussed in France in the 1960s (and these discussions were saturated with sexual over- and undertones).[93] Indeed, there is growing evidence that the war was a significant point of debate in the decade following Algerian independence and that forgetting (or attempts to forget) became more important to a sense of national identity only subsequently.

This historical *process* of memory also demands alternative strategies by which to document histories, including searching for silences and gaps. "When the present has given up on the future," Fisher writes, "we must listen for the relics of the future in the unactivated potentials of the past."[94] Queer postcolonial temporality provides the possibility of building alternative strategies to counter state-sanctioned approaches to the institutionalization of memory—mechanisms that profoundly affect which traumas count or matter in the "official" historical record. In looking to historical palimpsests, my hybrid methodology is not dissimilar from Ann Laura Stoler's method of reading along the grain, which reveals "condensed sites of epistemological and political anxiety."[95] It reads between the lines, facilitates intracategorical thinking, and analyzes works that record the experiences of those silenced, forgotten, or otherwise left out of the troubled historical record of the war. This approach allows me to consider modes of affiliation and disaffiliation, identification and disidentification, and the ways in which the borders of the self—formed in conjunction with but also in resistance to hegemonic institutions (including law, language, and citizenship)—fluctuate with the environment in which that individual is situated.

The "duty to remember" has, however, also been emphasized in postwar and postgenocide contexts like the French-Algerian conflict. Functioning in a cautionary capacity, this duty is aimed at avoiding any repetition of the horrors of the past. However, forgetting is not always malicious and may even be salutary. As early as 1882, French historian Ernest Renan famously declared: "Forgetting, I would even go so far as to say historical error, is a crucial factor in the creation of a nation."[96] While Renan's thesis that forgetting the past is a prerequisite for the establishment of a coherent (national) identity has been refuted, the value of memory versus forgetting continues to be debated. In response, I avoid setting up or supporting a binary opposition between remembering and forgetting wherein the former is celebrated and the latter is demonized. Similarly, I concur with María del Pilar Blanco and Esther Pereen when they warn that the "danger in marking all remembering with the affective registers of melancholia is that we may come to understand memory as working solely on the basis of repetition and negativity, rather than on its progressive (future) productivity."[97] In this sense, regarding forgetting as a form of rupture may also offer an opportunity for creative self-determination both in constructing one's past and in imagining one's future. Indeed, I make no assumption that remembering is preferable to forgetting (or vice versa) and maintain that interrupting linear time can be queer and productive. Jack Halberstam echoes this call for reconsidering our relationship to forgetting: "To say that we might want to think about memory and forgetting differently is in fact to ask that we start seeing alternatives to the inevitable and seemingly organic models we use for marking progress and achievement; it also asks us to notice how and whether change has happened."[98]

To avoid these oppositional dynamics—those of remembering versus those of forgetting—I instead embrace the approach suggested by feminist theorist Karen Barad, who reconceptualizes memory as a practice of "re-membering" that references its corporeal and psychic aspects: "Remembering is not a process of recollection, of the reproduction of what was, of assembling and ordering events like puzzle pieces fit together by fixing where each has its place. Rather it is a matter of re-membering, of tracing entanglements, responding to yearnings for connection, materialized into fields of longing/belonging, of regenerating what never was but might yet have been."[99] Inspired by this "reconfiguring anew [of] seemingly disparate parts" as described by Barad, I see this as a way of reconstituting and taking memory back from national projects of memorialization and looking toward loose cultural networks of individuals trying to cope with living, remembering, and forgetting in the context of post-decolonization Algeria and France.[100] The intergenerational aspects of the transmission of trauma in the French Algerian context—a trope that appears throughout *Hybrid Anxieties*—inevitably means that it also refers to memories of events not directly experienced. That is, re-membering could be a tool with which subsequent generations might creatively work with and through the memories of the war passed on to them by preceding generations. For me, re-membering is a queering of the memory/oblivion dichotomy, and as gerunds, both re-membering and queering point to (the power of) incompleteness and to a constant process of becoming.

The fact that memory cannot be reduced to linear coherent narrative structures is also reflected in the form that all texts analyzed in this book take: disruptive, fragmented, partial, mysterious. They are also marked by the achronological, which manifests itself in phenomena such as haunting, unconsciousness, and repetition. Haunting, a trope that appears and reappears—indeed, haunts—the texts, blurs the temporal divide and collapses any possibilities that past, present, and future could ever be separate. In communicating "the depth, density, and intricacies of the dialectic of subjection and subjectivity," as Avery Gordon writes, haunting affectively draws us in.[101] The texts I analyze capture our attention, whether in the apparent pursuit of a mystery or to piece together divergent parts of a deconstructed narrative. In some, plots are difficult to follow or do not make any sense at all, inviting us to participate by puzzling the stories together. In others, texts repeat and relive the same story over and over again. This approach also permits the creation of links with (our own) affective memory, approximating what Jill Bennett describes as the power of images in their "capacity to address the spectator's own bodily memory; to touch the viewer who feels rather than simply sees the event, drawn into the image through a process of affective contagion."[102] Reading and viewing become intra-active processes whereby meaning and matter are co-constituted, leaving neither intact and both constantly changing.[103]

Book Overview

This book is structured as follows. Part 1, "Masculinity and Memory," explores the concerns and anxieties and the hopes and fears of the postwar period and its (ongoing) extended aftermath. While the majority of academic scholarship attuned to the gendered aspects of the war has focused on Algerian women, less attention has been paid to masculinity.[104] The first two chapters approach the themes of masculinity and memory by examining the central place of both physical and symbolic violence in discussions of the French-Algerian War. Both chapters highlight the damaging effects of memories on maintaining a hegemonic and normative French masculinity and also gesture toward alternative modes of masculinity.

Chapter 1, "Haunted Masculinity and the Wounds of War," takes up Alain Resnais's *Muriel, or the Time of a Return* (1963), a highly fragmented film that, through its disjointedness, speaks to the psychological and bodily pain inflicted on Algerians during the war, as well as to the anxieties of French soldiers upon their return from Algeria. As the title of the film suggests, Resnais is interested in the story of "Muriel," an Algerian woman who was tortured and murdered by a French army unit. This title character, however, never appears in the film, and her absence highlights the multitude of silences surrounding the war and French remembrances of it. While the torture scene is not represented visually, its absence haunts the entire film as a metaphor for the ways in which Algerian women were used as screens onto which white French men could project their anxieties around colonial power and masculinity. While touching upon memories of destruction and rebuilding (both figurative and symbolic) after World War II, the film's principal narrative is concerned with Bernard, one of the soldiers responsible for Muriel's torture and death, who falls into a psychological crisis upon his return to France. He knows no other way to deal with his guilt toward the incident than to gather "evidence" in the hope of eventually telling Muriel's story. Bernard's efforts will, however, ultimately prove unsuccessful, revealing the intransmissibility of the war and its relationships to masculinity as experienced by many French conscripts. I pair *Muriel* with an analysis of Laurent Mauvignier's stylistically compelling novel *The Wound* (*Des hommes*, 2009), as it builds upon Resnais's film and reveals the long-lasting trauma and the multiple ways in which the conflict is still so palpable today. Whereas the first part of the chapter examines the fractured experiences of a French conscript returning to 1960s France, this section engages with constructions of masculinity in twenty-first-century postcolonial France. Although published as *The Wound* in English, the translation of Mauvignier's French title—"Men" or, alternatively, "Of Men"—highlights the importance placed on masculinity when writing about and remembering the war. This multivalent title also provokes a host of questions: What does it mean to be a man? Who can be considered a man? What is "man" capable of? Although Algeria is not even mentioned until a third of the way into the novel and is often referred to as "over there," it is always just beneath the surface, occupying the space of the unsaid. Both Resnais's film and Mauvignier's novel grapple with the ways in which these individuals are haunted and suggest that this haunting may also allow for different ways of embodying identity and subjectivity.

Chapter 2, "'You'll Never Give Me a Bad Conscience!': Masculinity and Postcolonial Guilt in *Caché*," similarly engages with masculinity, memory, and violence, this time as presented in Michael Haneke's film *Caché* (2005). Through its portrayal of the bloody events of October 17, 1961, in which as many as two hundred Algerians were drowned in the Seine River in one of the most hidden acts of colonial violence ever exercised on European soil, the film signals how individual and collective memories are inextricably linked. While other works have been interested in reconstituting the events of October 17, 1961, and its aftereffects in France and Algeria, *Caché* takes the notion of French colonial violence a step further and makes the massacre metonymic of a whole host of forms of state-imposed violence and hidden national memories that are not unique to France. Haneke's film also reveals a complex process in which gendered subjectivity informs and is informed by acts of physical violence and the symbolic violence that works to silence them. Through its exposure of the complex ways in which memory has been negotiated and renegotiated in a neocolonial, post-9/11 global era of surveillance, *Caché* highlights the conundrums of postcolonial amnesia, affecting not only memory but also conflicts over citizenship and human rights, concerns that also reverberate in more recent events whose postcolonial resonances have been overlooked—particularly the terrorist attacks on *Charlie Hebdo*. Drawing a comparison between the events of October 17, 1961, and January 7, 2015, this chapter argues for a more nuanced view on contemporary violence in which the ongoing effects of the French-Algerian War are recognized.

Part 2, "Queering Postcolonial Legacies," shifts attention to the redemptive and resistant possibilities that reconfiguring identity holds by analyzing work that eschews linear paths, defined lines, and heteroreproductive futures. These productive and deconstructive maneuverings rethink the hegemonic and dominant hold over ways of doing masculinity and performing memory by engaging with queer diasporic cultural forms and engaging in disidentificatory practices. The texts analyzed also question traditional narrative genres and structures and underscore the transformative potential of looking toward the queerer aspects of the war's aftershocks.

In chapter 3, "Eros and Eden: Pierre Guyotat and Queer Pleasures," I focus on sex and sexuality—queer sexualities in particular—as a way to subvert notions of modern subjectivity. I ground my analysis in *Eden, Eden, Eden* (1970), written by the highly controversial French novelist Pierre Guyotat, who underscores the transformative potential that sex holds within revolutionary movements, but I also reach out to the work of both Herbert Marcuse and Michel Foucault to illustrate the transformational possibilities that are opened by rethinking the notion of the subject, a process I identify as inescapably queer. Together, these three writers offer a supplement to poststructuralist, feminist, and queer forms of critique that have acknowledged the fractured nature of being and the profoundly decentering effects of language and culture. Banned in France and considered pornographic because of its depiction of male brothels, queer sex, and extreme violence, Guyotat's text presents the body as a battleground for both violence and liberation and speaks to the war's intense destruction and destructiveness. Set in a postwar Algerian desert, the almost hallucinatory novel also subverts form and genre by virtue of being composed, in its entirety, of one single sentence. While most fictional and nonfictional work about the war focuses on the past, *Hybrid Anxieties* gives due credit to the present, here exemplified by Guyotat, who makes a statement about temporality by only writing in the present tense.

Chapter 4, "Queer Palimpsests and October 17, 1961: Memory Politics in Leïla Sebbar's *The Seine Was Red*," revisits the Paris police massacre of October 17, 1961, explored in chapter 2. Here, I turn to French Algerian writer Leïla Sebbar's *The Seine Was Red* (1999), a novel that grapples with remembering the events of that night. In the struggle for independence from France, the FLN called for a peaceful demonstration to protest a curfew that forbade Algerians from leaving their homes at night. Tens of thousands of Algerians marched through the streets of Paris to assert their place as French citizens. But what began as a peaceful demonstration soon turned into a bloody massacre, with thousands injured and hundreds killed. Vocalized through a group of three young individuals who are attempting to come to terms with the event thirty-five years later, the novel asks how migrants and diasporic subjects engage with memory in the postcolonial city. Together these three characters retrace the 1961 protest—a retracing that is reminiscent of the urban redrawing that occurred in the actual event. In their physical and temporal journey, the novel's protagonists leave subversive commemorative traces, writing with red paint over World War II plaques in order to mark the Algerian protesters' actions and lives. In addition to highlighting and accounting for silenced voices, the palimpsests or countermonuments that they leave behind queer temporality and symbolize the palimpsestic nature of memory itself.

In the final chapter, "Queering Identity, Embracing In-Betweenness: Disidentification and Re-membering in Nina Bouraoui's *Tomboy*," I further explore gender, racial, and national hybridity through an analysis of Nina Bouraoui's *Tomboy* (2000), an autobiographical novel that lays bare the ambiguity and in-betweenness felt by many postwar subjects. As with nationality, gender becomes blurred for the novel's protagonist, Nina, and her male alter ego and friend, Amine, who, like Nina, is a child of the war—someone for whom neither Algeria nor France represents home. Nina, who narrates the novel, attempts to find a way to express a certain masculinity, despite a changing female body that seems to betray this gender identity. Bouraoui's text also defies traditional narrative structures, thereby mirroring the nonnormative experiences of the protagonist, whose gender ambiguity and queer desire may reinforce a difficult process of unbelonging. In addition, the narrative also demonstrates the productive potential that queerness holds for disrupting conventional thinking. *Tomboy* unites memory and embodiment to further establish the entangled and critical relation between trauma and masculinity and transforms the remembering/forgetting binary into a process of re-membering, a counterhegemonic practice that points to both the subject-forming capacities of memory and the vulnerability of the fractured body.

The book concludes with yet two additional examples that contend with a present postcolonial moment marked by changing understandings of gender and sexuality. I juxtapose Merzak Allouache's feature film *Chouchou* (2003) with the vitriolic debates around marriage equality in France in 2013, both of which can be read as exposing deep anxieties about national identity as diffracted through a conflation of fears of migrants and gender and sexual minorities. As a whole, this book aims to lay bare the entanglements of race, nationality, gender, and sexuality as vectors that shape postcolonial legacies while consequently underscoring their productive potential to reimagine social engagements and reorder temporalities. With a focus on the reconfiguration of both memory and masculinity, *Hybrid Anxieties* adds a new impulse to the question of how to rethink hegemonic notions of gender, sexuality, and nationality. Without losing sight of the trauma of this particularly violent chapter in history, the book proposes a new kind of hybridity that, however anxious and anticipatory, puts emphasis on the productive force of a queer desire—a desire for deconstructing any teleological relationship between the past, present, and future.

PART 1 Masculinity and Memory

1 Haunted Masculinity and the Wounds of War

Alain Resnais's *Muriel* and
Laurent Mauvignier's *The Wound*

> Whenever we are trying to recover a recollection, to call up some period of our history, we become conscious of an act sui generis by which we detach ourselves from the present in order to replace ourselves, first in the past in general, then in a certain region of the past—a work of adjustment, something like the focusing of a camera.
>
> —Henri Bergson, *Matter and Memory*

Muriel, or the Time of Return (*Muriel ou le temps d'un retour*, 1963), the third feature-length film from acclaimed French director Alain Resnais and his second collaboration with screenwriter Jean Cayrol, attempts to make sense of a fragmented past and present that have been torn apart by international wars and domestic conflicts. Taking the recently concluded French-Algerian War (as well as the slightly more distant World War II) as its point of departure, the film interrogates a postwar amnesia and its far-reaching effects on bodies and minds. As in his previous films, *Hiroshima mon amour* (1959) and *Last Year at Marienbad* (*L'année dernière à Marienbad*, 1961), Resnais maintains a stylistic agenda of innovation in cinematic form and uses a variety of techniques to reflect the uneasiness and anxiety felt by his characters, who are, for the most part, average French citizens coping with the anxieties of the period. In this way, they are representative of the psychic and physical struggles occurring for this particular class in the wake of a conflict that saw hundreds of thousands of deaths and witnessed the use and abuse of interrogation techniques performed under the guise of French national security interests.

Throughout his career, Resnais showed a marked lack of interest in making verisimilar films, forcing his viewers to become active spectators who must constantly work to grasp content and meaning: "My goal is to put viewers in a state that in a week, six months, a year later, faced with a problem, they can't cheat but are required to react *freely*. . . . What is necessary is to shake people's certainty, wake them up, make them accept that given values are not intangible."[1] While Resnais never fully embraced the Nouvelle Vague movement in cinema, his eschewing of unity and coherence was undeniably New Wave–esque. In *Muriel*, for example, we must make sense of repeated contradictions in character and plot, drawing connections where there may actually be none. Rapid montage and pervasive lingering shots create an atmosphere of fragmentation that makes the film nearly impossible to summarize, indeed comprehend, in any coherent way. Dialogue is often illogical, questions posed are rarely answered, and awkward silences are ubiquitous. Characters often appear to be having conversations only with themselves, refusing to conform to the unstated rules of interpersonal communication. Despite the fact that the film has been deemed "one of the most technically innovative and thematically ingenious films to have been inspired by the Algerian war," it is still, as one reviewer puts it, "difficult to seize, let alone write about."[2] Susan Sontag echoes a similar sentiment, describing the film as "designed so that, at any given moment of it, it's not about anything at all."[3]

The film's title positions a particular individual (Muriel) as its prime topic of investigation, an Algerian woman who was tortured and killed by a French army unit during the war. This character will, however, never appear in the film, and this conspicuous absence of the Algerian female body centers the French male body. Given that the film has been critiqued for solely exposing the experiences of the French soldier and civilian, it follows that its true investment is in confronting its survivors rather than its victims.[4] Indeed, I propose that *Muriel* is most interested in representing the pitfalls and paradoxes of a changing French national identity complicated by France's wartime crimes and its ultimate relinquishment of l'Algérie française. It is through its disjointedness that it speaks to the anxieties that French soldiers experienced upon their return from Algeria in the early 1960s. However, I argue, it is through these same cinematic techniques that it also alludes to—if not quite explicitly represents—the psychological and bodily pain inflicted on Algerians during the war. Thus, we may interpret Resnais's aesthetic choices as obliquely addressing issues at the heart of the French-Algerian conflict, including public secrets such as censorship, torture, and war crimes.

The epigraph from Henri Bergson's *Matter and Memory* summarizes the sort of memory work that is occurring for the film's protagonist, Bernard, a French soldier involved in Muriel's torture who becomes obsessed with his haunting memories of this woman and with documenting her story. Bergson's metaphorical camera is echoed by the ubiquitous camera that Bernard totes as he attempts to reconstitute memory while calling out those guilty of her murder. However, this evocation simultaneously forces the viewer to question the role of the camera filming this feature film. In encouraging a presumably French audience to confront issues of colonial violence and torture (even if they are visually absent), Resnais's camera can be interpreted as a tool through which to accept collective responsibility for the actions taken in the name of the French Republic.

While the French government denied its use of torture and even censored films and books that suggested it advocated such tactics, there was no question that torture techniques were being employed on both sides of the Mediterranean.[5] The goal of torture was not always to force insurgents to reveal information about the resistance; instead, it was meant to function as a form of psychological warfare, with both revolutionaries and civilians being targeted in an attempt to destroy morale and win support for continued French governance of the region.

In his essay "A Victory," Jean-Paul Sartre stated that "in the case of torture, this strange contest of will . . . the torturer pits himself against the tortured for his 'manhood' and the duel is fought as if it were not possible for both sides to belong to the human race."[6] Torture, as Sartre implies, is necessarily tied to gender, and while the intention of torture was often, as Marnia Lazreg signals, "to rebuild the native 'suspect' or combatant from the ground up in a psychological action based on sex, masculinity and femininity," there were also heavy stakes for the torturer, who was often performing a certain degree of masculinity through this act of violence.[7] In the context of Resnais's film, the French male body informs the sort of violence that could and would be enacted on the Algerian female body. While the violence will ultimately destroy this woman, it will also have lasting effects on the bodies (and particularly masculinities) of her torturers.

Practices of memory evasion such as forgetting and denial and, conversely, attempts to remember (and even hyperremember) also play out in particular ways that intersect with gender. Not unlike Elaine Showalter's still pertinent assessment that shell shock is "the body language of masculine complaint, a disguised male protest not only against war but against the concept of 'manliness' itself," many men returned home from the French-Algerian War broken, attempting to piece together their lives and to reclaim some semblance of postwar masculinity.[8] Bernard knows no other way to deal with his memories and guilt than to gather "evidence" (in the form of photographs and "documentary" footage) in hopes of eventually telling Muriel's story. Unsurprisingly, his efforts will prove unsuccessful, as he is powerless to change what happened in Algeria or to be understood by his family and friends at home in France.

In the pages that follow, I first map out the ways in which representations of destruction and rebuilding (figurative and symbolic) around both the French-Algerian War and World War II inform my reading of *Muriel*. I then go on to examine how the film's form and content subtly reveal memory and masculinity as being tied up in this postwar identity crisis, exemplified by Muriel's haunting absence/presence and other visual disappearing acts. By way of an extended conclusion, I juxtapose the fractured experiences of *Muriel*'s French conscript returning to 1960s France with the wartime ghosts that haunt the French men of twenty-first-century postcolonial France, as detailed in Laurent Mauvignier's stylistically compelling 2009 novel *The Wound* (*Des hommes*). The interrelationship between memory, masculinity, and violence is complex for the protagonists of both Resnais's film and Mauvignier's novel, both of whom are former conscripts named Bernard. These portraits of evolving masculinity also underscore how gender is constructed in relation to postcolonial anxieties. At first glance, these two Bernards might seem to negotiate their wartime memories in different ways: Resnais's Bernard hyperremembers his wartime actions and their consequences, whereas Mauvignier's Bernard buries his memories at all costs, even as they constantly bubble under the surface and appear in violent ways. However, because we encounter these two characters at different moments in their lives—the former just after his return from Algeria and the latter almost five decades later—I suggest that we read them as intimately connected, as extensions or evolutions of one another. More generally, this chapter's engagement with haunting (one of the key conceptual anchors of this book), which appears, disappears, and reappears through spectral figures that reflect the persistent effects of the war, highlights a queering of temporality in the disjointedness, spiraling, and mingling of time that occur in the two narratives.

Layered Memories and Failing Frenchness

Jean Cayrol's screenplay begins:

> This story should take place in a reconstructed city. There now exist only a few islands of ruins, old ruins that have aged badly. Cement sparkles. Houses open onto indefinable rooms, full of straw, debris, gardens with dead trees. But these little domains from an old war can only be discovered by accident. . . . The rest of the city is brand new, stupidly new. Straight roads intersecting at right angles, streetlights giving off an orange glow, avenues ready for the next war, allowing for the easy passage of tanks. Empty stores for rent. Parking lots. Cinemas whose sound never stops. Blank walls. Lots of television antennas . . .⁹

Muriel's protagonists play out their own troubled relationships to time and place against the backdrop of a destroyed city haunted by its newness. Ruins, although often well hidden, are constant reminders not only of a lost past but also of the magnitude of force (i.e., aerial bombardment) that caused such utter devastation. The city has been partially rebuilt after the destruction of one war but is simultaneously ready for another, as the new urban geometry allows for the easy passage of military vehicles. While there are inconspicuous ruins to be found throughout the city, a shiny novelty pervades it. Bright lights point to rapid modernization, juxtaposed against blank walls and empty storefronts. These stimuli cannot overpower the emptiness that remains, giving the city the feeling of what one of the film's characters terms "a martyr city." Similarly, in the eerily vacant streets of this rebuilt city without a center, no path ever seems to lead to either level ground or a feeling of stability.[10]

The film is set in the northern French city of Boulogne, a region decimated by the Germans in 1944 but now completely rebuilt, with modern block-like structures populating the urban landscape. As Kristin Ross has expertly detailed, the 1950s and 1960s were a period of newfound optimism and confidence for France's burgeoning class of baby boomers; new technologies and increased buying power allowed these "technocrats" access to a more comfortable way of life filled with appliances and automobiles, seemingly ensuring happier times ahead.[11] This future-directed hopefulness that occupied the period known as *les trente glorieuses* (the glorious thirty) was, however, enacted during a period of troubled relationships with the previous decades. As the colonial project failed, focus was directed to a slightly more distant, albeit quasi-mythical, past wherein France emerged victorious. The French-Algerian War remained obscured at this moment when memories of World War II, during which the French valiantly fought to fend off their Nazi occupiers, were crystallizing in the collective imagination, thereby aiding in the construction of a postwar national identity.

In *Muriel* these issues of remembering and forgetting around World War II and Algeria are present in both form and content. While there appeared to be a collective amnesia around the war, we are left to wonder: Could World War II commemorations provide a protective layer to shield the public against confronting the atrocities committed under the French flag? Could celebrations of the French Resistance to Nazi occupation hide their own war crimes? Could an eight-year struggle that saw intense conflict in both Algerian and French cities and villages really be forgotten so quickly, and if so, what sorts of repercussions would this have on bodies and minds? *Muriel*'s two intersecting narratives grapple with these questions and expose the imbrication of these two twentieth-century conflicts.[12]

In the film's first and, for the purposes of this chapter, more significant narrative, Bernard maintains a strained relationship with the past. Back in France for eight months after serving in the army for almost two years, he is haunted by the French-Algerian War, just as his stepmother, Hélène, is haunted by distant memories that revolve around World War II. In this second story line, Hélène (played by award-winning actor Delphine Seyrig) is a thirty-eight-year-old woman who, according to Cayrol's character sketch, should look both twenty and forty-five years old. She is an antique dealer and a compulsive gambler who lives among the dusty antiques that she sells from her apartment. Her obsession with the past becomes all the more clear when we learn that she has invited Alphonse to her home, a now middle-aged man with whom she had an affair twenty years prior. In this strange reunion, both Hélène and Alphonse seem invested in communicating a particular version of the past (often at odds with each other), especially concerning World War II, when their affair took place. Uncertainty, instability, and deception characterize their interactions (and the film as a whole), and we never know what to believe. The viewer is soon met with other uncertainties, as Hélène's true motivations for setting up this two-week visit are opaque. No one (including Hélène) will understand why she brought about this reunion, highlighting a confusion that is emblematic of the film's plot as a whole. Like Hélène, Alphonse also has a problematic relationship with the past. His past and present are a series of lies, beginning immediately upon his arrival, for he has brought with him Françoise, a young actress whom he introduces as his niece but who is actually his present mistress.[13] He also presents himself as having been a successful restaurateur in Algeria, saying that the fifteen years he spent in North Africa were the happiest of his life and that he only left because of the escalating conflict. The truth, as we will later learn, is that he never even set foot in Algeria.

In *Muriel* Algeria is spoken about, yet it never truly congeals into memories that can be adequately grasped and communicated. Commenting that in the film "there are two memories . . . each marked by a war: Boulogne and Algeria," Gilles Deleuze underscores the confusion inherent in the presentation of this temporal moment: Algeria refers to both the location in North Africa and the Algerian War, while Boulogne refers to the French city but must also refer to World War II and the destruction it unleashed upon this city.[14] A problematic relationship to the past, particularly to the overlap of World War II and the French-Algerian War, is made evident through a rapid montage technique of moving back and forth between these two moments. Street signs commemorating the French Resistance are presented alternately with images of newly built structures that symbolize the modernized city. This juxtaposition maps the two historical moments onto one another, emphasizing their urban overlaps, as well as their temporal proximity. However, through the choice of images, the film simultaneously evokes the idea that World War II was (and continues to be) highly commemorated, while the French-Algerian War is not.[15] Even though the conflict exists in the memories and imaginations of the film's characters, the city has no plaques to commemorate this war. The film can only represent the recent colonial past obtusely through the contemporary technologies and structures so emblematic of this technocratic society of the late 1950s and early 1960s—a newly imagined world order that was very much constructed in the face of decolonization. In Boulogne, as in other French cities, the narratives of decolonization and modernization became inextricably linked to one another in both time and space.

In a 1961 interview, Resnais spoke of the importance of fragmentation in the structuring and style of his films: "Modern life is full of ruptures, it's felt everywhere. Painting and literature bear witness to it, so why wouldn't cinema do so as well, instead of sticking to a traditional linear narrative?"[16] This "modern life" of which Resnais speaks is modernity at a very specific moment when both French and Algerian society were still reeling from destruction and decolonization. In a war that saw upward of one million casualties, those bodies that survived were literally and figuratively marked by the eight-year conflict. Some of those tortured were obliged to live with the scars and burns left on their bodies by the violence inflicted upon them. Others had no visible evidence to mark their simulated drownings and repeated electrocutions, for the military became increasingly vigilant about *not* leaving any trace of the violations inflicted on these bodies. French soldiers returning from the war also had to deal with traumas, both physical and mental, and many returned to a more modernized France with missing limbs, broken bodies, and haunting memories of the violent acts that they regularly witnessed and performed. French soldiers like Bernard were coming home to urban spaces that looked quite different from the way they had prior to the soldiers' deployment. Indeed, rebuilding for the future often requires replacing, razing, or even reinventing, and the reconstructed city of Boulogne provides the backdrop for this process of negotiating past, present, and future.

A patchwork of shattered and fragmented memories, Algeria cannot be related in any coherent language. In a similar vein, Lazreg writes of the linguistic challenges of speaking about a conflict that relied on an impossibility of being named:

> The grammar of euphemisms contained torture by sinking it below the level of consciousness, repressing its disturbing intrusion on the oft displayed stage of France's "civilizing mission." It released torture from its special status as an uncivilized method and floated it as one of many anonymous "exactations," reflecting the namelessness of the war itself. French officials and the press alike referred to the war as "Algeria's incidents." ... Tangled up in this orgiastic name-fixing was the French unease with acknowledging Algerians' identity. A French department (Algeria's official status) was inhabited by *French* people. But every French person knew that Algerians were not quite French, yet they needed to be thought of as such for France's own sense of identity.[17]

Bound up with the process of naming and misnaming, French identity shows itself to be rather tenuous and, in a Hegelian dialectical fashion, dependent on the construction of a lower hierarchical status for Algerians. In the film too, it becomes complicated to speak about Muriel, and stand-ins proliferate for this ever-absent woman, whose visual absence renders her ever-present. For example, before we learn who she actually was, Bernard speaks to Hélène of his supposed fiancée in the first minutes of the film:

BERNARD: I'm going to see Muriel.
HÉLÈNE: You'll be back for dinner, I hope.... Where did you meet this Muriel? Such a strange name.
BERNARD: She's ill now.
HÉLÈNE: Ah!
BERNARD: No, she isn't ill.[18]

The obscure dialogue suggests that mystery surrounds this woman, her name, and her health. Only later will we come to understand that *this* Muriel, the conflation of a murdered woman with a make-believe lover, is a figment of Bernard's imagination. In a way, this made-up relationship evidences a certain queerness, much in the way that Elizabeth Freeman writes that queer is about "living aslant to dominant forms of object-choice."[19] Nonetheless, this dynamic also evinces a point made by Emma Kuby that the contemporary postwar climate was marked by an anxiety that torturers would bring home to France diseased and sadistic forms of sexuality. This problematic construction, Kuby contends, also relied on a logic of displacement whereby attention was directed away from the suffering of Algerian victims to portray French torturers and families as those who were most damaged by torture, which, I contend, is also detectable in Resnais's choice to focus on the war's survivors rather than its victims.[20]

Muriel was not in fact the name of the woman to whom the word refers, and she was only given this French-sounding moniker (even if Hélène finds this to be "such a strange name") by those who violated her. While her agency and identity were symbolically and physically stripped (through both this misnaming and the violence inflicted on her body), calling this woman Muriel also created a certain proximity to Frenchness, even as her torture and death simultaneously highlighted the impossibility of her ever being truly "French." Lazreg refers to this as a failed Frenchness: "Torture was meant to beat the 'primitive' out of the failed Frenchness of the victim. The Algerian was seen as having been created by France, but failing to become French. Torture was meant to remake him [or her] into an obedient French colonial subject."[21] Despite her murder, Muriel will be posthumously made into such an obedient French subject: in the form of Bernard's imaginary fiancée. It is through this queering of kinship relations that he can ironically appear to embody a "healthy," heteronormative masculinity rather than a pathological manliness wherein he participates in this same woman's torture and murder. This desire to reconstitute his masculinity might also explain why "Muriel" might be used as the name of an imaginary girlfriend; she can live on as his fictional partner without causing his family and friends to question her ethnic background, as they will never meet.

Resnais's Modernist Mise en Abyme

Throughout the first half of the film, several oblique and vague references are made to Bernard's time as a soldier in Algeria and to the woman (mis)named Muriel, but it is not until halfway through that we finally learn from Bernard who she was.[22] His monologue begins as follows:

> Nobody knew this woman.... I can still see it. The shed was in the back, with the ammunition. I didn't see her at first. I stumbled over her as I went up to the table. She looked asleep, but she was trembling. They said her name was Muriel. It couldn't have been her real name. There were five of us around her discussing it. She had to talk before nightfall. Robert bent down and turned her over. Muriel moaned. She had her arm over her eyes. He let go, and she collapsed like a sack. Then it began again. She was dragged by her ankles to the middle of the shed. Robert kicked her. He pointed a flashlight toward her. Her lips were swollen and flecked with foam. Her clothes were ripped off. She was propped on a chair, but she fell. One arm was sort of twisted. It had to be finished. She was beyond talking, anyway. I hit her too. Muriel groaned under the blows. My hands hurt. Muriel's hair was all wet. Robert lit a cigarette and went up to her. She screamed. She stared at me. Why me? Then she closed her eyes and began to vomit.... I went back later. I lifted the cover. As if she'd been a long time in water... like a sack of potatoes split open. Blood all over her body, in her hair... burns on her breast. Muriel's eyes were open. I almost didn't care. Maybe I didn't care at all.[23]

The gravity of Bernard's description is undeniable. Muriel's body is at the center of his story; her raw corporeality (her eyes, lips, arm, and hair) and her bodily fluids (blood, vomit, and sweat) still obsess him. However, while her body is central, it is only the object of the story. The subject, as demonstrated by the use of the subject pronoun "I," is Bernard: "*I* can still see it," "*I* hit her too," "*I* went back later," "*I* lifted the cover." After he admits to slapping Muriel, the focus becomes the pain felt in *his* body, not hers. In a shift from the beginning of his monologue, when it was Muriel's gaze that singled him out, partway through, as he stares at her, she becomes the object of *his* gaze. It is precisely because he had found himself as the object of her gaze that here he feels the need to escape guilt by shifting the frame of reference, yet again removing her agency.

At this moment, there is a profound disconnect between the words we hear and the images we see. The film's screen literally becomes the screen for another film composed of very different images. Bernard's "confessional" and admission of his role in this woman's death is told to a mysterious old man dubbed Old Jean and is set against the backdrop of home movies. These images occupy the entire frame, seemingly inserted into the fictional film as documentary footage, but they are instead amateur videos presumably shot by Bernard during his time in Algeria. Yet this film-within-a-film is not composed of images of Muriel or of tortured bodies but rather, as Cayrol describes in the screenplay, of "blurry images of North Africa, very postcard-like."[24] Cayrol's choice to describe the images in this way is significant, given the appearance of actual postcards earlier in the film. During his first night in Boulogne, Alphonse, Hélène's guest, finds himself alone in her apartment, Hélène having strangely departed with her current lover. He begins to snoop around and comes across postcards of what appear to be the Algerian landscape, complete with sunny skies and palm trees. This leads him to a stack of documents belonging to Bernard: notes, journals, military papers, photographs. Most significant to this scene, however, is that we are given a preview of the above story of Muriel's torture and death, with Bernard's handwritten journal revealing what happened. As Alphonse flips through the pages, we can only attempt to piece together these linguistic fragments: ". . . grave very quickly. I lifted the cover. Muriel's eyes weren't closed ... It was with Muriel that everything really began, that I understood. Since Muriel I can't really live ... I'm lost. I think I want to die. Anyway, I'm no longer afraid of it ..."[25] The discrepancy between images and words in the scene containing Bernard's monologue and admission also highlights a certain impossibility of truly telling the story of Muriel or, more generally, telling the story of torture. Bernard can say the words, but there are no appropriate images to match his narrative. Emmanuel Levinas's elaboration on the relationship and break between the visual and the auditory is helpful in illuminating this discordance: "In sound, and in the consciousness termed hearing, there is in fact a break with the self-complete world of vision. . . . In its entirety, sound is a ringing, clanging scandal. Whereas, in vision, form is wedded to content in such a way as to appease it. In sound the perceptible quality overflows so that form can no longer contain its content. A real rent is produced, through which the world that is here prolongs a dimension that cannot be converted into vision."[26] For Levinas, the hermeneutics of sound is privileged over the hermetics of vision. Vision, associated with rationality and knowability, strives to capture what it represents, whereas sound always goes beyond, defying any attempt to contain it. In Levinasian terms, *Muriel*'s sounds of war elude representation, especially in light of the dissonance between the auditory and the visual. Additionally, for Levinas, sound moves us, and we feel its vibrations in our body. We feel Bernard's words, but his monotony of voice both betrays and magnifies the gravity of his narration's content. Even though the story he tells is contained, the reverberating narrative—itself located at the exact midpoint—bleeds through the rest of the film into all that precedes and follows.

Resnais's cinematic devices and the elliptical nature of the film's plot leave the viewer feeling unsettled and disturbed, much as Bernard felt upon his return to France. Yet despite the ability to portray violence, Resnais did not film the most serious form of violence contained in the film: the torture of Muriel. The violence of the unrepresentable is echoed in the violence of Resnais's filming and aesthetic strategies, particularly in the pairing of Bernard's narration of Muriel's torture and death with the screening of his amateur film footage. However, the modernist mise en abyme that is Bernard's film creates a metafiction: the internal duplication in *Muriel* allows it to talk about itself, adding a self-referential quality to Resnais's and Bernard's films, to the act of narration, and to the use, misuse, and abuse of images. The medium of cinema also allows that Muriel be conspicuously absent, that she *not* be seen. The absence of both torture and the title character is a glaring omission, but one that could be interpreted as Resnais pointing out a larger absence in the national consciousness.

We later encounter another discrepancy between the visual and the auditory that equally reinforces Muriel's visual absence. Toward the end of the film, Alphonse's lover Françoise comes across one such piece of evidence: a tape recorder belonging to Bernard. She jokingly asks if it contains "secrets or confessions," a question that prompts Bernard to slap her across the face (echoing the slap he confessed to having given Muriel), thereby suggesting that he may in fact be hiding something. Further complicating the situation, she then accidentally starts the tape, playing what we can assume is a recording of the torture session. The recording is not of screams of pain; instead, analogous to the images in Bernard's film, it contains sounds of soldiers laughing. Just like Bernard's retelling of Muriel's torture, the sound recording from the "interrogation" defies representation. In fact, Algeria (and all significations it carries with it) thwarts speech, always forestalling any capacity for true comprehension. It is this mise en abyme that, while evading and avoiding representing torture, subtly alludes to governmental silencing around the French-Algerian War. Indeed, Raphaëlle Branche has shown that the absence of torture scenes in the film resulted from direct censorship.[27] Although state censorship had been abolished with the founding of the Fifth Republic in 1958, declaring a state of emergency allowed for the reinstatement of that censorship. Numerous works depicting scenes of torture would be banned, including films such as Jean-Luc Godard's *The Little Soldier* (*Le petit soldat*) and texts such as Henri Alleg's *The Question* (*La question*).[28] During the war, Resnais also had personal experience with censorship. Before directing *Muriel*, he had commissioned Anne-Marie de Vilaine to write a story about Algeria in which "politics was articulated with sexual relations."[29] The screenplay about a young couple torn apart by the war would never be produced, however, for the censor's intervention forced him to abandon the project.

Returning to the scene in which Bernard confesses his role in Muriel's death, the "blurry images of North Africa" that provide the backdrop to the story recounted by Bernard are composed of film footage of troops firing heavy artillery, images of mosques, and depictions of quotidian activity of French troops joking among themselves. With the exception of the film's last scene, in which Simone (Alphonse's estranged wife) arrives at Hélène's home in search of her philandering husband, Bernard's amateur footage contains the film's only shots in which the camera is in motion. Resnais's aesthetic choice to shoot nearly the whole film in still shots speaks to a larger issue of psychological and somatic fragmentation in this social and political climate. In the post-Muriel epoch in which these characters live, they see themselves as immobile and unable to effect change in the past or present. They must stay in neat little boxes (which, ironically, are the sorts of structures that populate the landscape of the modernized city of Boulogne), just as they must stay within the frames of the film. Conversely, the use of moving shots suggests a freedom of movement of both body and camera. Like the blurry images and scenes of soldiers laughing, Bernard's handheld moving shots, albeit shaky, hark back to a recent past. The only other tracking shot used in the film does, however, open up some sort of hope for the future: although the film's main characters have dispersed around Boulogne or even fled the city entirely, Simone is able to move freely in the space, potentially demonstrating a break on the hold that the past has had on these memory addicts.

Blurred Bodies and Kaleidoscopic Consciousness

It is impossible to separate style and narrative in *Muriel*, for the film's fragmented plot is both reflected and exacerbated by its editing. Jump cuts, long takes, cutaways, oblique angle shots, and discontinuous cuts dominate, working to create a feeling of incompleteness, almost as if something has been omitted from the film. Through stylistic techniques such as rapid montage and lingering, almost voyeuristic, shots, Resnais's camera lends itself to reflecting on violence. His technique of using extreme close-ups of body parts, for example, has been read by some scholars as creating the effect of mutilation. The viewer is immediately confronted with this feeling of visual fragmentation and corporeal cutting in the opening sequence, as random objects rapidly alternate with hands and other body parts. These shots remove subjectivity and dislocate the camera's object from any living consciousness, yet they speak to larger social issues. According to Emma Wilson, "Through the intrusive cutting of the film, its restlessness, its challenge to order, its plangent music, *Muriel* appears to assault the viewer. This can certainly be read as a reflection on modern alienation and on the unease of this post-war French community."[30] Surprisingly, despite the film's obsession with memory and the past, there are no flashbacks—an absence that underscores the unrepresentability of memories.

While creating a feeling of unease for the viewer, the incoherent and, at times, kaleidoscopic filming simultaneously makes a strong statement about the film's topic matter. Bodies and psyches are broken, and the structure of the film itself describes the shattered existences of the characters. I will now turn to two such scenes that, through an overlapping of style and narrative, highlight the fragmentation of identity, including gender and nationality. The first scene is a brief moment, comprised of only seven seconds, in which we see Bernard through a kaleidoscope. The second is a bit more mysterious and depicts the fading into nothingness of a projected image of Algerian women. While the former highlights replication and duplication and the latter focuses on blurring and fading, they both point to the reality of the period's fractured existences.

Sandwiched between two much longer unrelated scenes, the kaleidoscope scene seems incongruous (as if any scene in the film actually "fits"). We quickly see an image of Bernard's actual girlfriend, Marie-Do, pointing a kaleidoscope in his direction (see fig. 1). The film's frame then shifts to what she is perceiving as she looks through the kaleidoscope's viewer: a colorful array of images, moving and shifting as she turns the kaleidoscope, that we can easily decipher to be Bernard.

This scene substantiates the film's investment in exploring the relationship to not only shattered but also indistinct and infinitely replicated and replaceable existences. In its kaleidoscopic approach, the entire project of *Muriel* might also, to use a Foucauldian framework, subvert the

1. *Muriel*: Bernard as seen through a kaleidoscope. Courtesy of Argos Films.

art of surveillance and refigure the diagram of power that existed both during and after the war.[31] Instead of setting up surveillance and power visually, like a pyramid or hierarchical structure, *Muriel* constructs it as a kaleidoscope, a circle, or a horizontal "plane," perhaps in an effort to diffuse the all-seeing, fascist-like gaze that existed in periods of censorship into a subjective, more democratic, yet, therefore, also less coherent visual experience. Bernard's earlier film-within-a-film also successfully draws attention to the fact that the film itself is a development process: you cannot see what is going on while you are experiencing it. In this way, the entire film (aided by the self-containedness of its static frames) functions as negatives from a roll of film, showing the inverse of the panoptic approach to filmmaking and questioning what a guard in Bentham's tower would have caught on tape. In *Muriel*, technologies (even "primitive" technologies like the kaleidoscope) diffuse power in order to create a direct tension with a systematic way of disciplining bodies. Despite the absence of the body of the tortured, the film and the film-within-the-film may represent a counter to official history.

2. *Muriel*: Projector scene. Courtesy of Argos Films.

In another curious scene later in the film, Hélène grows concerned about Bernard after fellow conscript Robert approaches her to inquire about Bernard's whereabouts. Against the backdrop of a foreboding and cacophonous soundtrack, she goes looking in his atelier and turns on a film projector. An image of several veiled women at an outdoor market flashes onto the wall, but immediately the image blurs and then disappears into nothingness (fig. 2).

A few seconds later, Bernard walks in and seems agitated to find his stepmother there:

BERNARD: It's strange to see you here.
HÉLÈNE: Will you show me a film?
BERNARD: I don't want to be a filmmaker. I'm gathering proof, that's all.
HÉLÈNE: Proof? Against whom?
BERNARD: You wouldn't understand.[32]

Bernard then stands in front of the screen onto which the images had just been projected, in effect replacing or standing in for the disappearing women's images that had faded moments before his arrival (fig. 3). He angrily tells Hélène to leave, but before exiting, she says: "You've been back for eight months, don't forget," an allusion to his inability to integrate back into society since his return from Algeria.[33] Bernard strangely utters: "Muriel isn't here, you know. Can you lend me three thousand francs?" To this Hélène responds: "I'm only interested in Muriel because of you."[34] Even though the image of the Algerian women had just strangely disappeared before her eyes, she does not seem disturbed or surprised and is only concerned with what directly affects her family, perhaps not dissimilar from the ways in which many French citizens preferred to turn a blind eye to the atrocities that were being committed across the Mediterranean Sea.

Ranjana Khanna writes of the ways in which representations of Algerian women were made to function in cinema: "The screen of visuality we observe in film is to be understood in terms of both what is seen and what is unseen on the scene of representation. . . . In many films about or from Algeria, the figure of woman encapsulates how filmic representation gestures toward that which it cannot represent. Its very constitution is made invisible."[35] Khanna's words approximate Resnais's project while also signaling linkages between representation and gender. The disappearance of the veiled women in the film found by Hélène, combined with Bernard's physicality in front of the disappearing image of Algerian women, suggests a larger crisis of masculinity occurring at this historical moment. As Fanon famously made clear, Algerian women had been used in particular ways by all sides of the conflict, and the female body itself was (re)colonized to function as a weapon used by men.[36] Algerian female bodies, I argue, also served as screens onto which French men could project their anxieties around colonial power and masculinity. In describing how this fits into larger dynamics of colonialism, Edward Said's concept of Orientalism becomes key: "European culture gained its strength and identity by setting itself off against the Orient as a sort of surrogate and even underground self."[37] As Sandra Ponzanesi and Marguerite Waller write, the inferiorized Orient became "the screen onto which Europe could project its own disallowed fears and desires. The

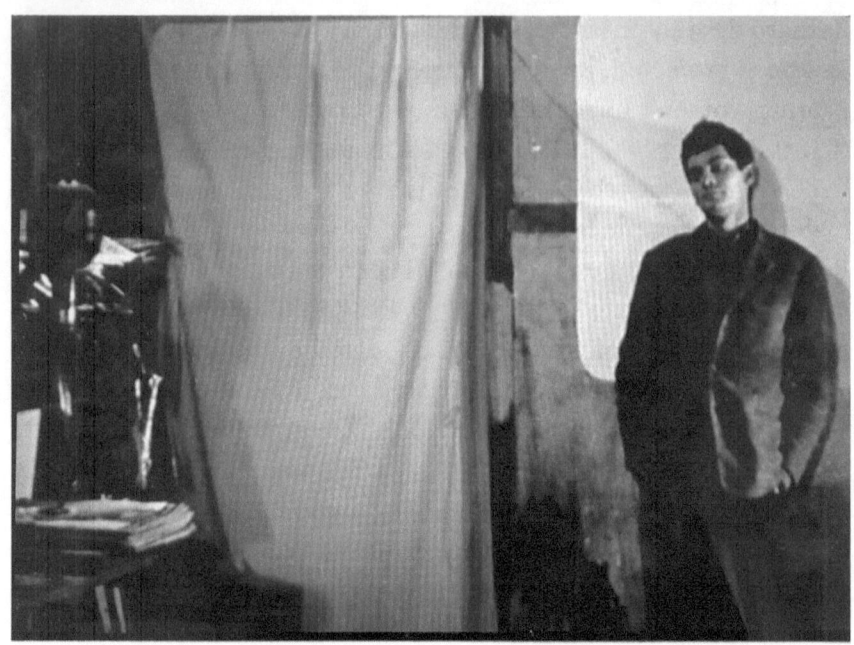

3. *Muriel*: Bernard in front of the projector screen. Courtesy of Argos Films.

representation of the Arab or Asian as mysterious, exotic, and seductive was coupled with the idea that they were inherently barbaric, criminal, and dangerous, set outside the frame of modernity, poised in a timeless space."[38] This literal and figurative projection thereby positioned French male soldiers as being able to discount or dispose of Algerian women's agency while simultaneously reinforcing, through military rank and the use of violence, their own status as virile men. Yet here, in the scene depicted in figure 3, it is curiously the opposite, as Bernard steps into the place where these images had been projected. He positions his body in the exact spot where the projected image of Algerian women faded away, underscoring the notion that (French) hegemonic masculinity was being (re)constructed against (Algerian) femininity and its dissolution. It is this reversal that allows us to see his fragility as he strives to embody some semblance of a healthy masculinity. However, the fissures and anxieties in this uncertain and unstable system are made clear as Muriel imprinted herself on him, causing him to fail at this form of colonial masculinity.[39]

Haunted, or Masculinity in Crisis

In *Ghostly Matters: Haunting and the Sociological Imagination*, Avery Gordon compellingly writes of the power possessed by ghosts, who are themselves not merely the dead or missing but social figures. She elaborates how ghosts' modus operandi—haunting—shapes subjectivity and affect: "The way of the ghost is haunting, and haunting is a very particular way of knowing what has happened or is happening. Being haunted draws us affectively, sometimes against our will and always a bit magically, into the structure of feeling of a reality we come to experience, not as cold knowledge, but as a transformative recognition."[40] Bernard is, in Gordon's terms, haunted by Muriel's ghost and by all for which she stands as she pulls on his emotions, provoking in him such a transformative and affective recognition. In his recounting, Bernard is particularly fixated on that instant at which he and Muriel locked eyes, for it was then that she saw him for who he was: a representative of the French colonial project and a torturer. She stared at him imploringly, forcing him to make a choice about saving her from the inevitable torture to follow, but he did nothing, and now he is haunted by her condemning gaze and her destroyed body. Although he seems to feel some responsibility for not halting the torture, his self-interrogation ("Why me?") has the potential effect of erasing the possibility of guilt in its suggestion that there is no reason for him to be singled out. Via his introspection (which will continue to haunt him), Bernard positions himself as both subject and object of the scene, for he knows there could be a reason why she stared so intently at him. While the question demonstrates the possibility of replacement (i.e., Why me? Why not another?), it simultaneously signals the singularity of his situation. He *felt* her stare so profoundly that it remained with him even upon his return to France. Hence, Deleuze's commentary makes sense: "The character in Resnais' cinema is Lazarean precisely because he returns from death, from the land of the dead; he has passed through death and is born from death, whose sensory-motor disturbances he retains."[41] To cope with what Deleuze would identify as the war's death-giving forces and to manage anxiety about his own annihilation, Bernard must work to save Muriel's memory and expose the injustices done to this woman and her tortured body, even as he struggles to rid himself of the sensory-motor disturbances that haunt him.

Bernard's existence becomes consumed by telling Muriel's story, which will come in the form of an indictment of his fellow soldier Robert, who forced him to be implicated in this act that would result in him being, as he puts it, "disfigured by the war." This disfigurement proves the most threatening, as Bernard will search for a way to reconstitute his masculinity, which eventually results in him committing a deadly act: he murders Robert. The fact that Bernard will never be successful in exposing the story of Muriel's torture is symptomatic of the larger diversion of memory and a preference to forget war crimes committed, as well as other memories that threaten (the façade of) a self-assured national identity and robust masculinity. Indeed, his quest often looks more like a search for absolution for his own crimes rather than an attempt to bring any justice to the situation. While Bernard will not be successful in exposing the information we are yearning for (i.e., who murdered Muriel and why), the act of assassinating Robert will do a different sort of work—that of shoring up a sense of masculinity that Bernard seems to have lost with the death of Muriel. Through his earlier sensitivity (often stereotyped as "feminine") to Muriel's pain and his figurative and literal detachment from his fellow soldiers (who participate in "masculine" activities like firing artillery, while he prefers to be behind his camera), Bernard has also distanced himself from what it means to be a man in this postwar period of international crises. He appears less interested in engaging in the violent acts that Robert embraces and more invested in exposing the fragility of human bodies and psyches. Having perhaps failed at "being a man," he attempts to restore a veneer of masculinity, perhaps a more self-righteous version, by acting as a whistleblower and incriminating his fellow conscripts, who killed at least this one individual.

Robert states early in the film, "You want to tell Muriel's story? But Muriel can't be told," and then later, "Algeria is all over for us. . . . We're in France. The main thing is for every Frenchman to feel alone, scared. He'll erect barbed wire around his little ego. He doesn't want trouble." These words again call attention to the inarticulacy and amnesiac tendency of war, for Robert places Muriel's story (and others like it) "in the realm of the *intransmissable*, or more particularly in the realm of that which will be repressed and silenced on return to France."[42] Here, Robert is simultaneously pointing to the fact that Frenchness (or perhaps French masculinity) is crucially at stake and is tied up with fear and individual and collective identity and accountability. Robert's statements become a wake-up call for Bernard, as he realizes nothing can be done to change the past and that perhaps no one *wants* to know Muriel's story. Despite Bernard's intention to incriminate those responsible for her torture and murder, Robert's words, combined with the realization of his powerlessness to change the past and repair the future, have drastic consequences for him. Instead of exposing the fact of Muriel's torture and death, Bernard later tracks down Robert, the only link he still has to his time in Algeria, and shoots and kills him, an act that seems to only reinforce his own complicity in the crimes of war.[43]

It is, however, with tears streaming down his cheeks that he assassinates Robert, the only individual in Boulogne who had shared with him those horrors. After killing Robert, Bernard renounces his efforts to represent the torture by throwing his ever-present camera into the sea, erasing any possibility that he might be able to bring Muriel's story to light. Like Françoise's half-joking statement that planted in the viewer a seed of doubt over what else Bernard might have done in Algeria, this act also forces us to question what might have been on that camera of which he rid himself. Might it have contained images of Muriel's tortured, destroyed, and dead body?

Muriel uncovers how guilt, collaboration, and the committing of unspoken (and unrepresentable) acts such as torture during the French-Algerian War led to the fragmentation of selves, bodies, and minds. Resnais's film speaks to the ways in which memory is structured and how images are repressed so as not to disturb the façade of sanity and national cohesiveness, a process in which masculinity becomes key. It was not haphazard that Resnais chose to focus on a female torture victim, nor was it an oversight to never actually represent her in the film. Although the torture scene is not represented visually, its haunting presence also echoes the idea that the Algerian female body functioned as a screen onto which French men could project their anxieties around colonial power and masculinity. Just like the replicable structures built up throughout the city of Boulogne, the film's impenetrable characters appear as mere façades without interior consciousness moving through the world. However, this appearance of emptiness is false and is instead a defense mechanism and self-preservation strategy to cope with this generation's process of self-searching in the wake of war, decolonization, modernization, and changing masculinities. These representative characters are projectors, casting violence onto colonized others, who serve as screens on which the characters can work through their anxieties. Yet these characters are also screens themselves, being imprinted upon and inevitably absorbing the pain and upheaval circulating throughout this period of decolonization.

Epilogue: *The Wound*

As Alain Resnais's *Muriel* makes clear, soldiers returning to France struggled to convey the unspeakable nature of war while simultaneously wanting to bury their shame about crimes committed during the conflict. By way of an extended conclusion, I want to build upon these themes to further explore the interrelationship between memory, masculinity, and violence. Whereas Resnais's film examined the fractured experiences of a French conscript returning to 1960s France, the novel to which I now turn engages with constructions of masculinity in twenty-first-century postcolonial France.

In Laurent Mauvignier's award-winning novel *The Wound*, we fast-forward to the late 2000s to tell the story of another former soldier, also named Bernard, who is in his midsixties and is silently grappling with the trauma of serving in North Africa decades earlier. While the characters' shared given name may be coincidental, this Bernard seems almost an extension of *Muriel*'s Bernard. These two Bernards—which I read as one—exemplify the fractured subjectivity confronted by an entire generation, a destabilization that would go on to have profound implications for thinking about identity, particularly gender, sexuality, nationality, and race. Mauvignier summarized this crisis over identity currently taking place in postcolonial France: "The Algerian War is not over. The National Front, that's the Algerian War. The comments that we hear today, this racism, the idea that a French person can't be Algerian—and an Algerian can't be French—it's really the original question of the war. And we can see how in France today this question isn't settled."[44] Prior to *The Wound*, his seventh novel, Mauvignier had received critical acclaim for earlier works, most notably *In the Crowd* (*Dans la foule*, 2006). Throughout his oeuvre, he has maintained an agenda of stylistic innovation while exploring the themes of loss, mourning, and the limits of language. *The Wound* builds upon these motifs and, through its enigmatic style, interrogates the ways in which the French-Algerian War emerges decades later and poses larger questions about what it means to live in a postcolonial epoch.

While centering on the current lives of former French conscripts who served in Algeria, the novel also uncovers the memory problems that the war still poses for later generations, including Mauvignier himself, who was not born until five years after the conflict had ended. Although his father served in Algeria, he did not speak of his time there, and Mauvignier would rely on his mother's little knowledge of her husband's ordeals to make sense of what he had undergone during his time in North Africa. His father later committed suicide, and from this personal tragedy emerged *The Wound*, as Mauvignier attempted to use writing to make sense of the war and his father's death: "It took me years to say that, perhaps, the fact of having participated in the war and having seen those things contributed to his suicide. He spent twenty-eight months there, that's not nothing. I also heard stories about guys who went crazy. It might seem like a cliché, but I was also interested in finding a way, technically, to speak about these clichés."[45]

Although published as *The Wound* in English, the exact translation of Mauvignier's French title, *Des hommes*—"Men" or, alternatively, "Some Men" or "Of Men"—highlights the importance placed on masculinity in testimonies and fiction about the war. The title of the English translation is taken from the epigraph, a quote from Jean Genet's *The Tightrope Walker* (*Le funambule*): "And your wound, where is your wound? I wonder where it is hidden, the secret wound where every man runs to take shelter if his pride is violated, when it is wounded. That wound—which has become his inner self—is what he will inflate and fill. Every man knows how to find it and inhabit it so completely that he becomes the wound itself, a kind of secret, aching heart."[46] Pain, heartache, and masculinity cannot be separated for the characters of Mauvignier's novel, nor could they have been for the protagonist of *Muriel*; by inhabiting these wounds, men become them.

Mauvignier's multivalent title suggests that, despite the level of violence seen and enacted, these soldiers still remain *simply men*. Nonetheless, they will be constantly compelled to prove their masculinity both during and after the war, whether through enacting violence or by burying the scarring emotions that the war carved into their consciousness. The text also poses larger questions about humanity and what "man" is capable of, as the following lines highlight: "Because, it's, to do what they did, I don't think you can say it, I don't think you can even imagine saying it, it's so far from anything, to do that, and yet they did that, men, men did that, without pity, without anything human, men took an ax to kill, they mutilated the father, the arms, they ripped off his arms, and they opened the mother's belly and—."[47] A similar sentiment is echoed earlier in the novel: "What kind of men can do that. The people who do that are not men. And yet. They are men."[48]

The overall structure of the text is rather rigid: told in four "acts" ("Afternoon," "Evening," "Night," and "Morning"), the narrative complies with standards for a tragedy and takes place over the course of twenty-four hours. Despite this clear structure, the text often eludes comprehension in its temporal spiraling as it attempts to pinpoint the origin of troubling behavior in the present, plunging further into night and its senseless (and enumerated) violence, where, like in a dream, nothing makes sense. While Resnais stated that the characters of *Muriel* "will be seen from the outside. We will never penetrate the thoughts and minds of our characters. These will show themselves only through their actions," in *The Wound* we plunge headfirst into the consciousness of several protagonists in this quest for explanations.[49]

The novel opens with a party for Solange, who has just retired and turned sixty. The mood is light and jovial until the arrival of Bernard, Solange's sixty-three-year-old brother, whose mere presence disrupts the celebratory atmosphere. Bernard, once a quiet and romantic young man with ambitions to open a garage in Paris (a hope that far exceeded that of his peers from the insular village in which he grew up), has disappeared behind the moniker Woodsmoke (Feu-de-Bois), a nickname that describes his horrid stench. After he returned from his required military service in Algeria, his life began to fall apart. His pent-up rage resulted in him slowly destroying his family life, eventually causing him to abandon his wife, Mireille, and their two children and to insult one of his sisters on her deathbed. Now a clochard, or vagrant, he is a stigma to his small French village of La Bassée. Upon arriving at this party, much to everyone's surprise, he offers Solange, the only remaining family member from whom he is not estranged, a gold brooch, a seemingly simple act that ignites a series of events that will take us back to the source of Bernard's troubled existence decades earlier. Solange refuses the gift, as she (and everyone else) assumes it must be stolen, since Bernard could never afford such an object. Furious over this refusal, Bernard gets into an altercation with Chefraoui, a local villager of Maghrebi origin, which ultimately prompts Bernard to commit violence toward this man's family. In the next section of the novel, entitled "Evening," we witness Bernard break into Chefraoui's house and terrorize his family, nearly raping his wife.

The first half of the novel is narrated by Rabut, Bernard's cousin and fellow conscript with whom he served in Algeria. Bernard's present behavior provokes Rabut to recall a forgotten past: the twenty-eight months they spent in Algeria are the key to explaining Bernard's tumultuous history, as well as his recent explosive behavior, demonstrating how traces of the war remain just under the surface and constantly threaten to emerge in violent ways. Through Rabut, we learn that Chefraoui reminds Bernard of Abdelmalik, a *harki* who betrayed their battalion during the war.[50] This realization results in a host of memories flooding the text as we begin to see possible explanations for Bernard's present violence and slowly witness how his life spiraled out of control following his time spent as a conscript in Algeria.

In the first two sections of the novel, the writing is nervous and polyphonic, often difficult to follow. Unfinished sentences abound, and the text constantly moves between oral and written language, between monologue and free indirect discourse, reflecting a larger hesitancy to speak coherently about a shameful past. Although Algeria is not even mentioned until a third of the way into the novel and is often only referred to as "over there" ("là-bas"), it is always just under the surface, occupying the space of the unspoken. This sentiment is summarized by Rabut, the narrator, as he attempts to explain why Bernard would have targeted Chefraoui and his family: "It's impossible to know. But we already know. We've known all along. Since, I mean—ever since—but that's something else, that time back there. Just something, something I'm thinking, which slips in and blurs this moment of our personal history when all of a sudden it's there, like a forty-year-old score to settle, forty years, the age of a mature man, when we look at ourselves and tell ourselves no, it's not over, we thought it was over but it wasn't."[51] As evidenced by this passage, the novel's stylistic agenda speaks to the many silences—governmental, historical, and personal—as it attempts to represent the language-defying nature of the war in particular and memory in general. Soldiers returning to France struggled to convey the unspeakable nature of the war, to express themselves, to speak in coherent speech while simultaneously wanting to conceal disgrace surrounding crimes committed during the war.

The Wound then moves from the growing darkness of "Evening" to pitch-black "Night," and with it there is a temporal and geographical shift to Algeria, 1960. This night sequence brings us back to the past and mingles time in such a way that we can no longer fully separate present from past or even future. While I will more fully explore queer and postcolonial temporality in chapters 3 and 4, it is already worth noting here that the French-Algerian War offers an exemplary site for exploring the fiction of linearity and teleological progress, a hallmark of both queer and postcolonial approaches to memory and temporality. In the text's slow, psychoanalytical descent into the origin of Bernard's present-day behavior, we are, true to the title of this third act, plunged into "Night," the time of day when we dream and have nightmares. The narration becomes more lucid as an omniscient narrator takes over from Rabut. First focalized through Bernard, the omniscient perspective then shifts back to Rabut and eventually to Février, another fellow soldier from the same village in which they all now reside. Not only are we presented with a clear portrait of the novel's principal characters several decades earlier, we also become privy to their thoughts and feelings as they arrive for military duty. Their lives changed as soon as they boarded the boat that took them across the Mediterranean, exemplified in this passage focalized through Bernard: "He senses a longer, louder sound resonating in the very depths of his being, it seems to him, it even makes his hands sweat and for once he meets the livid gaze of another draftee who, like him, like them, knows that from that moment on, his whole life will be perforated by the sound of the siren announcing their departure."[52] The naivete of the soldiers is highlighted through the general ignorance they display toward the land in which they are to spend more than two years of their lives. Among the violence, however, there remain moments of innocence—like when we see that their only pleasure is taking out of their wallets photos of their girlfriends or fiancées—and we are reminded that many of these men are barely twenty years old.

Yet perhaps even more touching is the friendship we learn that Bernard developed with a young Algerian girl named Fatiha whose family lived on the army base and aided the French military. In an attack that was likely the result of Bernard's and Rabut's actions (they caused their platoon to return late to their base following a four-day leave), Fatiha and her family—along with several of Bernard's comrades—were brutally murdered by Algerian freedom fighters. When Bernard returned home to his own village years later after having abandoned his wife and children, he only brought with him photos taken during his time in Algeria (including photos of Fatiha), with which he decorated his walls. Seeming to momentarily forget the constant silence surrounding their time in Algeria, Rabut describes the shock and anger he experienced when he first saw those photos twenty years after the war: "[Bernard] dared to frame them, hang them on the wall, show them there, and not say a word about them, say nothing, as if they were vacation pictures, say nothing about them to me, to me, who he'd seen so often over there and shared the—"[53] However, as Marianne Hirsch reminds us, photographic images are more than merely indexical; they are also symbolic and indicative of our needs and desires.[54] As they did for *Muriel*'s Bernard, the photos reference the hopes, desires, and anxieties these men continued to carry. Also similar to the protagonist of *Muriel*, who visually documented his time spent in Algeria, Rabut too used photography as a survival tool in order to attempt to escape his wartime reality: "I thought that in Algeria I had put the camera in front of my eyes only to prevent myself from seeing, or only tell myself I was doing something—let's say, useful. Maybe. Afterward, I never took pictures again."[55]

From there, the text seems to evolve into a film, as the next sequences, in which these young soldiers are thrust into a series of incomprehensibly violent acts, are told with cinematic focus and detail. In the first episode, French soldiers invade an Algerian village, running and screaming "to buck themselves up, to frighten . . . surprised that with guns in their hands they're the ones who seem frightened."[56] Demanding information on the location of rebel munitions, they then begin to interrogate a young boy, who cannot understand them because he does not speak French. Even after threatening torture, they learn nothing and eventually leave. However, moments later, one of the soldiers returns and shoots the boy in the head. A litany of senseless acts follows—soldiers kicking random women and children while their village burns and a lieutenant grabbing a baby by the neck, asking where its father is, and then throwing the baby on the ground "like a pit you spit out after rolling it around in your mouth for a long time."[57] In many ways, this section is like an endless nightmare of violence or, as Norbert Czarny terms it, "a litany, a parade of horrors, a sort of perpetual nightmare."[58] The next line of the text typifies the level of violence French soldiers and Algerian civilians encountered every day: "And then they'll keep going, to the next village."[59]

The interminable violence that Resnais's protagonist encountered and enacted during his time in Algeria was not unlike the brutal and life-altering experiences of the former soldiers of *The Wound*. Following the nightmarish sequence of "Night," we awake with Rabut from these horrid memories, but they never truly disappear: "Even if I wake up and get out of bed, neither the anxiety nor the images go away."[60] In the next and final section of the text, "Morning," we return to the present as Rabut reflects on these forgotten memories while attempting to come to terms with how the war continues to mold the lives of this generation of men, who served decades earlier. Like *Muriel*, the novel concludes with an uncertainty about the past, present, and future:

> I would like to see if Algeria exists and if I, too, had left something more than my youth back there. I'd like to see, I don't know. I'd like to see if the air is as blue as in my memories.... I'd like to see something that doesn't exist but lives inside yourself, something you keep like a dream, a resonant, palpitating world, I would like to, I don't know. I never knew what I wanted, there, in the car, just not hear the bombardments or the screams anymore, not know what a charred body smells like anymore, or the smell of death—I'd like to know if you can begin to live when you know it's already too late.[61]

Rabut's desire to "see" (*voir* in French), which he repeats four times, leads to a desire to "know" (*savoir* in French, containing the same root): his hope is that seeing Algeria will be the key to knowing if he can finally live. His speech, however, is choppy, broken up, and filled with short clauses and ellipses, reminding us that he still lives in the post-Algeria epoch, where language is uncertain and violent acts often replace articulate speech. Although they have attempted to forget, these men are haunted by the still-present past.

Together, *Muriel* and *The Wound* reveal the long-lasting trauma and the multiple ways in which the French-Algerian War remains so palpable today. Reading the two texts in succession gives us some indication of how the lives of *Muriel*'s characters might have developed, as well as how the shattering of masculinity and subjectivity continues to have an impact decades later. *Muriel* and *The Wound* are also concerned with the burden of being a witness to—but also of participating in—literal and symbolic acts of violence in the name of the collective (e.g., nationality) and the personal (e.g., masculinity). While these men are unquestionably traumatized, I want to propose that we think instead about the ways in which these individuals and subsequent generations are *haunted* and how this haunting may allow for new and different ways of embodying identity and subjectivity.

Here I turn once again to Gordon's *Ghostly Matters*, in which she uses the metaphor of ghosts and haunting as a way into a theoretical exploration of the idea that "life is complicated."[62] Gordon continues by pointing to the productive potential of haunting, "precisely the domain of turmoil and trouble, that moment (of however long duration) when things are not in their assigned places, when the cracks and rigging are exposed, when the people who are meant to be invisible show up without any sign of leaving, when disturbed feelings cannot be put away, when something else, something different from before, seems like it must be done."[63] Although haunting is a frightening experience that marks social violence, it is distinguished by its capacity to instigate change and transformation.[64] Both *Muriel* and *The Wound* similarly haunt us, producing a "something-to-be-done" from which we cannot look away in this postcolonial era, a theme that will be more fully explored in the next chapter.

2 "You'll Never Give Me a Bad Conscience!"

Masculinity and Postcolonial Guilt in *Caché*

In Paris on October 17, 1961, one of the most hidden acts of colonial violence exercised on European soil occurred, claiming the lives of hundreds of Algerian-born French citizens. Occasionally called the Paris Massacre of 1961 or the 1961 Paris Pogrom, the event was, according to historians Jim House and Neil MacMaster, "the bloodiest act of state repression of street protest in Western Europe in modern history."[1] Only recently have memories of October 17, 1961, begun to enter the French public consciousness and historical memory. Historical accounts and testimonies have started to appear, and restrictions on access to related police archives have been relaxed. Memory activism has taken many forms, with associations like In the Name of Memory (Au nom de la mémoire) and October 17, 1961: Against Forgetting (17 octobre 1961: contre l'oubli) emerging and creating websites to post testimonies of both participants and victims of the massacre. Even a song by French rapper Médine was devoted to the event ("17 octobre").

The efforts made by writers, artists, and historians to rescue from oblivion colonial acts of violence such as October 17 reflect a much more global cultural and literary obsession with remembering (and forgetting) the past. While this "memory boom" may appear as a new phenomenon, its legacy can be traced back to sociologist Maurice Halbwachs's early twentieth-century work, which posited memory as a collective rather than an individual experience. In the preface to his seminal *On Collective Memory*, Halbwachs states: "If we enumerate the number of recollections during one day that we have evoked upon the occasion of our direct and indirect relations with other people, we will see that, most frequently, we appeal to our memory only in order to answer questions which others have asked us, or that we suppose they could have asked us. . . . Most of the time, when I remember, it is others who spur me on; their memory comes to the aid of mine and mine relies on theirs."[2] This chapter reflects on this tension between individual and collective memory—and the corollary, individual and collective amnesia—in a recent treatment of October 1961: Michael Haneke's 2005 film *Caché (Hidden)*. While other works have been interested in reconstructing the events of October 17, Austrian director Haneke's French-language film takes the notion of French colonial violence a step further, making the massacre metonymic of multiple forms of state-imposed violence and hidden national memories that are not unique to France. Like other texts I analyze throughout this book, *Caché* struggles with the hauntological confluence of past, present, and future, signaling how the silencing of the massacre would go on to have direct effects on both French and Algerian masculinity while simultaneously exposing how individual and collective memories are inextricably linked. The film leaves the viewer uncertain about what to do with this troubling information, but I argue that it is through such destabilization that colonial ghosts intervene in the present historical moment, which, as I discuss in the epilogue, has come in the form of deadly terrorist acts such as the 2015 attacks on *Charlie Hebdo*. While many have linked these acts of terrorism to the emergence of radical Islam on the stage of world politics, such argumentation overlooks a key component to any understanding of the attacks: the French-Algerian War.

Between Citizenship and Statelessness

After years of war, the French relinquishment of Algeria seemed almost a foregone conclusion by late 1961. Nevertheless, the last months prior to Algerian independence saw an increase in attacks and bombings in both the colony and the metropole. On October 5, Paris Police Chief Maurice Papon (who had previously served as prefect of the Constantine department in Algeria and two decades prior to that had played a key role in the deportation of approximately fifteen hundred French Jews under the Vichy regime) announced the introduction of a curfew that forbade Algerians from leaving their homes at night. While the curfew targeted "Algerian Muslim workers," "French Muslims," and "French Muslims of Algeria," the new law in effect became a form of racial profiling, as any individual who *appeared* Algerian was subject to arrest if found in the streets at night—and this was despite the fact that Algerians were French citizens. Nearly two centuries after the ratification of the Declaration of the Rights of Man and of the Citizen (1789), Algerians' rights (which had already been slowly stripped away over the course of the war) were undeniably violated by the curfew's establishment and subsequent strict limitations of movement. Tens of thousands of Algerians marched on October 17, 1961, to protest against the curfew, but the peaceful demonstration soon turned into a deadly massacre at the hands of French police forces.

Hannah Arendt's seminal work on the twentieth-century failure of human rights has been instrumental in allowing us to think about the relationship between transnational political crises, citizenship, and statelessness.[3] For Arendt, statelessness equals rightlessness, and rightlessness places one's membership in the human community under question. Algerians, by virtue of their ambiguous status at this historical moment, could be characterized as "stateless," and their loss of citizenship resulted in a loss of humanity that deprived them of rights. Drawing upon Arendt, Susan Maslan comments on the relationship this formulation has with the category of "the human": "For Arendt, the tragic irony of human rights is that when one loses one's status as a citizen—a process that often entails a loss of fixed residence, a loss of community, a loss of occupation or profession, a loss of one's place within a known social structure—one ceases to be human."[4] Indeed, with the instatement of the curfew, Algerians risked losing all of this, and, due to such deprivation, they were metaphorically and literally (although not exactly legally) confronted with the loss of citizenship. It is also worth noting that many Algerians arrested during and after the events of October 17, 1961, were sent back to Algeria, the land that France was trying so desperately to hold on to. This "immediate repatriation," as it was termed, becomes rather ironic and prompts the question: How can one be repatriated from France to Algeria when Algeria is French?

In *The Origins of Totalitarianism*, Arendt discusses the Nazi persecution of German Jews: "The point is that a complete condition of rightlessness was created before the right to live was challenged."[5] Applying this statement to French Algeria, many Algerians also found their right to live threatened by being deprived of the benefits of French citizenship. In having their rights slowly stripped away, Algerians were seen as increasingly less "human" and more "animal." *Raton*, or "rat," for example, became a common pejorative term with which to refer to North Africans.[6] Thus, this animalism also conveniently served as a justification for less than equal treatment. As an Arendtian formulation would argue, it was this process of dehumanization that made Algerians seem more disposable.

Returning to the events of October 17, the French branch of the FLN called for a peaceful demonstration to protest the curfew, and approximately thirty to forty thousand Algerian men, women, and children marched along the *grands boulevards* of central Paris to assert their place as French citizens deserving of liberty, equality, and fraternity. The FLN's loftier goal was to attract domestic and international attention to the injustices that the French government was imposing on its own citizens while simultaneously claiming physical space that had been restricted. What began as a peaceful protest (by all accounts, the demonstrators were unarmed, as demanded by the FLN) soon turned into a bloody massacre; many police officers, all of whom were armed with sticks capable of fracturing a skull with a single blow, were encouraged to take matters into their own hands and violently handle their personal "grievances" with Algerians. Papon gave carte blanche to his police force: "Settle your affairs with the Algerians yourselves. Whatever happens, you're covered. . . . Even if the Algerians are not armed, you should think of them always as armed."[7] Still surprising, however, is the extreme level of violence enacted by the police that night. Numerous unconscious demonstrators were infamously thrown into the Seine River, hands tied, and left to drown.[8] A total of 11,518 individuals were arrested (totaling 14,000 by the end of the week), and many of them were rounded up and transported to large stadiums, such as the Palais des sports.[9] Police made sure, however, that all prisoners were evacuated by October 20, when a Ray Charles concert was scheduled to take place there. On the day of the concert, *France-Soir* wrote: "Ray Charles will be able to sing tonight. After having been disinfected, the Palais des sports returned to its usual appearance."[10] In an event that, by FLN estimates, resulted in 200 Algerians killed, 400 disappeared, and 2,300 injured, not one police officer was ever prosecuted. French police reports only acknowledged three deaths, two caused by police agents in self-defense, and the other due to cardiac arrest. Years later, an officer involved in the massacre would continue this public denial: "Drowning Algerians? That never existed.... When we were in pursuit of the leaders of the FLN on the banks of the river, it sometimes happened that they threw themselves into the Seine while trying to flee."[11]

Despite the FLN's efforts to emphasize the violence and prejudices systematically directed at Algerians, the protest and the massacre were virtually forgotten on both individual and collective levels. Even Algerians seemed to have a strong desire to forget this day, as one of the main characters in Leïla Sebbar's *The Seine Was Red* (which will be treated at more length in chapter 4) states: "Who wants to listen to the story of that day, October 17, 1961? Who? Neither the French nor the Algerians, neither immigrants nor native-born nationals."[12] Yet this forgetting adds another layer of symbolic violence to the event. Indeed, literary scholar Jonathan Crewe is right when he summarizes one of the significant implications we can draw from Halbwachs's theory of collective memory, namely, that "the alienation or exclusion of any individual from social memory will be tantamount to both social extinction and deprivation of identity."[13]

Postcolonial Haunting

While leaving conspicuously absent many official and unofficial historical details of October 1961, Haneke's film highlights the pervasive divergence of postcolonial temporality and emphasizes how European colonialism continues to constitute memory, space, and the very idea of Europe. While Algeria is largely unnamed in *Caché*, the colonial massacre and the issue of collective responsibility haunt the narrative, demonstrating the episode's far-reaching effects many decades later. Garnering three awards at the Cannes Film Festival and starring two of the biggest stars in French cinema, Daniel Auteil and Juliette Binoche, the film was marketed as "a psychological thriller about a TV talk show host and his wife who are terrorized by surveillance videos of their private life."[14] Despite this marketing campaign, which portrayed the film as yet another blockbuster tale of suspense, writer and director Haneke professed that the film is ultimately about a more universal concern: the relationship between the repression of collective memory and the suppression of personal memories.[15]

Caché opens with a three-minute-long take of a gated home on a mundane Parisian street, immediately transmitting a sense of mystery and voyeurism. The next scene follows a man (played by Auteil) emerging from the gated home (this time in darkness) to look around concernedly. The film then returns to the original shot but begins to rewind itself, revealing that we were watching a video-recorded image all along. In this opening sequence, Haneke abandons traditional principles of film structure and composition, leaving the viewer unsettled about who is in control of the camera. Soon after, we are introduced to the Laurents, a Parisian bourgeois family who one day received on their doorstep the mysterious videotape that we just watched. Similar monitoring tapes soon arrive, which are followed by childlike drawings depicting bloody scenes of violence. Confusion turns into fear as the previously insular lives of Georges, Anne, and their adolescent son, Pierrot, are threatened by the inexplicable surveillance they are now under. New tapes and some detective work on the part of the couple lead Georges to a housing project, where, as secretly suspected by Georges, he finds Majid, an Algerian man of a similar age. Georges hides the meeting from his wife, telling her that the apartment is unoccupied—a lie that is soon uncovered when the family receives a videotape of heated dialogue between Georges and Majid. Thanks to this initial encounter, as well as a conversation that Georges has with his bedridden mother, we learn that Majid was the son of an Algerian couple who worked for Georges's family decades earlier when the two were young boys. A brief yet explanatory allusion to the French-Algerian War is made halfway through the film when Georges finally tells his wife how he knows this man, whom Georges believes to be the author of the tapes: "His parents worked for us. Dad liked them. I guess they were good workers. In October '61, the FLN called all Algerians to a demonstration in Paris. October 17, 1961. Enough said. Papon. The police massacre. They drowned about two hundred Arabs in the Seine. Including Majid's parents most likely. They never came back."[16]

Certain memories—real, fantasized, mediated, recuperated, and forgotten—complicate the postcolonial safe space in which the Laurents reside and in which anything unpleasant is kept out of the frame of viewing. Much as Alain Resnais uses the mise en abyme in *Muriel* (see chapter 1), Haneke deploys this cinematic strategy to ultimately subvert this insular sense of security. In his incisive study of *Caché*'s postcolonial dimensions, Hamish Ford analyzes the film's investment in showing how the contemporary Western world inhabits an unreconciled postcolonial moment, specifically as related to other films in a tradition that rewrites the visual and virtual relationship between France and its colonies.[17] Indeed, as a postcolonial film, *Caché* uncovers how French discriminatory and violent practices (on both small and large scales) during the French-Algerian War continue to have effects decades later, effects that are further exacerbated by the denial and repression of colonial memories on the individual level.

Employed as a television commentator, Georges is accustomed to editing his appearance, but once turned into an object of surveillance via the video monitoring, he appears utterly powerless to control his affective responses. The film also exposes Georges's unconscious through a series of disquieting images in the form of nightmares and daydreams, invading his attempts at sleep or distraction. His body defies mastery, and his general anxiety points to a fracturing and fragmentation of dominant masculinity. Like that of the two Bernards in chapter 1, Georges's white French masculinity threatens to disintegrate under the pressures of the French-Algerian War's ghosts that invade the present moment, beckoning us to act.

In addition to Georges's uncontrollable memories, other flashbacks appear as randomly inserted between scenes in the film, seemingly having no psychic source. The ambiguity of their origin, similar to that of the surveillance tapes, could suggest a certain unreliability (after all, we have no idea of their source), but it may also intimate their applicability to other (colonial) contexts. Despite the absence of agency behind the gaze and the disjointedness of these images, we are slowly able to reconstruct Georges and Majid's relationship. Following the disappearance of Majid's family, Georges's parents decide to adopt the boy, but six-year-old Georges suddenly feels threatened by this new familial arrangement and resolves to have Majid sent away by telling his parents that he saw him coughing up blood. When the threat of tuberculosis does not work, he decides to trick Majid into getting himself banished by telling him to cut off the head of the family's rooster, a request that the young Majid obeys. The plan works, and having no guardians or parental figures, Majid is sent to an orphanage, a decision that will dramatically alter his life path, denying him certain forms of cultural capital and resulting in him now living in the sparse apartment where Georges meets him again many decades later. Now, more than forty years after the event, not only have the disturbing circumstances of October 17 come back to torment Georges, but so too have a whole host of postcolonial anxieties spurred on by his own actions in preventing a blended, hybrid family life with an Algerian brother.[18]

Margrit Shildrick argues that, when confronted with the body of the othered and marginalized, subjectivity is threatened: "Faced with the reappearance of its pre-subjectival phantasies that should have been banished . . . the subject is endangered by the putative failure of its own boundaries of distinction and separation."[19] Georges is similarly faced with the reappearance of such presubjectival desires, hopes, and fears, which should have been expelled when the body of Majid was likewise banished from Georges's childhood home. Crucially, they do not fade away but remain under the psychic and corporeal surface. Reading Georges in this way offers a possible explanation or account for his behavior, as he reveals himself to be potentially shattered by this failure of, in Shildrick's words, his "own boundaries of distinction and separation" when he comes back into contact with his almost-brother.

The receipt of more tapes and the false suspicion that Majid has kidnapped Georges's son, Pierrot, ultimately lead Georges back to Majid's apartment four times. Each time Georges tries to intimidate Majid, uttering statements such as "if you try to interfere with my life, scare my family, or damage me, you'll regret it, I swear." Then Georges receives a phone call from Majid requesting him to come over. What follows is a violent and shocking scene that becomes all the more unexpected because, up until this moment, the slow pace of the film had almost contradicted its classification as a thriller. On this fifth visit, Majid states: "I called you because I wanted you to be present," upon which he slits his own throat and dies right in front of Georges's eyes. On the one hand, as Paul Gilroy has convincingly argued, the scene can be read as "Haneke's collusion with the comforting idea that the colonial native can be made to disappear in an instant through the auto-combustive agency of their own violence."[20] On the other hand, through this scene, Majid's body, previously relegated to an invisible sphere when it threatened young Georges's familial security (and French national security), now becomes hypervisible through his shocking suicide. Georges is literally touched by this body's blood as it spurts across the room, echoing the sanguinary fear that the young Georges had manipulated in order to get Majid expelled from his family circle. The scene's camera angle, the same that we have come to associate with the surveillance tapes, suggests indeed that the encounter has been taped, creating indelible proof of the event, as well as evidence that Georges may have something to hide.

Even though *Caché* has been marketed as a thriller and whodunit, the source of the surveillance tapes and harassing drawings is never revealed. Because we never know who is behind the terrorizing, and none of the available candidates seems particularly plausible (both Majid and his son deny any participation, and we are sympathetically led to believe them), the images seem to take on a life of their own, functioning apart from any human control or volition. Indeed, the goal of the film is not to uncover the culprit, for the tapes actually serve to force Georges to look at his past actions and their ramifications. However, through constant lies, evasions, and statements such as "I am not responsible," "I am not to blame," and "What do you want me to do, apologize?" Georges refuses to take responsibility for the violence he had previously enacted while also seeming condemned to repeat those violent enactments in revised form. His inability to confront the meaning of the past also proves allegorical of the far-reaching individual and collective repercussions of European colonial projects and their subsequent denial.

Anxiety, or the Disappearance of the Black Cyclist

Violence appears in complex and multiple forms throughout *Caché*. Physical violence and bloody images (both real and imaginary) pervade: the cartoonish depictions of violence and murder sent to the Laurents, the flashbacks of young Majid slitting the rooster's throat and then, as an adult, doing the same to himself, and the evocation of October 17, 1961, all point to the physical violence of that historical event and to its violent sequelae. Although the massacre resulted in the deaths of hundreds and, as the film thematizes, forever altered the lives of many more, violence also functions on another, overlapping level. The surveillance and disciplining of bodies that disobey, question, or violate prescribed norms, combined with the hiding and forgetting of the past, substantiate the myriad ways in which violence is symbolically incorporated and reenacted by postcolonial subjects.

Like physical violence, symbolic violence takes various modalities in the film, including, for instance, Georges's parents sending Majid away, which denied him access to resources such as education. Following Pierre Bourdieu, I use symbolic violence and domination here to refer to the unconscious process of imposing modes of thought, perception, and behavior by the dominant group or class on dominated individuals or groups. As Bourdieu states: "The effect of symbolic domination (sexual, ethnic, linguistic, etc.) is exerted . . . below the level of the decisions of the conscious mind and the controls of the will."[21] Like symbolic domination, symbolic violence is intricately linked to the reproduction of social and cultural norms, and its modus operandi involves those with more symbolic capital wielding power over and shaping the thoughts, actions, and even bodies of those possessing less capital. In Bourdieu's framework, symbolic violence especially perpetuates itself through the school system, the mode of social and cultural reproduction par excellence from which Majid had been excluded.

Another form of symbolic violence in the film's narrative presents itself through the surveillance under which this seemingly in-control bourgeois family finds itself, a surveillance that seems to violate the security and privacy that they believe to be an inherent right by virtue of their social class. The sort of violence perpetrated against the Laurent family, however, is subversive. Michael Rothberg reminds us that Alexis de Tocqueville wrote of surveillance in the early colonial era in his *Rapport sur l'Algérie* (1847): "French colonialism in Algeria was driven by the desire to 'put under surveillance' the Algerian people, so as to 'penetrate their techniques, their beliefs, and . . . the secret to governing them.'"[22] The surveilling lens, formerly an instrument of power used by the French during the war to regulate and control, is, however, turned on the "colonizer" in *Caché*. In both form and content, the mysterious tapes subvert the desire to look away, as they literally and symbolically force Georges to look at himself (and to look at himself being looked at). The panoptic gaze has shifted, resulting in the dominant group's inability to locate the source of the "terrorizing" gaze and provoking anxiety about their uncertain future.

As some have pointed out, despite the Laurents' feeling of being violated, it is Georges who can be read as the real figure of violence in the film.[23] Indeed, he can be read as a symbol for France and its inability to come to terms with (or even to confront at all) its colonial and racist past *and* present.[24] On several occasions Georges is, in fact, urged to confront his racism, prejudice, and privileged status as French, upper class, heterosexual, white, and male, each time by a figure somehow representative of France's colonial past. Invariably, Georges gets angry and attempts to shift blame from himself to the other. This gesture is highlighted in an early scene when Georges and Anne go to the police in order to find a solution to the intrusion of privacy and the "campaign of terror" they see being waged against them through the videotapes and unsolicited mail. As they are leaving the police station, they begin to cross the street without looking and are nearly hit by a black man on a bicycle (fig. 4). Georges immediately becomes outraged, accusing the man of carelessly almost running into them. The cyclist looks directly at Georges, who lectures him on his disregard for others, their space, and their boundaries. While Georges cannot believe that he could be invisible to someone else's gaze, this attitude sits in stark contrast with his paranoia of being overexposed to the unknown surveilling gaze of the anonymous taping. Despite the fact that Georges and Anne were the ones in the wrong, they still lay claim to the public space as their own.

4. *Caché*: Georges, Anne, and the bicyclist. © Les Films du Losange.

This scene also illustrates Sara Ahmed's characterization of whiteness as a bad habit, "a series of actions that are repeated, forgotten, and that allow some bodies to take up space by restricting the mobility of others."[25] Georges's habitus—his unconscious dispositions and movements—and the expectation that others will defer to him constitute another form of inherited symbolic capital, a sign of his privilege and symbolic power. In this scenario, however, the cyclist (a figure representative of the formerly dominated) questions the distribution of symbolic power, prompting Georges and Anne to quickly turn away, seemingly unable to look him in the eye, despite the fact that they are the ones accusing him. The confrontation soon escalates, and the cyclist eggs Georges on: "Yell at me, yell at me some more." His words and bodily disposition speak to the changing power dynamic, impelling the viewer to question the unstated privilege that Georges unconsciously carries with him as a white French male in his everyday movement through the world. In the face of this newly empowered postcolonial subject, Georges can only walk away, unable to confront either the underlying power structures and their history or the simple fact that in the present circumstance, he is in the wrong. Moreover, in their sideways glance, Georges and Anne echo a wider turning away: they become metaphoric of France's inability to confront the repercussions of its imperial past, including struggles around citizenship, immigration, and racial and ethnic diversity.

This scene is even more revelatory of the way in which fear and anxiety are both distinct and overlapping. Invoking Fanon's analysis of fear and movement, Ahmed details how fear becomes located or contained in the body of the black man, a notion that is built on histories of racial discrimination and colonialism. Ahmed explains that as an object of fear, the black man may pass by precisely because "his proximity is imagined then as the possibility of future injury."[26] Yet at the same time, he becomes even more threatening *if* he passes by (even though he is precisely able to pass by *because* he is constituted as an object of fear): "*It is the movement that intensifies the affect.*"[27] If we take Ahmed's point seriously, then we might read Georges's behavior not as entitled and careless but as threatened and fearful. After the cyclist passes by, the situation shifts from fear to anxiety for Georges. He is shaken by this interaction, which has revealed cracks in the embodiment of his hegemonic masculinity. This dynamic is also repeated in his later encounters with other representatives of postcolonial otherness, (e.g., Majid and Majid's son), provoking a general sense of anxiety, which, in contrast to fear, is an intransitive affect that takes no object.

This image of Georges and Anne with the cyclist (like that of the blood spatter of Majid's suicide) has in fact become iconic of *Caché* and has been used in various publicity campaigns. After a quick online search of posters and other marketing materials for the film, one notices, however, that in some versions of the image, the cyclist actually disappears, photoshopped out. He has passed by, leaving anxiety in his wake. The decontextualized image consists of only Georges and Anne looking off into the distance. In this version, Georges's stance now takes on a multivalence. Is he pointing or gesturing? Might his outstretched hand in this image even be interpreted as welcoming or inviting? Underlying this choice of imagery is, however, the continued erasure of the uncomfortable colonial past and its postcolonial legacies through the deletion of the black man.

Another moment at which Georges must face his privilege and prejudices occurs in one of the final scenes, when Majid's son (the film's only main character who is not named) arrives at the television station where Georges works and confronts him. As his father has just committed suicide, he wants to know "what it feels like to have a man's life on [Georges's] conscience." Georges is evasive and attempts to dismiss Majid's son from Georges's professional space, where Majid's son's nonwhite body will attract attention. Citing Nirmal Puwar's notion of white bodies as somatic norms that make nonwhite bodies feel like strangers within certain spaces, Ahmed again proves useful in understanding how regimes of whiteness are also straightening devices: "When bodies arrive that seem 'out of place,' it involves disorientation; people blink and then look again." However, as Ahmed elaborates, this has queer resonances: "The proximity of such bodies makes familiar spaces seem strange.... Such proximity has, in other words, a queer effect: things are no longer 'in line.'"[28] In line with *Hybrid Anxieties'* broader aims of applying a queer lens, the film can be interpreted as laying bare a certain queering of bodies and spaces through its depiction of these moments in which racialized bodies disrupt hegemonic norms.

In order to protect his self-cultivated image of liberal television commentator and to maintain the whiteness of the space, Georges attempts to hide this encounter from his colleagues and escapes to the bathroom, where Majid's son follows him. When Georges becomes aggressive and increasingly attempts to avoid blame for Majid's suicide, his son demands violence, yelling, "Go ahead, hit me!" Georges responds with "You'll never give me a bad conscience about your father's sad or wrecked life!" and then quickly turns his back to Majid's son before stating: "You're sick. You're as sick as your father!" The scene is, in fact, one of the most violent in the entire film, but not because of Majid's son's words or presence. Instead, the ultimate form of symbolic violence manifests itself through Georges, who, having been made to feel powerless by his repressed guilt, refuses to take responsibility for the effects that his actions have on other individuals and on future generations. In his attempt to make Georges acknowledge the past, Majid's son explicitly draws attention to the violence that is exerted on both individual and collective levels when denying certain populations access to resources and forms of real and symbolic capital. Because the educational system is the motor of social and cultural reproduction, unsurprisingly, it is education that Majid's son alludes to as the way in which Georges destroyed his father's life: "You deprived my father of a good education. The orphanage teaches hatred, not politeness."[29] He also states that his father managed to raise him well despite his father's limited means, instilling in his son politeness, not hatred, despite the wrongdoings done to him. Through this emphasis on "politeness," Majid's son plays with the language of the colonizer: his words counter the oft-accepted narrative that when the dominated cease to tacitly accept certain conditions, they will be framed and perceived as impolite and disruptive. This notion inevitably harks back to France's self-described *mission civilisatrice*—the idea that it sought to "civilize" and "educate" the colonized—but in this process, Frenchness is revealed to be an inherently "white project." Elisa Camiscioli has also shown how, despite the education and indoctrination that colonial subjects received under the civilizing mission, they were refused access to French citizenship, as ultimately it was suggested that they "could not be made French by merely adopting French language, customs, and values."[30] Despite the fact that Algerians *were* French, they could never actually *be* French. Although culture consistently trumped citizenship in this framework, it paradoxically uncovers the emptiness of Frenchness as a signifier.

Symbolic violence is further replayed through acts of forgetting, perpetuating an avoidance of responsibility. Whether carelessly walking across the street or, much more dramatically, playing a role in the death of another individual, the scenes analyzed above demonstrate that, even in the face of the racialized other's challenges, Georges is an apathetic figure in his refusal to take responsibility for his actions, but he is also—not dissimilar from other French men of his generation and perhaps, more specifically, like the Bernards in chapter 1—marked by fear and anxiety stemming from the war. Repeatedly, his way of coping is to take a sleeping pill (a *cachet*, pronounced the same as the film's title, *caché*), close the curtains, and go to bed. However, as the film's penultimate scene reveals, even in sleep, Georges cannot flee. His nightmares of a young Majid being forcefully dragged from his home and taken off to the orphanage invade his only hope of a space wherein he is free from emotional baggage.

While Georges's denial appears in multiple forms throughout the film, some of these instances interpellate us as viewers and our own patterns of complicity. For example, Haneke's use of mise en abyme forces us to reflect on how domestic crises may occlude instances of violence that occur far away but from which we are by no means detached. This is made clear late in the film, when Georges and Anne become highly concerned about the whereabouts of their absent son, Pierrot. They begin to anticipate the worst: that he has been abducted by Majid (which proves to be untrue). Meanwhile, they are completely unaware of the drama unfolding on the television screen in front of them: images from the Iraq War (and more specifically, the Abu Ghraib torture scandal), followed by coverage of the Israeli occupation of Palestine (see fig. 5).

The scene is strategically shot with the television in between Georges and Anne, suggesting that current events are constantly mediating and interfering in our interpersonal interactions, even if we choose to ignore or turn away from them. *Caché* accordingly presents an allegory for both French colonial history and present American domestic and international policy. Through visually and narratively juxtaposing Iraq and Algeria, as well as by suggesting spectator guilt and compelling a process of self-reflection, the film pulls the viewer in. The mutilated bodies of Iraqi prisoners tortured in Abu Ghraib recall that of Majid, who, like those on television, is a "casualty" of colonial oppression, albeit delayed. Additionally, the images on the screen also raise questions of human rights. With the Israel-Palestine conflict and the events of Abu Ghraib on the television between them—which respectively hark back to France's settler-colonial past and to the use of torture during the French-Algerian War—we cannot help but recognize how statelessness continues to work as—to use Achille Mbembe's formulation—a necropolitical strategy today.[31]

Postcolonial Gender Constructs

Underlying the film's discussion of violence, memory, and responsibility is a less developed commentary on postcolonial gender constructs, although it is not immediately evident. While female characters are largely absent from the film, the limited deployment of women is,

5. *Caché*: Domestic and international crises in *Caché*. © Les Films du Losange.

however, significant. The only notable female presence is that of Anne, who is kept in the dark and, because of her husband's lies, is unable to see the "truth" and react accordingly. Georges's mother also makes a brief appearance, but as previously stated, she claims to barely even remember the young Majid and does not comprehend why Georges would want to think about him these many years later. While the actual status of women is certainly more complex than the film suggests, the limited portrayal of female characters presents women as guardians of an untroubled space of security (not so different from an idealized domestic space) wherein unpleasant postcolonial repercussions are brushed under the carpet. While Anne claims to want answers to the family's bizarre surveillance, she is also hesitant to dig deeper or to press Georges for more details, thereby drawing attention to another mode of being where ignorance could be bliss. Conversely, Georges's mother actively pushes out traces of France's colonial past (perhaps even more violently than Georges, who at least struggles on some level—even against his will—with the haunting past). Not only did she have Majid forcibly removed from the family home, she has erased all memories of the boy who almost became her adopted son.

Although the film speaks in a glancing way to the roles of women in the postcolonial moment, it is even more interested in commenting on contemporary masculinities. Not dissimilar from that of the two Bernards in chapter 1, Georges's fragile masculinity is threatened in his regular encounters with the postcolonial other. His sighs, twitches, heavy breathing, night sweats, and general corporeal tension uncover the fault lines running through a dominant masculine presence. Indeed, his anxiety becomes a regular feature of his disposition and is enacted through his body, producing what Ahmed has described as the feeling of fear, "press[ing] us into that future as an intense bodily experience in the present. One sweats, one's heart races, one's whole body becomes a space of unpleasant intensity, an impression that overwhelms us and pushes us back with the force of its negation, which may sometimes involve taking flight, and other times may involve paralysis."[32] A colonial masculinity that had previously aimed to surveil and discipline colonized bodies fails in the postcolonial epoch, where the previously colonized can subvert the instruments of oppression, terrorizing the terrorizer and asserting agency through control of their own bodies, even if that comes in the form of self-annihilation, as it did for Majid. While Majid's suicide enacts what Foucault understood as a uniquely modern form of power that usurped the sovereign's authority, Georges's only recourse to protect some semblance of masculine mastery becomes an active refusal of any awareness of his role in the perpetuation of symbolic violence.[33]

Haneke offers no resolution in *Caché*, even suggesting that the story has only just begun. As the title suggests, its meaning is hidden.[34] While it is not in the scope of this chapter to grapple with the film's conclusion, it is worth mentioning that the final scene quickly subverts any outstanding expectation we might have had of discerning the author of the tapes.[35] On the front steps of a school, the quintessential mark of symbolic capital, we see Majid's son walk up to Georges's son and begin talking, although, up until this moment, we had no reason to believe that they knew each other. Perhaps most significantly, the scene is shot with a still camera and has the marks of another surveillance tape. Indeed, *Caché* itself seems to evolve into the videos that it includes, forcing us to reflect on both our own viewing practices and our contemporary political climate.

Epilogue: Contemporary Violence and the Legacy of the French-Algerian War

In its prompting of a reflection on how prior actions may set off a chain of events that strip away others' life chances, *Caché* mirrors the ways in which the colonial past continues to haunt a postcolonial present in contemporary Europe. It is worth noting, for example, that *Caché* opened just weeks before France's infamous riots of November 2005. Caused by festering frustration and rage over racial profiling, high unemployment rates, and unequal representation, the riots laid bare some of the ways in which issues of race, gender, and class continue to complicate discussions of what it means to be French.

The series of protests, riots, and car burnings that occurred in several housing projects in metropolitan areas throughout France was in many ways provoked by attempts at defining (and limiting) who is "French" and who has the right to access the privileges conferred upon this national identity. While often portrayed as an "immigrant issue" by the media, a closer look at the riots reveals something quite different. The majority of the participants may have indeed been boys and young men of North and West African descent, but they were also French citizens. In fact, most were born and raised in France. Hence, the threat made by Nicolas Sarkozy (who was then minister of the interior and who would later become president) to deport those responsible for the violence became irrelevant. Despite the incontestability of these youths' citizenship, questions of race and national identity were at the forefront of this social and political debate, which itself is undoubtedly a legacy of France's colonial past. The protests and riots were also popularly framed as a distinctly "masculine" response to racism and oppression. As in *Caché*, the social unrest was presented as originating in male bodies—violent acts like car burnings and bombings could only be seen as the work of men, while women's activism was relegated to the sidelines. The coincidental timing of the film's opening also forces the realization that France—or any former colonial empire, for that matter—cannot escape the repercussions of oppressive actions, much like Georges can never truly shut out his past.

Fast-forwarding ten years, we see a clutch of events that similarly hark back to France's unresolved colonial past, including the January 2015 attacks on satirical weekly magazine *Charlie Hebdo* that resulted in 12 deaths; the deadly terrorist events of November 13, 2015, in which 130 people were killed and hundreds injured when a series of coordinated attacks were carried out in Paris and the city's suburb Saint-Denis; the incident of a truck ramming into a crowd in Nice on Bastille Day in 2016, leaving 86 dead; not to mention the even more recent attack in Strasbourg that left 5 dead in December 2018. While I would not go so far as to suggest that France's colonial past can solely be blamed for each of these acts of terrorism, I would argue that the attacks on *Charlie Hebdo* specifically cannot be grasped without some sense of how French imperialism and Western (particularly American) neo-imperialism shaped the conditions for these brutal killings to occur. While the magazine's blasphemous cartoons mocking Islam are often regarded as the cause of Chérif and Saïd Kouachi's murderous acts, the satirical images were only one of many instances of the discrimination and stigmatization French Muslims of North African descent face on a daily basis. Hence, Didier Fassin's commentary on the attacks rings true: "These caricatures were just one more sign of the stigmatization they endured as Muslims, but also as children of immigrant families, as members of low-income households, as school dropouts. . . . The caricatures were one more affront in a long list. Indeed, whereas satire has long been a way to mock and challenge the powerful, in the case of the French magazine, it only added insult to injury, targeting an already stigmatized and discriminated group, constantly exposed to Islamophobia as well as racism and xenophobia."[36]

The majority of mainstream media outlets, however, have presented the attacks as just another manifestation of radical Islam, a framing that helps bolster the already systemic violence directed against Muslims, which intensified with over fifty anti-Muslim incidents reported in France during the week after the attacks. Such quick explanations are dangerous, as they fail to recognize the colonial resonances of this recent act of terrorism. Rather, these attacks must be placed in the context of colonial and postcolonial treatment of North African (specifically Algerian) colonial subjects and eventual immigrants, with whom France has maintained a troubled relationship since its invasion of Algeria almost two hundred years ago. While media reports did make connections to Algeria early on, these were typically used to trace the brothers' "path to terror." Similar to the media's framing of the November 2005 riots, which named the protesters as foreigners, Chérif and Saïd Kouachi were also initially assumed by media outlets to be jihadi terrorists from North Africa or the Middle East. They were, however, not foreign—they were French citizens, born in France to Algerian immigrants. And not unlike the character of Majid in *Caché*, they were sent to orphanages and foster homes after their mother's death.[37]

As but a few journalists covering the shootings have shown, nothing happens without a past.[38] Mark LeVine puts it well: "If Charlie Hebdo reminds us of anything it is that the arc of blowback can stretch for decades, growing more uncontrollable as the political, economic, social and technological chaos of the contemporary world increases."[39] Indeed, there are numerous parallels between what happened in Paris on January 7, 2015, and what had occurred in the same city in 1961, even as perpetrators and victims (insufficient as such categories are) may have shifted. Moreover, it is not a coincidence that two of the most deadly terrorist acts in Paris—the *Charlie Hebdo* attacks, which killed twelve people, and a train bombing that killed twenty-eight people in June 1961—can be traced through a legacy of French colonialism.[40] While the *Charlie Hebdo* shootings involved Muslim extremists, the earlier act of domestic terrorism was perpetrated by the French dissident OAS, which virulently opposed France relinquishing Algeria toward the war's end. That same year also witnessed, of course, the Paris police massacre of October 17, which resulted in at least ten times as many deaths.

Continuing the parallels, it has been largely forgotten that the FN, now considered a Far Right French nationalist political party, was born out of militant calls to hold on to French Algeria during the war; indeed, it was originally named Front national pour l'Algérie française (National Front for French Algeria). As detailed in this book's introduction, the party has gained increasing ascendancy in recent years (and hopes to reach even more voters throughout Europe in its recent rebranding as the Rassemblement national, or National Rally). These political processes are happening alongside anti-Muslim movements across Europe and other forms of state-sanctioned Islamophobia.

Undoubtedly, there are also divergences between the events of October 17, 1961, and January 7, 2015, particularly regarding their subsequent representations. While the latter was a constant presence in media reports during the days after the killings, the former was virtually absent in newspapers despite the fact that hundreds of people were killed or had been disappeared. This points to a larger divergence in what is allowed to enter collective memory. In the immediate aftermath of the *Charlie Hebdo* shootings, both the French nation and Europe as a whole gathered together, with upward of two million people marching in the streets of Paris and with politicians from all over the continent on the front lines. Meanwhile, collective memory seems to have actively rejected the events of October 17, in which hundreds of Algerians lost their lives. Nonetheless, the brutal acts of the Kouachi brothers emerged precisely from this long trajectory of previous violence—both physical and symbolic—against colonial and postcolonial Algerian subjects. To this we can add the impact of contemporary US neo-imperialism in the Middle East. During the 2008 trial that sent him to prison for three years, it was observed that Chérif Kouachi's interest in radical Islam could be traced to his anger over the US invasion of Iraq, particularly the abuse and torture of Muslims held at the Abu Ghraib prison, an event that also made an appearance in *Caché*.[41]

Despite the fact that the international "Je suis Charlie" movement, which emerged after the attacks, seemed built upon the idea of freedom of expression, both human rights and free speech prove to have limits within the context of the global "War on Terror." In addition to the Islamophobic and anti-Muslim rhetoric that emerged in both news sources and social media after the attacks, we must also pay attention to another aspect of its aftermath: the numerous arrests due to a French antiterrorism law enacted in 2014. In January 2015 alone, approximately seventy people were prosecuted for comments such as "I am proud to be a Muslim, I do not like Charlie, they [the brothers] were right to do that" and "The Kouachi brothers is just the beginning; I should have been with them to kill more people"—statements that were punished with significant jail time.[42] This allows us to return once more to *Caché*, specifically to its thematization of surveillance. The French government continues to pursue expansion of surveillance and wiretapping, not unlike measures already in place in the United States and elsewhere.[43] While *Caché*'s characters were suspicious of—and threatened by—a surveilling gaze meant to expose colonial violence and provoke the (re)surfacing of postcolonial memory, in the aftermath of the *Charlie Hebdo* attacks, surveillance has again become, as it always was, a state instrument of discipline and control and, one might add, of which the Muslim other is not allowed to be suspicious, as any criticism of such an act would likely be seen as compliance with terrorism.

As *Caché* makes clear, in the face of postcolonial diversity, there is a growing tendency to retreat behind walls (both literal and figurative) in hopes of protecting physical safety, domestic privacy, and national identity. Yet when colonial pasts are repressed, physical and symbolic violence intensifies. In this sense, both Haneke's film and the *Charlie Hebdo* attacks and their aftermath reveal that perpetrators and victims can quickly turn and, most importantly, that the boundaries between them are often blurry and ambiguous (a phenomenon that is also evident in the parallels between World War II and the French-Algerian War that haunt this entire book). France's turning away from—and active forgetting of—the colonial past has resulted in racial discrimination and a steady festering of the wounds inflicted upon the previously colonized, culminating in (although not solely responsible for) acts of terrorism and violence, of which the *Charlie Hebdo* attack is only one of the most recent. It has, however, also resulted in new, alternative subjectivities that queer nationality, gender, and sexuality and open up to the redemptive possibilities of enacting novel modes of relationality and embodiment that repudiate the fixed identity categories and the thick dark colonial histories that they bear—a potential that is already detectable in the works discussed thus far, particularly in their referencing of the disintegration of the protagonists' white French masculinity. It is to such alternatives that I turn in part 2 of *Hybrid Anxieties*, beginning with a radical interrogation of subjectivity and sexuality in the wake of the war.

PART 2 Queering Postcolonial Legacies

3 Eros and Eden

Pierre Guyotat and Queer Pleasures

Partially inaugurating the field of queer theory, Gayle Rubin, in "Thinking Sex: Notes for a Radical Theory of the Politics of Sexuality," famously explicated the relationship between politics, oppression, and institutional forms and norms of sexuality as follows: "The realm of sexuality has its own internal politics, inequities, and modes of oppression. As with other aspects of human behaviour, the concrete institutional forms of sexuality at any given time and place are products of human activity. They are imbued with conflicts of interest and political maneuver, both deliberate and incidental. In that sense, sex is always political. But there are also historical periods in which sexuality is more sharply contested and more overtly politicized. In such periods, the domain of erotic life is, in effect, renegotiated."[1] In addition to emphasizing the historicity of sex, Rubin gestures toward an underlying tension between sex and sexuality. Here, sexuality speaks to the complex processes of identification, whereas sex implicates preidentitarian formations. That is, while sexuality refers to identity and is hence at risk of being pathologized, sex is corporeal and offers, in Michel Foucault's words, "a possibility for creative life."[2] Sex as raw corporeality also has the capacity to subvert the power relations within which inhere modes of subjectivity and ideologies under which we assume identities and become subjects. In short, sexuality is more concerned with *being*, while sex is about *doing*.

A central concern of queer theory has been the ways in which sex and sexuality are products of human activity that are, as Rubin writes, laden with politics. In the context of post-decolonization France and Algeria, this fundamental concern is also at the crux of the relationship between discourses of sex and questions of subjectivity at a critical point provoked by decolonization—a moment when sex, sexuality, desire, and erotic life were indeed renegotiated.[3] This chapter looks to avant-garde writer Pierre Guyotat's 1970 *Eden, Eden, Eden*, a censored text in which colonial violence cannot be separated from desires, pleasures, and sexual acts. The text serves as an example that unsettles the system, a case that portrays a world in which the processes of subjectification and identification are radically disrupted and imagined through sex and violence.

For Guyotat, who consistently advocated an indissoluble link between sex and politics, sexual revolution was spurred on by the French-Algerian War, decolonization, and their concomitant silences.[4] Offering a counterpoint to the troubled masculinity that chapters 1 and 2 evidenced as prevalent in the war's wake, Guyotat's work imagines a world in which France's loss of empire provoked a new excess of libinality and a rethinking of sexual freedom and repression.[5] His *Eden, Eden, Eden* also questions norms and underscores the transformative potential of nonnormative or queer forms of sex and gender. Banned in France and considered pornographic because of its depiction of male brothels, queer sex, and extreme violence, Guyotat's *Eden, Eden, Eden* speaks to the war's intense destructiveness. Set in a postwar Algerian desert, the almost hallucinatory novel—which may be better described as an antinovel in its eschewing of all conventions—also subverts form and genre in that it is composed of a single interminable sentence. In this landscape, the body is a battleground for both liberation and domination and has the potential to write narratives that counter official history and destabilize, dissolve, or, indeed, queer subjectivity. A growing body of work has highlighted how contemporary French political discourse was laden with sexuality during and after the war, but I want to push this line of thinking even further to link this coupling of sex and decolonization to a radical rethinking and questioning of subjectivity itself, a process that Guyotat illuminates in his text.[6] *Eden, Eden, Eden* upends and rejects hegemonic norms of subjectivity precisely at a moment when identity politics were so vitriolic and contested.

This chapter begins by looking to the work of political theorist Herbert Marcuse in order to elucidate the libidinal potentialities offered by *Eden, Eden, Eden*. I then trace the complicated story of Guyotat and his text, focusing on the scandal and censorship that characterized the reception of the novel, which allows me to draw out the relationship between sex, violence, and the Algerian cause as the centerpiece of Guyotat's work—a theme that he explores in an undiluted poststructuralist format. From there, I move to a discussion of Foucault, who himself identified *Eden, Eden, Eden* as offering a radical proposal regarding sexuality and subjectivity. Theories of subjectivity have long been central to philosophy, literature, and art, particularly as crises in identity and subjecthood haunt the twentieth century. However, in advocating for the dissolution of the subject at this particular moment, the trio of writers that I group together in this chapter—Foucault, Marcuse, and Guyotat—offer a supplement to poststructuralist, feminist, and queer forms of critique that have acknowledged the fractured nature of being and the profoundly decentering effects of language and culture. Staging a conversation between these three thinkers provides tools with which to grasp the potentiality for transforming social relations opened by rethinking the notion of the subject—a process I identify as inescapably queer.

Marcuse: Liberation through Polymorphous Perversity

For Herbert Marcuse, the aim of theory must be to inform practice and action, and he believed that a robust theory of subjectivity attuned to erotic, embodied, and aesthetic dimensions was necessary for real social transformation to occur. In his reworking of Freud's *Civilization and Its Discontents*, Marcuse compellingly (yet also utopically) depicted the social construction of the subject in *Eros and Civilization* (1955). Affiliated with the Frankfurt School and aligned with New Left politics, Marcuse has been celebrated for his work on Hegelian ontology and Marxist theory (of which he was both a critic and a proponent). In outlining his methodology and motivations, he explains that the philosophical approach he employs is one centered on the social and the political. In his view, the traditional borders between psychology, on the one hand, and political and social philosophy, on the other, are obsolete in contemporary society, and thus psychological problems become political problems. Marcuse argued that cultural and social factors shape desires and freedom, yet he also believed that their historical construction could be transcended.

Predating poststructuralist critiques, one of Marcuse's primary arguments was that the notion of the modern subject must be destabilized, as dominant forms of subjectivity are oppressive and limit our access to freedom. It becomes our task, then, as Douglas Kellner paraphrases Marcuse, "to develop a new sensibility, qualitatively different than the normalized subjectivity of contemporary advanced industrial societies."[7] This new sensibility was encapsulated in Marcuse's radical subjectivity: an embodied, gendered, political, and resisting mode of being. Rather than being fixed or innate, it is always in production, developing, and fluid. Marcuse was also particularly attentive to grounding his conception of radical subjectivity in contemporary movements and struggles, which he saw as equally shaping identity. He was, for example, a strong critic of imperialism, speaking out against French colonial violence and other forms of injustice. In short, for Marcuse, subjectivity must be reconsidered and reconfigured in relation to social, political, and historical conditions.

Although Marcuse builds his argument both in opposition to and in conjunction with Freudian concepts, his ultimate aim is to uncover an alternative to the repressive model, which would then offer an entry point into the creation of a nonrepressive civilization that would lead to instinctual liberation. He critiques Freud for ignoring the fact that the ego is a sociohistorical organization of reality: Freud's reality principle falsely makes historical contingencies into biological necessities. One of Marcuse's central claims is that the subject is a product of normalization and is subjected to social domination. Desires and perceptions of reality are organized by society, which represses the individual's instinctual needs. However, in his reading of Freud, the human being can only tolerate so much repression and will eventually rebel and radically oppose society.

In embedding this argument in a sociohistorical framework, Marcuse also posits a theory of remembrance that interrupts teleological understandings of progress-oriented temporality. In "Anamnestic Totalization: Reflections on Marcuse's Theory of Remembrance," Martin Jay outlines Marcuse's contribution by writing that "the very notion of progress with its never-ending dissatisfaction with the present and impatient yearning for an improved tomorrow was one of the earmarks of a repressive society."[8] This approach to temporality is encapsulated in Marcuse's statement that "time would not seem linear, as a perpetual line or rising curve, but cyclical, as the return in Nietzsche's idea of the 'perpetuity of pleasure.'"[9] For him, transgression and revolt are rooted in collective memory, which he thereby regards as transformational.[10]

Marcuse utilizes several examples in order to show that civilization can evolve from free, libidinous relations and that in a nonrepressive civilization, activities and relations do not have to be sexual "in the sense of 'organized' genital sexuality" but can be libidinal and erotic. He builds his argument by referencing nonnormative societal relations, such as "desexualized, sublimated, homosexual love for other men," which, as Freud argued, were founded on both sublimated and unsublimated libidinous ties. He cites Sándor Ferenczi's notion of "genitofugal libido," which proposes that with the release of tension, the libido flows back from the object to the body, resulting in happiness.[11] No longer mere fungible parts in a well-oiled capitalist machine that directs energy away from sexual activities and toward work (i.e., Freud's reality principle), we must embrace the pleasure principle, which remains in our unconscious and has revolutionary implications.

In this framework, Marcuse depicts a sexual (and socialist) utopia wherein people would be equal, free from the confines of alienated labor, and able to pursue pleasures at will. Societal relations would be fundamentally altered in a nonrepressive civilization, and the division of labor would become reoriented toward the gratification of individual needs. No longer solely an instrument of labor, the body would become resexualized as an instrument of pleasure. In this radical transformation of the libido, the entire personality would thus become eroticized, institutions would disintegrate, and traditional kinship structures (i.e., the monogamic and patriarchal family) would dissolve. In other words, similar to Marx, Marcuse argues that once civilization no longer requires the repression of the pleasure principle and the control of sexual instincts to satisfy the society's needs through alienated labor, it will transform itself.

Given its liberatory aspirations, Marcuse's framework has been taken up by scholars in queer theory and sexuality studies. In *Homosexual Oppression and Liberation*, for example, Dennis Altman lays out the struggle of the homosexual subject (a figure that is historically contingent) for liberation. Altman utilizes Marcuse's *Eros and Civilization* to argue that "any real theory of sexual liberation must take into account the essentially polymorphous and bisexual needs of the human being."[12] Instead of being channeled into a heterosexual reproductive norm by a dominant and repressive social regime, Altman's conceptualization of polymorphous perversity depicts a world in which romantic couplings are reimagined and eroticisms are diffused. As a consequence of breaking apart sexual norms (including the homosexual/heterosexual binary), Altman envisions that binary gender will also be exploded (a reversal of other theoretical work that has suggested that a paradigm shift would first explode gender norms, and from this would follow a new, freer form of sexuality in which desire is no longer gender-based). By liberating the subject from modernist subjectivity through Eros, we will ultimately be free—from discourse and from our "selves."

Indeed, this aspect of polymorphous perversity provides the centerpiece to Marcuse's theoretical framework. To quote Peter Drucker, a panoply of relationalities would be fostered by "the liberated erotic energy of non-genitally-obsessed 'polymorphous perversity.'"[13] While Marcuse's belief that a resexualization of the body and reactivation of erotogenic zones would lead to a disintegration of institutions like the patriarchal family might appear rather idealistic, Guyotat's *Eden, Eden, Eden*—to which I now turn—presents a vision of such a world within one particular reality principle, namely, post-decolonization Algeria. Guyotat's project, like Marcuse's, aims to radically deconstruct subjectivity through sex as pure action while also reminding us that liberation itself cannot be separated from domination. Similar to his fellow Frankfurt School theorists, Marcuse was tremendously invested in the ability of artistic work to express something that language cannot, which he believed would trigger a radical form of subjectivity. Art and literature can play a vital role in rethinking subjectivity, as Guyotat's oeuvre instantiates through its similar aim of dissolving contemporary attitudes and understandings of the modern subject.

Guyotat: *Eden, Eden, Eden*

Pierre Guyotat (1940–2020) was one of France's most controversial writers of recent decades, and his work resides in the avant-garde and pornographic traditions of the Marquis de Sade, Antonin Artaud, Georges Bataille, and Jean Genet, all of whom enacted their own libidinal revolutions and overturned literary conventions. Eight years after the French-Algerian War had ended and Algeria had gained independence, Guyotat released—to both great acclaim and significant consternation—his scandalous *Eden, Eden, Eden*. The book was published by respected publishing house Gallimard and was prefaced by a trio of literary powerhouses—Michel Leiris, Philippe Sollers, and Roland Barthes—illustrating how *important* this work was.[14] Barthes echoed this sentiment and anticipated the book's groundbreaking status in the conclusion to his prefatory remarks: "Whatever the institutional peripeteia, the publication of this text is important: a whole body of critical and theoretical work will be carried forward, without the text ever losing its power of seduction: outside all categories and yet of an importance beyond doubt, a new landmark and a starting-point for new writing."[15] Indeed, the text marked a turning point—both socially and stylistically—and ignited a firestorm soon after its publication. Guyotat's work was radical in both form and content and would go on to send shockwaves through the literary world and the public consciousness. It rethought language, grammar, and syntax and pulled away the public's blinders to sex and war. Like Barthes, I read *Eden, Eden, Eden* as a watershed text that inaugurated a new way of writing in a post-decolonization era that exploded any coherence of textual and personal identity, which, in this sense, indexes the reification of a particular mode of subjectivity that locks individuals (and texts) into a specific idea of who (or what) they are or could be. Countering any structural dynamics that would curtail possibilities for multiplicity, Guyotat offers novel ideas about the plurality of forms that a text or a subject can inhabit.[16]

Sex, writing, and the limits of consciousness are intimately connected—both practically and thematically—in Guyotat's textual production.[17] Incidentally, Guyotat is perhaps most notorious for, first, his practice of masturbating while writing and, second, overwriting himself into a coma. Throughout his oeuvre, we also glimpse the ways in which memories of violence (inherited but also directly experienced) haunted him from early childhood, turning him into a fractured, plural, and sexually divided individual. Consequently, Guyotat has been read as an ambiguous figure—an image that he cultivated in his most recent writings. While he has often been classified as a "gay writer"—perhaps contrary to his own refusal to submit to this (or any other) categorization—Guyotat and his texts enact a dispersion of sexual acts and a deconstruction of subjectivity, a combination of "fluid divided selves ... yet overflowing sexual creativity," to use Owen Heathcoate's words.[18] Upon the release of *Eden, Eden, Eden*'s English translation in 1995, journalist Roger Clarke reiterated a conversation he had with Guyotat in which the author expressed his discomfort with and resistance to identity labels: "To be homosexual, to be anti-sex, pro-sex—'to be' something does not exist."[19] This tension between acts and identities echoes the ongoing project of queer theory and Foucault's *The History of Sexuality* as one of its cornerstone texts, which itself was published a few years after *Eden, Eden, Eden* and was likely shaped by it, not least as Foucault was, as I will go on to show, an obvious admirer of Guyotat's text.

Scandal and Censorship

Guyotat was no stranger to scandal and had already instigated controversy for his earlier novel, the genre-bending and gut-wrenching work *Tomb for 500,000 Soldiers* (*Tombeau pour cinq cent mille soldats*, 1967), which was set during the French-Algerian War and depicted brutal warfare and hallucinatory scenes of homoeroticism. In *Tomb for 500,000 Soldiers* (and in *Eden, Eden, Eden*), war is portrayed as an apocalypse in which sexual violence and desire play a pivotal role. In fact, the text was considered so scandalous that General Jacques Massu forbade French soldiers serving in North Africa from reading it.[20] Due to its exploration of senseless violence, libidinal excess, and nonnormative sexual acts, his subsequent *Eden, Eden, Eden* was met with even more severe treatment: a triple ban by the French Ministry of the Interior that forbade advertisement, display, and sale to minors. This partial censorship ignited a firestorm of controversy, with a number of public intellectuals signing a petition in support of the book, which they saw as a brilliant piece of literature written by one of the most talented voices of the post-Algeria generation. The petition was published in the newspaper *Le Monde*, and the original signatories included Simone de Beauvoir, Jean-Paul Sartre, Kateb Yacine, Marguerite Duras, Alain Robbe-Grillet, Jacques Derrida, and Jean Cayrol.[21] When it was eventually reprinted, the list required twenty-seven pages to include all the names of its signatories.[22]

While the triple ban on *Eden, Eden, Eden* has been described as inhibiting free speech and literary freedom, it was by no means the first text referring directly (or indirectly) to the French-Algerian War to be sanctioned. In fact, as also mentioned in chapter 1, censorship and silencing were central to French attempts to contain and manage how the conflict and its questionable wartime tactics were perceived by French and Algerian publics.[23] (A narrative of denial would of course continue for decades, as the government only finally acknowledged the war as such in 1999.) After a protracted struggle that involved a number of high-profile French intellectual figures, the ban on *Eden, Eden, Eden* was overturned in 1981 by President François Mitterand, just after Guyotat awoke from his aforementioned two-week coma.

The period in which Guyotat's text, which was written some years after France lost its most valued colonies and directly following the student and worker protest movements of 1968, was released was marked by rapidly changing social attitudes toward sexuality and the colonial past. Even still, *Eden, Eden, Eden*'s story of censorship exemplifies how violence, memory, and oblivion were carefully managed and how representations of gender and sexuality continued to be guarded. The ban on *Eden, Eden, Eden* has often been attributed to its portrayal of violence, but this narrative overlooks the central geopolitical context in which the text unfolds, that is, the barren Algerian landscape of the post-decolonization period. While violence was a central justification for the book's interdiction, I posit that the censorship stemmed even more profoundly from, first, the book's veiled critique of French actions in Algeria and the impacts of decolonization and, second, the text's subversion of normative ideas of sexuality and kinship through a depiction of queer sexual acts.

Thus far, insufficient attention has been paid to these aspects of the text and its censorship story. One of the few scholarly articles to purportedly analyze the place of Algeria—Stuart Kendall's "Eden and Atrocity: Pierre Guyotat's Algeria"—only addresses the context of Algeria in passing, despite its title. Instead, Kendall shifts the focus to make the point that Auschwitz haunts *Eden, Eden, Eden*—a stance with which I concur in the sense that, as stated at the outset of this book and elaborated in chapter 1, all texts about the French-Algerian War are inevitably *also* about World War II. Indeed, neither the Holocaust nor Algeria nor their attendant intergenerational horrors can ever be left behind, as both of these traumas prompted the French nation to rethink morality and subjectivity. Nonetheless, I posit that Algeria represents the most salient point of reference here. Guyotat was writing in the wake of an even more recent disaster of modern subjectivity, the French-Algerian War and fall of empire, which I interpret as more finely focused on decolonization than previous scholarship has acknowledged.

Guyotat was most certainly not the first to make a link between the French-Algerian War and nonnormative sexualities. In the wake of the war, other writers also identified the profound effect that the conflict had on understandings and enactments of sex, sexuality, and masculinity. For example, just one year before Guyotat's book appeared, Bernard Noël published *The Castle of Communion* (*Le château de cène*, 1969), and it too was met with government censorship. In the postface to this disturbing and sexually graphic novel (the postface was also published as a short essay entitled "The Outrage Against Words"), Noël argues for the inextricability of sexuality, censorship, and the events in Algeria. Noël confesses that his novel was written in response to the violent colonial atrocities committed by the French military and other authorities (including the massacre of October 17, 1961, which figured in the previous chapter and will return in chapter 4).[24] Further, Noël upends our reliance on traditional narrative structure to remind us that Algeria requires us to learn to read anew. As *Eden, Eden, Eden* does via its interminable sentence, *The Castle of Communion* also reimagined composition: Noël is said to have dictated the entire novel into a tape recorder over a period of only three weeks.[25]

Only one year after the release of *Eden, Eden, Eden*, Sartre's leftist journal *Tout!*, making a clear link between sex and decolonization, devoted its April 23, 1971, issue to the work of the Homosexual Front of Revolutionary Action (Front homosexuel d'action révolutionnaire, FHAR), which was inspired by contemporary social struggles, including civil rights, anticolonial, and gay liberation movements. The issue included a now well-cited quote by Jean Genet: "Perhaps if I had never gone to bed with Algerians, I could never have approved of the FLN. I probably would have been on their side anyway, but it's homosexuality that made me realize that Algerians are no different than other men."[26] Provocative in its linking of queer sexuality with support for the Algerian decolonization movement—and its confession that it was sex that led to his realization that Algerians are just like other (i.e., French) men—Genet's statement does, however, evidence the weight of "identity" at this moment. In *Disturbing Attachments*, Kadji Amin bolsters this argument by undertaking a critical analysis of writings by Genet and the FHAR that constructed the black or Arab sexual penetrator as a fetishized figure "through which the white bottom may enjoy his temporary release from the burdens of identity via self-shattering."[27] It is this intimate connection between sexuality and decolonization and this aspect of self-shattering in which I am interested, specifically, how writers like Guyotat increasingly called into question the notion of identity at this post-decolonization crisis point. Through queer sex, the Algerian male body became a screen or receptacle to rehearse or perform desubjectification, a convenient way to let go of the weight of standing in for the "colonizers" by leaving their identity as white French men at the bedroom door. And the censorship story continues here, for the aforementioned publication in which Genet made his controversial statement was banned and seized, and Sartre was charged with outrage to public decency.[28]

Queer Relationalities and the Algerian Cause

Guyotat was profoundly scarred by Algeria, and many of his works have been shaped by his experiences of colonial combat. At the age of twenty he enlisted, eventually spending nearly two years in Algeria, from 1960 to 1962. As Catherine Brun details in her meticulously documented biography of Guyotat, although he could have avoided military service, he saw this as a chance to escape his father's authority and assert his freedom. He began his service as rather apolitical, but the war quickly altered his views on imperialism and instilled in him profound and long-lasting anticolonial sentiments, succinctly summarized by Brun as follows: "Pierre came to the Algerian cause; he never left it."[29] During his time spent serving in North Africa, he was even accused of inciting soldiers to desert, for which he was punished with a sentence of three months in solitary confinement. He also became a great sympathizer with the Algerian cause, which eventually earned him the government-awarded title of "Friend of the Algerian People."[30] Years after the war ended, Guyotat returned to this land that had profoundly transformed him and traversed the Algerian desert as a nomadic ethnographer, immersing himself in the environment of the recently independent nation. It was upon this experience and his military service that he drew when writing *Eden, Eden, Eden*.

For Guyotat, fighting in the French-Algerian War was marked by class relations, on the one hand, and by nonheterosexual acts and troubled masculinity, on the other. In arguing that *Eden, Eden, Eden* is characterized by class struggle, Guyotat writes in his autobiographical *Littérature interdite*: "If there is violence in this text, then it is *class violence*, from the first to the last word—and this class violence is often signified by the terms of a *species to species* violence."[31] And if this period spent in Algeria was also marked by contingent homosexuality and frustrated male bodies, it became a profound lesson in masculinity for Guyotat and his comrades. For Guyotat, as for many of his generation, Brun writes, "the Algerian war was not only a war: it was also 'a moment of [his] youth,' as much as it was his initiation into becoming a man."[32] Guyotat admits that these combined elements—war, class relations, and sexuality—produced in him a state of "permanent anxiety": *l'angoisse permanente*, as he terms it.[33]

His subsequent writings were profoundly shaped by these violent, anxiety-ridden experiences. Coming to terms with the traumas of the war was not a conscious process for Guyotat, and it was through writing that he was fully able to understand and recognize their effects on his understandings of sexuality and class: "This entire Algerian period constitutes a semiconscious, but crucial, blockage: it is also possible that this 'arrival' of my contradictions in an extreme place ... led to their elucidation and *integration into politics*. But it wasn't until writing *Tomb for 500,000 Soldiers* that the effects of this shock could be detected: as far back as I can remember, the sexual drive has always, for me, overlaid the drive to the proletariat."[34] For Guyotat, *Eden, Eden, Eden* reflects a direct experience of struggle and deconstruction. In translating his experiences of the war, Guyotat offers what may seem to be the ultimate contradiction: a simultaneously utopic and dystopic postwar landscape of infinite couplings where subjectivity is effaced and no act is privileged over another. The revolution of the text (by text, I here mean both what it says *and* how it says it) mirrors the revolutionary moment of postwar Algeria. Text, sex, and revolution are, for Guyotat, inseparable and mutually constitutive. Specifically in *Eden, Eden, Eden*, this translates into an enactment of forbidden relationalities in its rethinking and reimagining of what gender and sexuality are (and could be) in the wake of mass violence and destruction. While Guyotat admits that "silence invades *Éden* bit by bit," it simultaneously attempts to break the silences and taboos that were so characteristic of a moment in which 1960s postwar technocrats ascended to prominence to rebuild a postcolonial future without thoroughly reflecting on the colonial horrors of the previous years.[35] Even in the irony of its government-mandated silencing, the almost hallucinatory text speaks back to this blinkered worldview by subverting form and genre via its single sentence—in fact, a sentence that *never* ends ...

The Death of the Modernist Subject: "I Destroy Rhetoric"

In a letter to his mentor Jean Cayrol written in 1962, well into his military service, Guyotat expressed the feelings that being in Algeria provoked in him. In words and style that uncannily resemble those included in the bleak sequences of *Eden, Eden, Eden* to which I will later turn, he wrote: "As I move through this time in Algeria, in this country and these men of Algeria, I understand what 'collective responsibility' is.... The nightmare persists. I drive through landscapes of war and murder where one can only imagine slaughtered cattle, men as ~~slaves~~ hostages, where each tree still standing seems to bear traces of bullets or blood, where every blackened ruin bears inscriptions such as 'France is strong, France remains,' etc. landscapes that we think about after the fact, like some 'bad' dreams."[36] His time in Algeria is haunted by war-torn landscapes and bloody nightmares. Nothing is untouched, with nature itself bearing the traces of ubiquitous murder and devastation. Rather than slaves (signaled by the strike-through), he sees those around him as hostages, a theme that will obsess *Eden, Eden, Eden* from its very first page. Moreover, the collective responsibility that he begins to feel will serve as an impetus to support the Algerian cause—and to write.

In a 1970 interview with Thérèse Réveillé, Guyotat addressed the relationship between the text and its specifically Algerian setting, stating that this relationship was

> directly produced by a biographical fact—not by chance, but historical constraint: conscription and the Algerian war.... [W]hen I was writing the text ... I revisited these subdesert and desert areas. These areas, I crossed, on the one hand, as semislave (second-class subject at the will of the officers, including interrogation and imprisonment), on the other hand, as a "nomad" noncitizen.... These two conditions of relative irresponsibility constitute the mental place from which unprecedented speech could be dared: the sexual act is, here, written, treated, so to speak, at a less immediate level, it is certain that "a writing that immediately takes all risks" could only have been produced from a similarly risky place. *Eden, Eden, Eden* ends, interrupts, dissolves into a place of general geography.[37]

The book was initially titled *Désert* (Desert) and then *Bordels désert* (Desert brothels), but the title ultimately chosen—*Eden, Eden, Eden*—communicates that one word will never be enough. This enumeration cultivates a sense of confusion, alienation, and detachment if not also a futile search for meaning at a moment when language no longer suffices. Further, Guyotat upends our prior associations with "Eden" as a biblical, premoral place of innocence, temptation, and knowledge, for, as Kendall argues, this "Eden to the third power" is "a place without God, where God has been replaced with a sinuous erotics of encounter, or hermeneutic delirium."[38] Indeed, the choice to map the novel onto the site of original sin is far from coincidental. This creation story also has clear gendered implications, for Eden is also the origin of sexual difference, where "man" and "woman" were, in a sense, created.[39] Guyotat captures the irony of the fact that this exemplar of heterosexual procreation is also a place of incest. In his own Eden, infinite sexual assemblages mean that kinship is reimagined. Couplings between humans and animals, for instance, are not suppressed, nor are queer bodies and acts. In locating pleasure outside socially normative practices and behaviors, Guyotat partially enacts the pleasure principle and libidinous revolution proposed by Marcuse. This is a site of polymorphous perversity where eroticism is diffused.

The text opens with an epigraph that appears to be a coded message indecipherable to the average reader. Comprised of slashes, dots, and symbols, this message sets the tone for the rest of the text. Yet what seems to be code is actually language, for this epigraph is written in the Berber dialect of Tamacheck and signifies "And now we are no longer slaves." Given that the text is heavily characterized by slavery and servitude (workers, prostitutes, slaves, and soldiers abound), this inscription suggests that freedom may at first appear contradictory.[40] Brun, however, offers two interpretations of this opening proclamation: either the text's figures are in fact free precisely because they exist in another space outside of ideology, or the epigraph is ironic in the same way, for example, that the motto *Arbeit macht frei* emblazoned at the entrance to the Auschwitz concentration camp is paradoxical.[41] The epigraph also forces the reader to question who is really "free": Are we all slaves? Are Algerians any more liberated now than they were prior to independence? Are the French who are responsible for this postcolonial apocalypse actually free? While Kendall remarks that the book is "hardly a narrative of liberation," it is perhaps the case that traces of our hostage status will, as suggested by Guyotat's strike-through in his above-cited letter to Cayrol, always remain.[42] Indeed, even if we are no longer slaves, we are still hostages. This dialectic between freedom and servitude runs throughout Guyotat's entire body of work and propels his investment in uncovering what freedoms might be revealed when we release ourselves from the strictures of identity, subjectivity, and norms.

Just as the foreign epigraph warns us that incomprehension will follow, *Eden, Eden, Eden*'s opening lines only further emphasize—through both syntax and thematics—the difficulty that this text will pose to any straightforward understanding. It begins with the following lines, which I quote at length to convey the intensity and unrelenting breathlessness that they evoke:

> / Soldiers, helmets cocked down, legs spread, trampling, muscles drawn back, over new-born babes swaddled in scarlet, violet shawls: babies falling from arms of women huddled on floors of G.M.C. trucks; driver's free hand pushing back goat thrown forward in cab; / Ferkous pass, RIMA platoon crossing over track; soldiers jumping out of trucks; RIMA squad lying down on gravel, heads pressed against flint-pitted, thorn-studded tires, stripping off shirts in shadow of mudguards; women rocking babies against breasts; rocking movement stirring up scents sharpened with bonfire-sweat impregnating rags, hair, flesh; oil, cloves, henna, butter, indigo, black antimony—in Ferkous valley, below breakwater heaped with charred cedars, barley, wheat, bee-hives, tombstones, drinks-stand, school, gaddous, fig-trees, mechtas, stone walls oozing spattered with brains, orchards blooming, palm-trees, swollen in fire, exploding: flowers, pollen, buds, grasses, paper, rags spotted with milk, with shit, with blood, fruit-peel, feathers, lifted, shaken, tossed from flame to flame in wind pulling up fire, from earth;[43]

The very first words—"/ Soldiers, helmets cocked down, legs spread, trampling, muscles drawn back, over new-born babes swaddled in scarlet, violet shawls: babies falling from arms of women huddled on floors of G.M.C. trucks"—make clear the extent to which the text subverts syntax, disregarding the traditional subject-verb-object order. The actors may be named (soldiers, women, babies), but it is unclear who is acting upon whom in this opening scene.

The text soon moves to a more graphic description of violence:

"soldier, chest crushing baby sucking at breast, parting woman's hair pushed over her eyes, stroking forehead with fingers covered in powdered onyx; orgasm spurting saliva from mouth, dowsing baby's buttered scalp; retracted member resting softening on shawls soaked up dye;"[44] Language and bodies are promiscuous—sublimation is clearly effaced. Frequent enumeration and numerous substantives are needed to express an idea (even though that idea remains elusive), and feelings can only be expressed through excess. Further, although the juxtapositions might appear crude (e.g., flowering orchards are paired with bodily fluids: "stone walls oozing spattered with brains, orchards blooming, palm-trees, swollen in fire, exploding: flowers, pollen, buds, grasses, paper, rags spotted with milk, with shit, with blood, fruit-peel, feathers"), they also collapse distinctions and hierarchies between humans, animals, and their natural surroundings.

The narrative also creates a sense of disorientation, as there appears to be nothing to guide the reader, and at times it feels as if we might never make it out alive. It is also littered with unfamiliar words (e.g., "gaddous" and "mechtas") and foreign place-names (e.g., "Ferkous valley"), but they begin to serve as scant clues regarding the time and place in which the narrative is set. These obscure flora and fauna, combined with references to landscapes and cultural practices, give astute readers cues that this is the North African desert.[45] Neologisms also abound, and in true poststructuralist fashion, the text conveys that language does not suffice. *Eden, Eden, Eden* is also a particularly challenging read because it mixes different languages and dialects. Argot, patois, Kabyle vocabulary, phonetically spelled words, scientific terminology, and technical language all play an equal role, deprivileging which language form is most valued. Additionally, the text's mixture of registers itself mirrors the postwar anxieties surrounding the hybridity of genre, gender, race, and nationality. In this leveling of hierarchies, the text enacts a queer approach that embraces the undoing and upending of norms. Guyotat stated that his mixing of languages and registers, as well as his use of archaisms, may push the reader to more directly engage with and work for the text, perhaps even having to consult dictionaries to understand a word's meaning.[46] The text demands something of us in that we must constantly strive for comprehension, engaging with a puzzle to which we do not seem to have all of the pieces. In this sense, attempting to read *Eden, Eden, Eden* is an intra-active process wherein the reader enters the text as the text penetrates the reader, neither leaving this encounter fully intact.

The opening passage also immediately signals that the disjointed narrative will unfold in an apocalyptic landscape where sex and violence occur among postwar remnants. Guyotat configures the desert and the army camp as primary exterior locations, whereas the male brothel is a strictly guarded interior space, with only male bodies allowed inside, leaving female bodies on the outside looking in. The brothel occupies the majority of the text, and sex scenes are only occasionally interrupted by camp and desert interludes. Nonetheless, these primary locations blend into one another, creating confusion and an inability to distinguish spaces and beings. This onslaught of dizzying pairings and sexually explicit acts is unrelenting; it is a penetration in all senses of the word. If the other locations allow for all sorts of bodily combinations, only man-on-man couplings occur in the brothel where male bodies are put on display. Even if the text thus deprivileges the male gaze, it is only males (and typically male prostitutes) who have access to proper naming in the text. Although norms have been exploded, this postwar masculine framework seems to continue to privilege masculinity. It is, however, not a centering of white (French) masculinity, as the prostitutes are Algerian. In this sense, the narrative faces similar problematics as those mentioned earlier in relation to Genet and the FHAR, namely, that white French masculinity is freed at the expense of black and Arab males.

A lack of characterization and a mix of body parts and fragments thereof further signal a loss of subjectivity. The dirty, dusty, military mise-en-scène communicates action and commotion, while enumeration, repetition, and silence convey a failure of language. In combination, they border on abject abuse not only of humans and animals but also of language itself. The clear army presence and combat sequences suggest an era of colonial occupation, while elsewhere we are led to believe that independence has been won. Is this war we are witnessing, or is this apocalyptic scenario merely evidencing the unending effects of the war?

Extreme abjection equally characterizes this world we are entering, with numerous forms of violence and domination creeping in (prostitution and slavery being the most prominent). Sex work and homosexuality, both of which figure so heavily in the text, escape normative reproductive circuits and enact queer relationalities that evidence a hybridity and an ability to break binaries. Brun stakes a similar claim: "In denying the tear (male/female, human/animal), the bipolar division, the hybrid nature of the prostitutes imposes, with the logic of 'two at a time,' a third term, neither mixed nor neutral, at once mixed and neutral, eccentric, irreducible, and 'outside the law.'"[47] Further breaking apart dichotomous structuring principles, the text refuses to distinguish between inside and outside and upends the idea that language is referential. With no clear narrator, there is no apparent perspective in the text, only a fluid and fluctuating subconscious that propels it forward. Guyotat pushes this decentralization to the limit through his extreme lack of characterization and emphasis on acts over thoughts or identities. Instantiating a poststructuralist and queer approach that views the subject not as universal but as produced via nexuses of knowledge and power, the text dismantles any stable subjectivity or "I."

Guyotat famously stated: "I destroy rhetoric."[48] Indeed, his text is not concerned with rhetorical style but rather portrays a cacophony of raw acts that exceed language. *Eden, Eden, Eden* deforms structure and grammar and subverts conventions, including the most basic, such as paragraphs, punctuation, and narrative coherence. The absence of conjunctions and transitions, which are replaced by commas and semicolons, creates an agrammatical text and a sense of extreme disorientation. In fact, even its single sentence remains unresolved, for the final line ends with a comma, signifying that both sexual and formal promiscuity will endure. The fact that the text cannot be separated into digestible parts mirrors the postwar moment, during which Guyotat perceived there to be no space between war and sex, filth and lust.

Yet even in the litany of sexually graphic and violent acts, there is a rhythm. Indeed, although the text may, on the surface, appear unrestrained, the formal character of the novel's prose has been celebrated and defended. Diarmuid Hester, for instance, asserts that it is "actually a work of exceptional complexity and formal rigor."[49] In pursuit of his deformation of both language and style, Guyotat skillfully employs a number of literary techniques, including parataxis (placement of phrases one after the other without any coordinating or subordinating clauses) and anthimeria (suppression of adverbs). Additionally, a radical syncope can be identified in the text. Indeed, the elimination or loss of sounds and letters further deforms language and comprehensibility.[50]

Typifying Marcuse's view of time as not linear but cyclical, critical to Guyotat's project is the choice to write *Eden, Eden, Eden* entirely in the present indicative tense, with no past or future. Distinctions of space and time collapse, and this extreme precision positions the text firmly in the here and now, with no before or after. In contrast to the other texts I analyze in this book—many of which are obsessed with revisiting, replaying, and revising the past—*Eden, Eden, Eden* is fully in the present, enacting what could be seen as queer theory's radical questioning of dominant modes of narration. Guyotat's use of the present tense also invokes a queer temporality that reorders past, present, and future while figuring the war as something that is still very much operating in the present. The constant use of the present further evokes simultaneity, which I identify as another mark of queer temporality in that it expresses the perpetuity of what *is* rather than what was or will be. This queerness resists future-dominated discourses that privilege reproductive futurity and curtail nonnormative desires. By only writing in the present tense, Guyotat admits that the present is all we have in these apocalyptic postwar times. To paraphrase queer theorist Lee Edelman, there is "no future."[51]

That said, this sort of approach (often regarded as "antisocial" in queer theory) is not the only way to read this text and the temporality it embodies. José Esteban Muñoz, for example, offers a different conceptualization of queer time that is equally applicable: "The present is not enough. It is impoverished and toxic for queers and other people who do not feel the privilege of majoritarian belonging, normative tastes, and 'rational' expectations." While Guyotat might at first sight seem at odds with Muñoz's reflections, I do not read the two as irreconcilable, especially if we read on: "Let me be clear that the idea is not simply to turn away from the present. One cannot afford such a maneuver, and if one thinks one can, one has resisted the present in favor of folly. The present must be known in relation to the alternative temporal and spatial maps provided by a perception of past and future affective worlds."[52] It is this move that I see Guyotat enacting: a hyperfocus on the present reveals something about those past and future affective worlds that continue to haunt legacies of the French-Algerian War. We cannot afford to turn away from this trauma and violence, which remains fully in the present but which must be conceived of as inextricable from other times and tenses.

Although I have by now commented at some length on the formal characteristics of the text, I am less interested in its style for style's sake than I am in how this form communicates something about (the loss of) subjectivity and sexuality in the post-decolonization moment. In other words, despite its precision and exactitude in abandoning the conventions of narrative structure and characterization, *Eden, Eden, Eden* disassembles, deforms, and distorts language, culture, and normative notions of sexuality and subjectivity—and inaugurates a new era. In terms of the implications for consequently thinking a more open and affirmative model of sex and sexuality, it is worth here turning to the work of Gilles Deleuze and Félix Guattari. Indeed, Guyotat previews what would come to be proposed by Deleuze and Guattari through their focus on corporeal disorganization and a mobilization of desire as fluid and without object or objective. Guyotat's conceptualization of sex not as internal but as directed outward also corresponds to Deleuze and Guattari's understanding of sexuality as expansive and as a network of flows and energies.[53] Margrit Shildrick interprets this dynamic as a deconstruction—a queering—of all bodies and subjectivities. Citing Deleuze and Guattari's *Anti-Oedipus*, she writes that this process entails "both 'taking apart egos and their presuppositions' and 'liberating the prepersonal singularities they enclose and repress.'"[54] Shildrick elaborates:

> In place of prohibition, repression and disavowal, Deleuzian desire is expansive, fluid, and connective, grounding sexuality itself as highly plastic and as no longer reliant on the terms of any binary opposition such as those of male/female, active/passive, or human/

animal. . . . At the same time, desire itself takes on a wider meaning that liberates it not simply from the bounds of genital sexuality per se, but more generally from the restricted parameters of what is usually defined as sexual relationality, whether that is accepting of, or challenging to, the conventions. Skin on skin in the bedroom is no more privileged than the sensation of fine sand running through my toes, or the sweet taste of a juicy peach on my tongue.[55]

This formulation also approximates what Guyotat suggests through a flattening of hierarchies and an equalization of practices. He radically deconstructs the unity and coherence of subjectivity and identity by deprivileging social structures that create hierarchies through the deployment of dichotomous thinking. Whether addressing sex or class, "the aim is the same," Brun writes, namely, the "refusal of hierarchization of clauses and utterances, substitution of parataxis by hypotaxis . . . refusal of the superiority of this or that category."[56] This refusal to submit to taxonomic stratification is encapsulated by Guyotat's statement that in *Eden, Eden, Eden* "[e]*verything is equal*: a kiss and vomit; horror, repugnance are defused."[57]

Rather than exclusively concerned with sex or desire, Guyotat's work is thus fundamentally invested in a deconstruction of hierarchies. In Guyotat's own words: "Here, there is no 'desire.' . . . [T]he movement is exclusively economic; there is no 'love.'"[58] In fact, *Eden, Eden, Eden* separates desire, sex, and sexuality, exemplifying Foucault's well-known turn to bodies and pleasures. In Guyotat, there is no sexuality, only sex. Indeed, the text illustrates some of the central tenets Foucault had begun to develop—and that would find their culmination in his multivolume study of sexuality. It is perhaps unsurprising then that Guyotat was lauded by Foucault, for as he described in *The History of Sexuality*, bodies and pleasures—not sex and desire—resist the apparatus of sexuality. Bent on avoiding the fixation of stable identities, Foucault's work—like Guyotat's—aspires to desubjectification.

Foucault: There Will Be Scandal . . .

"Tell me what your desire is, and I'll tell you who you are, if you are normal or not," Foucault famously stated in "The Gay Science," ventriloquizing the growing psychiatric-industrial complex.[59] Foucault's oeuvre—a seminal elaboration on knowledge, power, and subjectification that contributed to the eventual emergence of queer theory—attempted to decouple pleasure from sexual subjectivity and a psychological theory of desire, not least as he could not bear the word "desire," which for him suggested approval of theories that posited it as evidencing a deep-seated identity.[60] Whereas desire leads to subjectivities, sexualities, and individualities, pleasure does not carry the same psychological weight in that it resists pathologization. Indeed, as Arnold Davidson details, there is "no primacy of the subject in the experience of pleasure."[61]

At its core, Foucault's project was founded on a critical questioning of subjectivity that warns us of the traps of identity. He explicates how the normalizing discourses of gender and sexuality are completely bound up in subjectivity and the process of subjectification, which sets the terms for identity. Scientific and cultural norms, for example, produce the ways in which we are able to conceive of sexuality as a concept and as an identity. In a now well-rehearsed argument that pervades queer studies scholarship, Foucault identifies how the seventeenth century was often considered to mark the beginning of an age of repression, silence, and censorship concerning matters of sex and sexuality. In reality, however, there was a "discursive explosion." What characterizes the past three centuries is neither prudishness nor the need to hide sex but rather an institutional incitement and a dispersion of devices created to speak about it. A multiplicity of discourses on sex emerged, with biology, medicine, psychiatry, pedagogy, and political science all implicitly concerned with how reproductive futurity encouraged some forms of sex (i.e., heterosexual monogamy) at the expense of all other activities considered "abnormal" (e.g., same-sex sexual acts), which were discouraged or criminalized.[62]

Foucault aimed to dismantle the psychological subject that emerged from what he termed *scientia sexualis*—an axis that corresponded to sexology, demography, and psychoanalysis and that was correlated with the form of knowledge that constituted biopower. The result was the placing of sex into discourse, which led to both an incitement to speak about it and an uptick in "sexual heterogeneities" and "polymorphous sexualities." For Foucault, repression is but one mechanism among others that gives form to sexuality and hence power relations. Despite "a whole series of tensions, conflicts, efforts at adjustment, and attempts at retranscription" marking the eighteenth century onward, there also exists a framework of infinite possibilities for resistance.[63] For Foucault, transgression rests not in simply talking about sex but rather in defending the most "perverse" sexual practices and engaging in counterattacks that "counter the grips of power with the claims of bodies, pleasures, and knowledges, in their multiplicity and their possibility of resistance."[64] Power shapes sex and sexuality through "polymorphous techniques of power," which are both productive and repressive.

Guyotat's *Eden, Eden, Eden* stakes a comparable claim through its graphic enactments of libidinal excess. However, in contrast to Foucault, Guyotat suggests that France's long war of decolonization (combined with capitalism) profoundly impacted the modern subject. Even as he long maintained political commitments, Foucault, unlike Guyotat, showed a surprising lack of engagement with the topic of French colonialism.[65] Foucault's biographer David Macey notes that he held "vague sympathy for the Algerian cause but was not a militant supporter," even if, more broadly speaking, his work influenced the field of postcolonial studies.[66] What has, however, been overlooked in critiques of Foucault's detached attitude toward French colonialism was his engagement with Guyotat's *Eden, Eden, Eden*.

In September 1970 Foucault published an open letter to Guyotat in the magazine *Le Nouvel Observateur* entitled "Il y aura scandale, mais..." (There will be scandal, but...). For Foucault, Guyotat's enigmatic text was groundbreaking in its illustration of the dissolution of the subject, which he identifies as having been shaped by the Algerian experience and Guyotat's colonial military service. After explaining that the reception of *Eden, Eden, Eden* would most certainly differ from that of his earlier *Tomb for 500,000 Soldiers*—primarily due to the temporal distance and the fact that it "lacks the noise of war that allowed your first novel to be heard"—Foucault admits that the French-Algerian War and the attendant brutality were publicly framed as a parenthesis.[67] Even if it was scandalous in its own right, Guyotat's earlier novel was accessible in that it could be interpreted through the long shadow cast by World War II over Algeria, which shaped the narrative that emanated from the near-decade-long conflict and France's eventual loss of empire. However, despite stemming from similar concerns, *Eden, Eden, Eden* eludes the reader in a way that *Tomb for 500,000 Soldiers* did not, precisely because it could be more clearly mapped onto a war that most were well aware of yet unwilling to fully acknowledge. *Eden, Eden, Eden* is, by definition, "hors lieu" (out of place), Foucault argues, and "it is from below the body that your text comes to us: surfaces, splinters, openings-wounds, clothing and skins that turn and reverse, white and red liquids, 'streaming from the eternal outside.'"[68] Here, Foucault shows a hesitancy to embrace the body, which he calls "an elegance—materialistic—to save the subject, the ego, the soul," in other words, precisely those identity-based social structures that he had been striving to undermine and undo in his own work, much like Guyotat does throughout *Eden, Eden, Eden*.[69]

Foucault then turns to his primary concerns: sex, sexuality, and subjectivity. In a powerful statement, he acknowledges Guyotat as the first writer in decades to reconfigure a theoretical understanding of this triangle, that is, to treat sex and sexuality neither as an appendage of the individual nor as an (aspect of) identity. I quote his proceeding lines at length precisely because they summarize *Eden, Eden, Eden*'s revolutionary nature and foreshadow some of the central themes upon which Foucault would elaborate in his later work, including an explication of the links between the individual, sexuality, and subjectification:

> I get the impression that you are bringing together what we have known about sexuality for a long time but that we carefully keep apart in order to protect the primacy of the subject, the unity of the individual, and the abstraction of "sex": that it is not at the limit of the body, nor is it a means of communication; it is not even the individual's fundamental or primitive desire; the very texture of its processes exists prior to the individual. The individual is no more than its precarious prolongation, provisional, quickly erased; in the end, the individual is only a pale form that emerges

for a moment from a great stock that is stubborn and repetitive. Individuals—the quickly retracted pseudopods of sexuality. If we want to know what we know, we must abandon what we imagine of our individuality, our ego, our subject position. In your text, it is perhaps the first time that the relationships between the individual and sexuality are frankly and decidedly reversed: they are no longer characters who fade away for the benefit of elements, structures, or personal pronouns; sexuality moves to the other side of the individual and ceases to be "subjectified."[70]

Here, Foucault lays out what he identifies as one of the most provocative elements of *Eden, Eden, Eden*, namely, Guyotat's ability to avoid putting the subject on a pedestal and representing sexuality as "the fundamental or primitive desire of the individual." Foucault sees in *Eden, Eden, Eden* something different from what had overwhelmingly been conceptualized by the pervading scientific and cultural discourses: sexuality is no longer connected to subjectivity. Sex reverses and dissolves the move from sexuality to subjectivity, by which he means the internalization of forms of identity produced in relation to the institutions, structures, and discourses that surround us. Unsubjectified sex is pure action.

In equal measure, Foucault and Guyotat sought to pursue the dissolution of subjectivity, a diagnosis that Kendall summarizes as standing as "a scaffold for the Western tradition."[71] In the case of Foucault, this dissolution of subjectivity referenced his approach to the individual as nothing but a fading phenomenon, the product of power and knowledge, a manifestation of the political and social moment, and one that can be quickly erased or altered. In this respect, Foucault argues that we must resist the notion that we have an "identity" or stable subject position: "We must abandon what we imagine of our individuality, our ego, our subject position," he writes in his open letter to Guyotat. Indeed, Guyotat presaged a number of central concerns that Foucault would undertake in his seminal work on sexuality. In this sense, *Eden, Eden, Eden* prefigures and exemplifies Foucault's turn to bodies and pleasures and similarly presents a counterattack to the apparatus of sexuality.

At the same time, I read the novel as following up on Herbert Marcuse's *Eros and Civilization* via its focus on libidinality, repression, and resistance. Foucault and Marcuse have, however, been read by some as occupying seemingly irreconcilable positions, particularly since Foucault so adamantly rejected the psychoanalytical project in his later work. He implicitly targeted Marcuse in *The History of Sexuality*'s characterization of the "repressive hypothesis" and found Marcuse's Freudian-Marxist interpretation of power problematic, viewing it as one-dimensional in that it is configured as merely stifling preexisting desires.[72] In his view, Marcuse diagnoses society as operating under a repressive regime, which runs counter to his own theoretical underpinnings. That said, I find Foucault's interpretation to be overly dismissive of the complexities of Marcuse's framework, and a careful reading would counter Foucault's characterization of Marcuse as believing merely releasing sex would counteract power.[73] In fact, Foucault's focus on bodies and pleasures shares much with Marcuse's investment in libidinal utopias and his radical conceptualization of sexuality and revolution. In this way, I read *Eden, Eden, Eden* as bridging what some have seen as a theoretical mismatch, providing a connection that therefore makes an important contribution to queer theory in its take on subjectivity and identity. In a full-scale dissolution of the subject, Guyotat's *Eden, Eden, Eden*—through its endless speech—unites Marcuse's vision of libidinal release with Foucault's characterization of an incitement to discourse.

At their core, the texts by Marcuse and Guyotat—and even Foucault—are texts about revolution and change. They are also intimately linked to reconceptualizations of time and memory, which Martin Jay summarizes in his essay on Marcuse and temporality as follows: "Memory subverts one-dimensional consciousness and opens up the possibility of an alternative future. . . . Memory, by restoring the forgotten past, was thus a model of the utopian temporality of the future."[74] This vision of sexual liberation as dependent on a socially transformative and antinormalizing framework and as offering the proposition of an alternative future, a vision that would later be elaborated upon within queer theory and politics, is particularly evident in Guyotat's text and its questioning of temporality.

An Alternative to the World

Guyotat's *Eden, Eden, Eden* evidences the ways in which the French-Algerian War enacted a radical rupture in subjectivity, temporality, narrative, sex and sexuality, relationality, and rhetoric. For Guyotat, libidinal excess was intimately linked both to the war and to its postcolonial anxieties. The subject no longer existed. The grounds on which subjectivity had been built had to be destroyed. Yet how can we also read this book, which radically deconstructs identity and is so violent, as a force of political change? To me, *Eden, Eden, Eden* is simultaneously utopian and dystopian, dissolving both of these terms just as it dissolves subjectivity itself: it is—to borrow from Marcuse—a "great refusal" of modernism and everything that it stands for, including imperialism, identity, and the coherent subject.[75] It deconstructs the opposition between utopia and dystopia—it is not about how it *should be* but about how it *is*. In doing so, it makes an obvious postcolonial critique without needing a coherent subject to do so.

At the same time, I do not want to romanticize the pleasures and perversities of *Eden, Eden, Eden*, a text that is firmly about violence. Guyotat also confessed that his text was a critique of capitalism and imperialism, and the portrait he paints of these twentieth-century forces could hardly be read as utopian. While the post-decolonization period in France involved a grappling with violence (physical, institutional, and symbolic), it was simultaneously a period of reimagining sex and sexuality and a growing exploration of nonnormative sexual acts. Thinking and reading it from a queer perspective does not mean pushing to the side or obscuring those unpleasant aspects, nor does it mean picking and choosing the more desirable features, for the biopolitical and the necropolitical become inseparable in being two sides of the same coin. It is in this regard that Guyotat engages in a practice in which no aspect of the text is privileged over another: there is no beginning, no middle, and no end; there is no separation; everything is equal. Indeed, a kiss is vomit.

In a reworking of Marcuse's concept of the great refusal as a proposal for radical subjectivity, Muñoz writes that "queer utopianism is a great refusal."[76] Here, I am also reminded of Juana María Rodríguez's commentary on sex and corporeality as integral to queer praxis: "The sexual practices and fantasies of our perverse imaginations create a place and time of elsewhere, a utopian nexus of critique and potentiality, available to anyone, where sex and recognition touch and cum together."[77] *Eden, Eden, Eden* similarly presents an opportunity: the sentence without end allows us to contribute—to add to this ongoing project and to take things in different directions by radically rethinking subjectivity. Queer sexual encounters are here productive in destabilizing or queering subjectivity and theorizing alternative temporalities in relation to pleasure, desire, and violence. Guyotat's text, as Brun also reads it, proposes an "alternative to the world."[78]

As with many other texts I analyze in the course of this book, there is no clear story in Guyotat's *Eden, Eden, Eden*. Coherent narratives no longer make sense in the context of the French-Algerian War, where progress is neither teleological nor temporally configured. Coming after decolonization, independence, and the fall of empire, *Eden, Eden, Eden* works through impulses and forges on in a manner that allows us not only to alter the terms of our engagement with the past but also to create an alternative future. Published at a moment marked by a deafening silence concerning French colonial violence, it captures the senselessness of the war and its aftermath. It responds to this silence by talking endlessly, without breaks, without periods, and, most importantly, without straightforward linguistic coherence or meaning.

To conclude, I want to turn to a 2009 interview with Guyotat in which he described his own relation to sex, sexuality, and desire as follows: "I don't have a single 'sexual orientation,' I have inside myself a double desire, two sexualities that I have never put on the same plane. . . . The nonheterosexual impulse is for me a way of expelling the large part of desire, the biggest desire, the most animal, the most dangerous, in order to arrive at a desire that is softer, more profound, productive."[79] Countering the harshness of *Eden, Eden, Eden*, Guyotat here offers a new way of thinking about the power of queer desires to arrive at something more profound. Marcuse writes in *The Aesthetic Dimension* that "the truth of art lies in its power to break the monopoly of established reality to define what is real."[80] Works of art like Guyotat's induce emotion and depict an alternative view of both the world and subjectivity. Art becomes a form of radical subjectivity and a tool with which to liberate oneself beyond the narrow confines of identity as channeled through cultural norms. Queerness here allows us to imagine a future that might find peace with the contradictions of fixating on the present while simultaneously radically rejecting the here and now and instead gesturing toward Muñoz's proposal of queerness as horizon, a "warm illumination of a horizon imbued with potentiality," thus arriving at a desire that is softer, more profound, and productive.[81]

4 Queer Palimpsests and October 17, 1961: Memory Politics in Leïla Sebbar's *The Seine Was Red*

> Deviation leaves its own marks on the ground, which can help generate alternative lines, which cross the ground in unexpected ways. Such lines are indeed traces of desire.
>
> —Sara Ahmed, *Queer Phenomenology*

Postcolonial scholarship has been particularly influential in rejecting narratives of progress, teaching us to be weary of a linear historicism in which colonialism had a defined beginning and end, after which "postcolonial" time was suddenly inaugurated. John McLeod, for instance, explains how postcolonialism as a historical marker and an aesthetic critical practice "stresses *continuity* and *change* by recognising the continuing agency of colonial discourses as well as resistances to them."[1] By critically interrogating a linear model of time, queer theory similarly deconstructs temporality and the sort of progress-oriented narratives that seem to dominate the contemporary era. Jack Halberstam has suggested that queer time offers an alternative framework for theorizing "anticanonical knowledges of queer practices."[2] Queer and postcolonial theorizations of time and temporality offer us tools with which to think outside of such teleological narratives and to reconceptualize memory and the ethical imperatives it implies, thus offering new modes of consciousness. By refusing chronologically defined structures, queer postcolonial temporalities imagine time differently, allowing marginalized and disqualified voices to emerge.

As more and more work on the French-Algerian War and memory is produced, there is a pressing need to reconsider how forgetting also functions to shape subjectivities and identities. Indeed, the effects of a colonial past are evidenced not only via its memories but also in what is forgotten and left out of the historical record. In "Narratives of Recovery: Repressed Memory as Cultural Memory," Marita Sturken asks: "While the concept of repression suggests that we forget, it is also based on the idea that memory retrieval is not only possible but healing. Yet recovered memory demands that we ask: What is an experience that is not remembered? What is a memory that doesn't need an experience?"[3] These questions represent, in essence, the complex conundrums that I address in this chapter through an analysis of Leïla Sebbar's *La Seine était rouge* (*The Seine Was Red*, 1999), a novel that confronts and creatively works through memories without experiences, exposing the complex memory politics at the center of a violent episode—October 17, 1961—that most seem to want to forget.[4] This chapter helps to unsettle the dominant narrative that memories of wartime experiences must be recovered for any hope at productive healing. It does so by returning to the 1961 Paris massacre examined in chapter 2, engaging with a novel that examines the consequences this event would have for a diverse trio of young individuals, none of whom experienced the actual event. While referencing the massacre by merely its date might suggest that it came and went several decades ago, the characters of *The Seine Was Red* continuously remind us that its effects persist, exemplifying that the "post" of "postcolonial" does not mark an "after" or a bygone era and that memories can be recorded and processed in alternative ways.

A number of scholars have remarked how the French-Algerian War resists any sort of finitude or defined beginning and end. I need only to recall the previously cited words of novelist Laurent Mauvignier in chapter 1: "The Algerian War is not over.... [W]e can see how in France today it still isn't settled."[5] If the previous chapter was invested in a queering of subjectivity and sexuality, here I make a case for reading the concept of memory—which itself reconfigures temporality and reorders the path between past, present, and future—through a queer lens in the context of the French-Algerian War. In this respect, Carla

Freccero's conceptualization of a queer-inflected spectrality as "concerned not with recovering specific queer subjects in or from the past but with mobilizing the combination of queer thinking (with its emphasis on multiplying sites of affectivity and pleasure) and spectrality (as an anti-teleological and non-binary mode)" is fundamental to this chapter's assertion that achronological, nonhierarchical modes of time are politically and personally productive in imagining different pasts, presents, and futures.[6]

While chapter 2's analysis of *Caché* looked at the ways in which October 17, 1961, provoked a host of violent effects, this chapter takes as its point of departure the same event in order to uncover how memory and geography can be actively redrawn through subversive countermemories, which I term "queer palimpsests." Sebbar's novel, in proposing an approach that is concurrently forward-facing and backward-looking, rewrites the cartography of the city's history by literally inscribing October 17 back into history. Arguably, in its resistance to linearity and clear progression, memory is always already "queer." Thus, I adopt a queer reading method that is both palimpsestic and palimpsestuous in order to resist reducing texts to a single narrative in which a hidden past is recovered, thereby illustrating how memories of forgotten or hidden colonial violence may allow for a subversion of official history and colonial temporality.

Yet, in line with Sara Ahmed's epigraph, *The Seine Was Red* is also a novel about desire—traces of desire that evidence that deviation and difference are productive and create unexpected relations, "alternative lines, which cross the ground in unexpected ways."[7] Taking the path less trodden leaves behind traces that speak to the possibility of something more—something different. In this sense, I read this text in line with Donna McCormack's conceptualization of queer postcolonial narratives. Queer and postcolonial theories can be bridged in order to construct a lens through which to better understand texts and characters that diverge from expected paths and then "re-emerge along the same—and sometimes different—roads, but always desire and create something a little queerer."[8] It is neither the gender nor the sexuality of the characters that frames my queer reading; rather, I use this approach to enquire into the intersecting nature of memory, gender, and nationality and its potential to reconfigure temporality.

Countermemory, Postmemory, and Transfiliation

Born in Algeria to an Algerian father and a French mother, the novel's author has long eschewed identitarian categories in her personal life and in her literary production. In *Remembering French Algeria*, Amy Hubbell points out that Leïla Sebbar has often resisted claiming any identity label, instead favoring ambiguous terms such as *croisée* (crossed) and *bigarrée* (multicolored) that suggest a mixing of France and Algeria.[9] However, rather than interpreting this as an attempt to rejoin or reconnect a separated France and Algeria, as Hubbell does, I understand Sebbar's refusal (both in her autobiographical writings and in her fictional work) as a radical act of enacting fluidity that acknowledges an enduring *inseparability* between France and Algeria. In the post-decolonization era, neither France nor Algeria is distinct. Memories and identities are hybrid. For Sebbar, writing is reparative and is a medium through which she can negotiate the complex politics of remembering and forgetting, as well as their anxieties, hopes, and desires: "It is there and only there that I reassemble body and soul and that I bridge over the two shores."[10]

Sebbar's novel takes the Paris massacre of October 17, 1961, as a starting point from which to explore the possibilities and potentialities of writing the war differently. The text is focalized through three young individuals who are attempting to come to terms with the event thirty-five years later. While they could be respectively characterized as Algerian, French, and *beur* (French Arab), like Sebbar, each one consistently resists these labels and expresses unease with categories of race, ethnicity, and national origin. Their backgrounds do, however, allow the novel to represent the complex identity politics at work both in the 1960s and in present-day France. In this sense, the text interrogates hybridity and asks how diasporic subjects engage with memory in the postcolonial city. Together these three characters retrace the 1961 protest in an act reminiscent of the urban redrawing that occurred in the actual event, which, as indicated in chapter 2, was called for by the FLN to protest a state-imposed curfew that forbade

Algerians from being out of their homes in the evening. The FLN hoped to attract domestic and international attention to the injustices that the French government was imposing on its own citizens. Serving the dual purpose of claiming physical space and "redrawing colonial cartographies," the protesters attempted to rewrite citizenship in a reclaiming of visibility via their movement from the Parisian periphery to the city center.[11]

Despite a growing number of literary works that reference the 1961 massacre, Sebbar's novel is the first to take the event as its primary narrative and central story line.[12] Sebbar begins the text with a dedication to the victims of October 1961 and to those who have come before her in the struggle to resurrect memories of the massacre, including Didier Daeninckx, Jean-Luc Einaudi, Elie Kagan, Nacer Kettane, Mehdi Lallaoui, François Maspéro, Georges Mattei, Jacques Panijel, Paulette Péju, and Anne Tristan. In dedicating the novel to such writers, historians, journalists, and photographers, Sebbar immediately reveals the text to be informed by a collective contribution to reconstitutions of October 17, 1961—a polyphonic record of a violent event, the traces of which many have worked hard to uncover. The table of contents (which foregrounds the various testimonies included in the text through its list of characters, locations, and dates) serves as a physical and temporal map of the journey that the novel's protagonists eventually embark on. From FLN militant to Paris police officer, from French *porteur de valises* to *harki*, from nearly drowned victim to good Samaritan, from those involved in the protest to those attempting to reconstruct events that have been hidden from them, Sebbar's multivocal text lays bare the alliances forged and the conflicts waged between nationalist groups and political factions.[13] Yet—and perhaps more importantly—this literary strategy also points to the fact that one voice will never be enough to communicate the event, its legacy, and its corresponding (and conflicting) emotions. Anne Donadey reads the multitude of perspectives "across generations, genders, political persuasions, and ethnic origins" as a way of reconfiguring the remembering/forgetting binary: "Anamnesis becomes a way of resisting the occlusions created by official history, of recovering the traces of another, submerged history in order to create a counter-memory."[14]

This notion of countermemory lies at the heart of Sebbar's project. Published by Éditions Thierry Magnier, a publisher specializing in literature for children and young adults, *The Seine Was Red* also serves as a pedagogical tool, filling in the blanks left by the official history books. We may even read the novel as a preemptive antidote to the turning away from the realities of the French-Algerian War (and colonialism in general) that came in the form of a 2005 law that would have forcibly included in the national curriculum instruction regarding the "positive role" of French colonization. Article 4 mandated that "academic research programs must give the history of French presence overseas, particularly in North Africa, *the place it deserves*. Scholastic programs should recognize in particular the positive role of the French presence overseas, especially in North Africa, and give the history and sacrifices of French soldiers from these territories the prominent place to which they have the right."[15] While the 2005 law itself was short-lived, its motivation nonetheless suggests a nation still grappling with a relatively recent loss of empire. Politicians saw a need to highlight the so-called benefits of colonialism (read: colonial occupation), which itself becomes subsumed and obfuscated within the phrase "French presence overseas." The law also hides the detrimental effects of imperialism, including the fact that violence and forced assimilation—whether in North Africa or eventually in France proper—were regular features of the "civilizing mission" (*mission civilisatrice*). In educating a younger generation about events otherwise omitted, *The Seine Was Red* makes a critical contribution to a long-standing political and historical debate regarding nationality, memory, and intergenerational transmission.[16] By rewriting or supplementing the fallible official historical record to include violent acts underwritten by the state, the novel also suggests that history repeats itself, thereby belying any notion of "civilization" or "progress."

Evidencing the novel's investment in situating place, character, and time, the first chapter is entitled "Nanterre. Amel. October 1996" and begins: "Her [Amel's] mother said nothing to her, nor did her mother's mother. Mother and daughter see each other often. They chat in French and Arabic. Amel doesn't understand everything they say."[17] Although she is already a skilled philologist, Amel, the bookish sixteen-year-old protagonist, does not understand Arabic, the mother tongue of her mother and grandmother. Even though they have not passed their language down to her, they do instill in her a need to focus on scholarly pursuits such as learning Latin and Greek, which they believe will create opportunities that they did not have as immigrants in France. Indeed, Amel is a product of the French educational system, which takes as one of its primary aims the transmission of national identity. For Amel, this presents an obstacle to understanding her own hybrid and multicultural background, as we can be certain that the classical education she receives does not address historical events related to the French-Algerian War, which was not even acknowledged by France as a war at the time the novel was published.

As well, Amel's mother and grandmother speak in Arabic to keep her from the harsh truths of their own experiences: "If she were to ask them what they were saying in the other language, 'the language of the homeland,' her grandmother would say as she always does: 'Secrets, my girl, secrets you shouldn't know, that must be kept hidden. But you'll learn them some day, when you need to.'"[18] Her female elders seem to benefit from her limited comprehension of their native language—an ignorance that protects her from "the truth" (*la vérité*), which will, however, inevitably come with adulthood. They are all too aware of the fact that trauma is passed down, a process that they attempt to interrupt. Amel, however, cannot understand what could be so bad that it "must be kept hidden," especially in light of the fact that she lives in a multimedia world infused with images of unhappiness (*malheur*): "We see it every day on TV, we read it, I read it in books."[19] Her grandmother responds: "In books, on TV … It's not the same as what I'll tell you someday, when the time is right, and your mother will too."[20] The day Amel begins to learn these secrets soon arrives, but it is not her female elders who impart these hidden truths. Instead, it is Omer, a twenty-seven-year-old pessimistic Algerian journalist reluctantly living in exile in Paris after receiving death threats in Algeria, and Louis, a twenty-three-year-old amateur documentarian producing a film about October 17, 1961, who teach Amel what happened on that fateful day.

While foregrounding the significance of intergenerational matrilineal communication, the novel opens with an evocation of that which is left out, not understood, and not translated. Just as *Caché* forced us to ask questions about modes of communication between parents and children (see chapter 2), *The Seine Was Red* also speaks to the difficulties of accurately recounting the past to the next generation. Like *Caché*, which concluded with the sons of the colonizer and colonized speaking (although we were not privy to their conversation), the most significant dialogues and debates in *The Seine Was Red* happen among the younger generation. And despite the fact that both works expose obstacles to intergenerational communication, they hold out hope for intercultural communication.

This generation that takes center stage in Sebbar's novel also occupies a unique position by virtue of their ability to link and delink past, present, and future. They are, to use Marianne Hirsch's term, a "postmemory" generation—the children of those who most directly experienced the French-Algerian War and the violent colonial event of October 17.[21] Yet Amel, Omer, and Louis—as proxies of this generation—engage with history differently from their elders. Hirsch writes that "to grow up with such overwhelming inherited memories, to be dominated by narratives that preceded one's birth or one's consciousness, is to risk having one's own stories and experiences displaced, even evacuated, by those of a previous generation."[22] If we take Hirsch's point, we could read the characters of *The Seine Was Red* as actively *resisting* mechanisms of postmemory. They do so by nonlinearly weaving different memories and temporalities together: Louis's documentary film, the characters' tracing of the 1961 protest, the inherited memories, and the palimpsestic traces that they leave behind all complicate and undo the expected chronology between time periods. Each of these strategies to represent and to give voice to the massacre reconfigures time and queers memory, illustrating Max Silverman's point that the relationship between past and present "takes the form of a superimposition and interaction of different temporal traces to constitute a sort of composite structure, like a palimpsest, so that one layer of traces can be seen through, and is transformed by, another."[23] To this end, Sebbar also subverts genre. The work exceeds the bounds of a simple and conventional novel and more closely resembles a documentary screenplay in that it contains filmic passages and scene-setting directions ("outside," "inside, daytime"). In playing with generic conventions, Sebbar—like many, if not all, of the authors investigated in *Hybrid Anxieties*—evidences the ways in which style, syntax, and genre had to be reconfigured in the wake of the war. Mixing the genres of novel and film also serves the purpose of decentering categorical thinking and fostering hybridity.

The novel expresses an interest in "transfiliation," a concept that Denis Provencher uses to capture the engagement and movement between the transcultural and the transnational across generations and identity categories.[24] Like Provencher, I read this as a queer approach that reconfigures relationships and relationalities and creates stories and narratives that transgress and subvert a linear teleology that would emphasize normative kinship and reproductive futurity. Provencher elaborates on its transgressive potentiality:

> *Transfiliation* is inherently tied to the process of flexible accumulation and engages with the transcultural and the transnational. It also involves reaching across generations and is transgressive because of its potential to reverse the direction of the transfer of knowledge, tradition, and symbolic heritage between parent and child. It ushers in new forms of heritage and transmission—i.e., procreation through representation.... *Transfiliation* also entails moving across genres in speaking about and representing selfhood—oral tradition, literature, television, internet, cinema, digital photography, performance art, letter writing, etc. It deals with movement across identity categories such as gender, sexuality, race, and class. Hence it is also inherently intersectional.[25]

In the novel, Amel, Omer, and Louis break a chain of silence—one that many scholars have identified as symptomatic of first- and second-generation immigrants. While the unspoken serves as a motor and catalyst for the novel, the characters also engage in this transfilial dynamic described by Provencher, a negotiation that involves a complicated—and complication of—intergenerational transmission of both silence and language. In its reversal of generational lines of communication and movement between genres and identity categories, this transfilial process is also queer.

In contrast to Haneke's surface-level treatment of women in chapter 2's analysis of *Caché*, women play an integral role in Sebbar's narrative. In presenting the novel's protagonists as united through previous generations of women who fought for Algerian independence, Sebbar outspokenly confronts the role played by gender in determining both memory and experience. Whereas *Caché* treats women as willfully engaging in amnesia (as seen in the figure of Georges's mother, who has virtually forgotten the boy she almost adopted), *The Seine Was Red* presents women as the protectors of memory.[26] Louis and Omer are the respective sons of Flora and Mina, who are close friends of Amel's mother and grandmother. All these women played a role in and were profoundly affected by the events of October 17, 1961. Louis's mother, Flora, for example, was a former "suitcase carrier," or *porteuse de valises*, and spent years in prison for her anticolonial activism. Sebbar's text also reveals a silencing of women on another level. While the October 17 protest has begun to garner attention many decades later, there was another, less discussed protest that occurred three days after: the women's protest (*la manifestation des femmes*). Expunged from the dominant historical record, Sebbar cites the protest of October 20, 1961, in which Algerian women took to the streets to protest in front of prisons (including La Santé, which appears later in the novel) where their husbands, sons, and brothers were held. A total of 513 women and 113 children were arrested that day.[27]

The text also offers alternative modes of masculine action and embodiment. In dealing with memory differently, for example, Louis adopts a new version of masculinity by utilizing his privilege as a white French male to gain unfettered access to stories and archives. This sits in stark contrast to the masculinity models witnessed in part 1 of this book. In *Caché*, for example, Georges and even Majid's son attempt to assert their place by taking up physical space, threatening others, and speaking loudly. Conversely, *The Seine Was Red*'s Louis and Omer feel that their actions must nurture a more affirmative and sensitive masculinity, thereby countering this otherwise violent (and anxious) postcolonial masculinity. In addition, they both use their status to give voice to forgotten women. For example, Louis's interest in making a film about the role of women in the October protest and Omer's risky decision to publish previously untold stories and photographs of Algerian women from the war in the Algerian press (which resulted in him having to flee Algeria out of fear for his safety) demonstrate a continued investment by their generation to create different understandings of gender and new models for relating to one another.

For his part, Louis had also been kept in the dark about his parents' anticolonial activities—actions that ultimately led to his mother's arrest and his father being forced into hiding. His mother, Flora, for example, never wants to respond to his questions about the war, saying it is in the past: "We've forgotten; it will be vague, approximate, uninteresting, I promise. . . . Ask your father, you'll see."[28] In other words, people want to forget these stories: "How many of them want to forget, and they do forget," Flora states.[29] While collective amnesia provides the impetus for Louis to embark on his documentary project, he nevertheless continues to encounter resistance from his mother, who questions his motives for wanting to make a film about something he did not directly experience, echoing ongoing debates around identity politics about who can speak about what (and on behalf of whom): "Do you really need to make this film? It isn't your story."[30] Yet ultimately, Sebbar's text demonstrates that October 17, 1961, is the story of every French and Algerian citizen, regardless of their participation (or lack thereof) in the protest or massacre. Louis summarizes: "Exactly, I want to do it. I'll do it because it isn't my story. 1954–1962. October 17, 1961 in Paris and you in this colonial war. . . . I need to know, not everything, but I need to understand some of it."[31] Even though the novel's main characters—Amel, Louis, and Omer—were born years later, they each learn that the war was, and continues to be, *their* story too, and giving voice to the marginalized and disenfranchised thus rests in their hands.

Thanks to Louis's film, Amel begins to learn some of the stories that have been kept from her. Upon watching the film, which includes archival footage of the protest and the recorded testimonies of its participants, Amel finally discovers these secrets—the events of October 17, 1961, and the role that her family played in them (her grandfather, a high-level member of the FLN, was one of the organizers of the protest). She is particularly surprised to learn that Louis has convinced her mother to share with him her testimony (presented in six segments throughout the novel, each in a chapter entitled "The Mother"), in which she details her memories of the massacre through her childhood eyes. After repeatedly watching the film, Amel is moved to respond to what she has learned and takes Omer with her on a journey across Paris to retrace the protest, starting at Nanterre, the site of the bidonvilles where the protesters lived, by way of Concorde and La Défense, to the Pont Saint-Michel, where numerous Algerians were massacred and thrown into the Seine River. Their retracing of the protest is reminiscent of the urban redrawing that occurred in the actual event, as tens of thousands of Algerians previously relegated to the city's periphery descended on Paris to reclaim public space—space that was rightfully theirs as French citizens. In their physical and temporal journey, Amel and Omer will not only follow the October 17 route but also leave subversive countermonuments, or palimpsestic queer traces, by writing with red paint over World War II plaques to mark the Algerian protesters' actions and lives. Instead of taking the straight and narrow path (in this case quite literally, as it is a straight line from the Louvre via Concorde and the Arc de Triomphe to La Défense), they redraw the city by acknowledging its periphery, an area on the fringes of the city that remains to this day primarily occupied by large housing projects populated by people of color and immigrant communities. In addition to highlighting and accounting for silenced voices, the palimpsests that Amel and Omer leave behind symbolize the palimpsestic nature of memory itself. In their rewriting, they problematize the idea that "by the time memory has been prodded into coherent form, its veracity is no longer under consideration."[32] In fact, the pervasive blanks of "official history" (symbolized by the plaques) actually leave space for these amendments, even though their addition would necessarily lead to a complete overhaul of the historical record.

Imbricated Memories

As repeatedly suggested throughout this book, World War II undoubtedly occupies a significant place in France's twenty-first-century memory landscape. Likewise, Amel and Omer's mapping of the 1961 protest route reveals that it is nearly impossible to walk around Paris without seeing commemorations of World War II everywhere. In his study of memory cultures in France and Germany, Peter Carrier draws a distinction between empirical memory and inherited memory in relation to memorials:

> It is precisely the heuristic value of museums, exhibitions, or memorials that facilitates broad social participation in the formation and understanding of memory cultures.... [W]hile the individual memory of the Second World War derives from witnesses' direct experiences of events and their subsequent interpretations, public memory of this event is inherited entirely indirectly via symbolic and rhetorical communication, and may therefore be acquired by all those who relate to the history of the Second World War via images, symbols, words and resulting exchanges of ideas about these media and the events to which they refer.[33]

While many have no memories of the conflicts memorialized through such symbols, the public may nonetheless access these pasts through public memorials.

However, the proliferation of monuments has another effect: France's ubiquitous war memorials paradoxically lead to historical amnesia. Panivong Norindr, for instance, reveals that there are very few memorials dedicated to colonial subjects, and the ones that do exist leave victims nameless—simultaneously remembered and forgotten.[34] The ubiquitous war memorials portrayed within the pages of *The Seine Was Red* similarly demonstrate that the sort of social remembering inherent in monuments is always linked to social forgetting. It is this other diversion of memory—or, as Donadey has termed it, the "Algeria syndrome"—to which Amel and Omer actively respond by creating their own memorials to October 17: "countermonuments" that literally rewrite history and challenge the grounds on which these original monuments have been erected.[35] Their first intervention occurs outside of Louis's apartment, which is situated next to the ironically named La Santé (Health) prison, a site of multidirectional memory where members of both the World War II Resistance and the Algerian Resistance were incarcerated.[36] They come upon a white marble plaque:

> ON NOVEMBER 11 1940
> IN THIS PRISON WERE HELD
> HIGH SCHOOL AND UNIVERSITY STUDENTS
> WHO, AT THE CALL OF GENERAL DE GAULLE,
> WERE THE FIRST TO RISE UP
> AGAINST THE OCCUPATION[37]

On the spur of the moment, Omer adds the following words with red spray paint:

> 1954–1962
> IN THIS PRISON
> WERE GUILLOTINED
> ALGERIAN RESISTERS
> WHO ROSE UP
> AGAINST THE FRENCH OCCUPATION[38]

The altered plaque with its overlaid text (see fig. 6) becomes a literal palimpsest.

While the syntactical and thematic similarities between the original plaque and this historically additive defacement are obvious, Omer's graffiti (itself traditionally seen as a subversive tool for the disenfranchised) evokes a number of differences from the earlier memorial. Although the actors in both commemorations are framed as activists, their identities are different. The actions of the Algerian "resisters" (*résistants*) in the amended plaque appear to be self-directed, while in the original, de Gaulle's call functioned as the primary motivation for high school and university students to protest against the German Occupation.[39] Moreover, in the original, the abusers (the Nazis) are implied but not stated, while in Omer's version, the occupier is clearly named as the French, even if the "occupation" (of Algerians) is actually going on in Paris as well. Another difference—but only evident in the original French—is the intentional choice to change "en cette prison" to "dans cette prison." While both signify "in this prison," in French they carry different connotations. Whereas *en* follows the formal language of memorialization, the more colloquial use of *dans* here marks the writer as younger while also signaling that acceptable ways of memorializing past events (here symbolized by language)

> ~~ON NOVEMBER 11~~ 1954–1962 1940
>
> IN THIS PRISON ~~WERE HELD~~
>
> ~~HIGH SCHOOL AND UNIVERSITY STUDENTS~~ WERE GUILLOTINED
>
> ~~WHO, AT THE CALL OF GENERAL GAULLE,~~ ALGERIAN RESISTERS
>
> ~~WERE THE FIRST TO~~ WHO ROSE UP
>
> ~~AGAINST THE FRENCH~~ AGAINST THE OCCUPATION

6. *The Seine Was Red*: Algeria and World War II as palimpsests. Courtesy of author.

are changing. Finally, the most conspicuous modification is the verb: "held" (*incarcerés*) becomes "guillotined" (*guillotinés*). The French specificity of the guillotine is notable, for this decapitation device, introduced during the French Revolution, was initially used to execute antirevolutionaries in the eighteenth century. Here, however, it is the revolutionaries (the Algerian resisters) who are targeted, thereby further emphasizing their lack of citizenship and exclusion from the French Republic. The severity of the violence is also underscored by the temporal duration in Omer's syntactical reversing of time and location. His choice to begin the new memorial with "1954–1962" contrasts the extended violence of an eight-year war with the oppressive abuses of one day. Finally, the original plaque's naming of November 11 serves to point out the absences of other, less remembered days—particularly those with which the novel engages. Armistice Day, for example, is hypermemorialized, while October 17 is not.

The genealogical approach theorized by Michel Foucault maps onto this more transgressive or queer practice of reading contradictions, confusions, and rewritings that is adopted by the novel's protagonists. In "Nietzsche, Genealogy, History," Foucault described genealogy as "the systematic dissociation of identity," which fragments what had previously been understood as unified and operates on "a field of entangled and confused parchments, on documents that have been scratched over and recopied many times." Sebbar's novel enacts such a genealogical mode of analysis and memory, seeking to uncover and expose the "substitutions, displacements, disguised conquests, and systematic reversals" described by Foucault.[40] It also gives voice to minoritarian subjects who decolonize the city, first by invoking the ubiquity of hidden colonial memories and then by reinserting them into the urban landscape.

Sebbar's text responds to the discordance and hierarchization between World War II and the French-Algerian War and reveals, to use Rothberg's phrase, the multidirectional nature of memory. While Rothberg does devote a portion of his compelling study to *The Seine Was Red* (and to *Caché*), his reading of the novel is imbued with a desire to expose the events of October 17 as intimately tied to the Holocaust. I propose a different approach, in which the overlapping nature of history and memory becomes key. I am more interested in the queer potentiality that results from the deconstructive impulses enacted by the novel's protagonists, that is, how they reveal what José Esteban Muñoz calls "ephemeral traces, flickering illuminations from other times and places."[41] These sites allow us to follow the unrealized potentiality and promise of queerness by harnessing a capacity to see something else beyond the dominant narrative.

The Palimpsest as a Tool of Queer Analysis

The countermonuments that Amel and Omer continue to create throughout the city could be classified as palimpsests. In a description remarkably similar to Foucault's characterization of genealogy, the *Oxford English Dictionary* defines the word "palimpsest" as "a parchment or other writing surface on which the original text has been effaced or partially erased, and then overwritten by another; a manuscript in which later writing has been superimposed on earlier (effaced) writing."[42] Thanks to his 1845 essay "The Palimpsest," the British essayist Thomas De Quincey is often credited with investing the palimpsest with metaphorical value or possibility. He describes its medieval origin as a writing surface that would be repeatedly written over—an economical way of using parchment or membrane so that successive thoughts could be documented. Yet the previous compositions could never be completely erased, leaving the traces of the earlier manuscript recoverable in each new composition. In detailing this process, De Quincey makes an analogy to thought and consciousness: "What else than a natural and mighty palimpsest is the human brain? Such a palimpsest is my brain; such a palimpsest, O reader! is yours."[43] Eventually taken up conceptually in poststructuralist theory, psychoanalysis, and cultural studies, the palimpsest has since become an apt metaphor to describe the slippage and ambivalence of memory itself. Indeed, it embodies a paradox in that the erasure that sits at its core actually allows for multiplicity and diversity, eschewing any notion of a superior or inferior text. As Shari Benstock argues in her study of women's writing and the Parisian expatriate experience, the palimpsest should not be read as hierarchical, with one layer considered primary and the other secondary. Instead, texts are "entwined and encoded in each other by the very fact that they are culturally produced."[44] The palimpsest preserves, even as it displays the cross contamination of one text by another. Texts are never fully erased, perpetually leaving overlapping (if not also competing) traces. De Quincey used the term "involuted" to describe this phenomenon, whereby "our deepest thoughts and feelings pass to us through perplexed combinations of concrete objects . . . in compound experiences incapable of being disentangled."[45] The palimpsest is in effect a queering strategy, providing a fabric upon which multiple, contradictory, and confused inscriptions and stories are intertwined and co-constitutive. Not only could "involutedness" be used to contest the fiction of linear history or stable memory, but this involuted approach also resonates with the queer reading methodology that I adopt throughout this book, looking to the silences, gaps, and traces.

In grammatical terms, from the noun "palimpsest" stem two adjectives: "palimpsestic" and "palimpsestuous." While "palimpsestic" characterizes the process of layering that produces a palimpsest and corresponds to an approach that seeks only to uncover or reveal, palimpsestuous reading is motivated by more deconstructive impulses in that it interrogates complex understandings of the logic and structure of the palimpsest.[46] In contrast to palimpsestic, palimpsestuous refers to the process itself whereby the underlying text, script, or phenomenon (re)appears. Gérard Genette specifically reads this as a transgressive or perverse phenomenon.[47] Indeed, we cannot but hear a phonetic similarity between "palimpsestuous" and "incestuous." In the case of Sebbar's text, a palimpsestuous reading would, for example, trace the incestuous imbrication of World War II and Algeria, signaling a certain perversity inherent in the relationship between these two events.

In "Reinscribing De Quincey's Palimpsest: The Significance of the Palimpsest in Contemporary Literary and Cultural Studies," literary scholar Sarah Dillon presents a provocative reading that couples the palimpsest and queer, accentuating both the queerness of the palimpsest and the palimpsestuousness of queer. Palimpsestuous reading, Dillon writes, "seeks to trace the incestuous and encrypted texts that constitute the palimpsest's fabric. Since those texts bear no necessary relation to each other, palimpsestuous reading is an inventive process of creating relations where there may, or should, be none."[48] Returning to Sebbar's novel, the palimpsests left by Amel and Omer perform dual tasks: they are both palimpsestic and palimpsestuous. They name the violence inflicted on Algerians during the war, and, through their acts of "writing over," they expose the lack of memorialization as reprehensible. They evoke memories of the physical violence while simultaneously naming the act of forgetting as shaping national identity and subjectivity. The palimpsests also make visible the fallacy of reading history as a progress narrative. Not merely identifying the erasures and oppressions of coloniality, a palimpsestuous reading here also uncovers the fabric of memory itself. Through their palimpsestuous nature, these palimpsests force us to see something perverse in the imbrication or hybridization of the French-Algerian War and World War II. Torture is turned around—the victim becomes the executioner. World War II haunts the French-Algerian War, and the two wars become, in a way, mutually informed and co-constituted. One contaminates the other in a cyclical and interconnected perverse chain of violence in which history repeats itself, even as the actors change. Yet these countermonuments are also acts of deconstruction. In Sebbar's novel, the palimpsestic and palimpsestuous countermonuments left by Omer and

Amel suggest that World War II can no longer be understood without its corollary, the French-Algerian War, and vice versa.

The Urban Memorialization Landscape and Queer Diasporic Reinscriptions

In their retracing of the October 17 protest, Amel and Omer encounter additional sites of memorial convergence that equally allow us to identify other possibilities and potentialities. Arriving at La Défense, for example, they cannot miss the imposing statue of Marianne, "a giant woman, standing, as if she were poised to face the enemy, courageous. She is holding a flag, the banner of victory? Defeat?"[49] Already at this point, Amel seems to have less patience for and interest in the particularities and details of the selective history of the French nation. She only quickly skims over, "skipping words and names" emblazoned on the statue, which is evidenced by the abundant ellipses left in the plaque's text as transcribed in the novel:[50]

> The statue
> THE DEFENSE OF PARIS
> INAUGURATED...
> to recall the courage of the Parisians
> during the terrible siege of 1870–1871.
> Reinstalled at its original site...
> It was inaugurated September 21, 1983...[51]

Perhaps Amel's impatience for such historical details also stems from the fact that a much less notable detail in the French historical record is that this statue was the official meeting point for Algerians on October 17. Marianne stands at the center of the French Republic, just as the Algerian protesters stood there, asserting their place in history.

From this starting place, many protesters took the métro to squares in various parts of the city, including Concorde, L'Opéra, La République, Richelieu-Drouot, Place de l'Étoile, and Bonne-Nouvelle. However, as Sebbar's novel reveals, upon leaving the stations, protesters met with extreme police violence. We are reminded of the video testimony of Amel's mother, Noria, who details her memories: "On the metro platform, men, Algerians, are being held with their hands on their head.

It's a roundup. They are going to be taken to detention centers just like my father who was taken to the Palais des Sports. They are brought as far as a famous hotel, one I had never seen. Flora told me the name of it; it sounds like 'Grillon.' Ask her; the cops rounded up Algerians."[52] The famous hotel—and an infamous site of police brutality—to which Noria refers is the Hôtel de Crillon. Thanks to Amel and Omer, there now exists a memorial to the attacked protesters at this site:

> ON THIS SPOT ALGERIANS WERE SAVAGELY BEATEN
> BY PREFECT PAPON'S POLICE ON OCTOBER 17 1961[53]

Continuing their trek, they come to the Saint-Michel fountain, but Omer's physical positioning hides a plaque laid there, and Amel can only read an incomplete version:

> IN MEMORY
> OF THE SOLDIERS OF THE FRENCH FORCES
> OF THE INTERIOR AND THE INHABITANTS OF THE Vth
> AND
> ARRONDISSEMENTS WHICH ON THIS SITE
> DEAD IN BATTLE[54]

Here, the body of an Algerian immigrant hides this memorial to the past, not allowing Amel to read the full text from her vantage point. No longer does he need to write anonymously over plaques to World War II—his corporeal presence asserts itself, demanding to be seen and accounted for.

Toward the end of the novel, Louis comes upon yet another trace at the Pont Saint-Michel surely left by Omer and Amel. It reads:

> ON THIS SPOT ALGERIANS FELL
> FOR THE INDEPENDENCE OF ALGERIA
> OCTOBER 17, 1961[55]

This new addition to the urban memorialization landscape is reminiscent of the infamous graffiti left at the same bridge after the October 1961 massacre: "ICI ON NOIE LES ALGERIENS" (HERE WE DROWN ALGERIANS).[56] There exists, however, a significant difference between the original spray-painted memorial and that left by Amel and Omer:

the former's use of the present tense implied that the drowning of Algerians would continue, while Omer and Amel's memorial commemorates the dead and places it in the past. While Guyotat's *Eden, Eden, Eden* resisted past and future tenses, these emboldened children of the colonized have taken power into their own hands and have strategically deployed the past tense to assert that they will no longer be drowned. This simultaneous forward-facing and backward-looking approach also positions Algerians as subjects rather than objects. The subject of WE DROWN (here, "WE" implies French) is transformed into an Algerian subject.[57] It is worth noting that two years after Sebbar's novel was published, Bertrand Delanoë, the mayor of Paris, placed a memorial plaque on the Saint-Michel bridge on October 17, 2001, to commemorate those Algerians who were murdered. This eventual memorialization has not, however, escaped controversy. The choice of a bronze plaque with bronze lettering requires of the passerby effort and intentionality to decipher its message. Moreover, as Laila Amine remarks, it was placed at the least visible corner of the bridge and has been defaced and replaced multiple times.[58]

Gayatri Gopinath refers to actions such as those taken in the novel as queer diasporic cultural practices. In *Impossible Desires*, she describes their workings as follows: "Queer diasporic cultural forms and practices point to submerged histories of racist and colonialist violence that continue to resonate in the present and that make themselves felt through bodily desire. It is through the queer diasporic body that these histories are brought into the present; it is also through the queer diasporic body that their legacies are imaginatively contested and transformed.... [Q]ueer diasporic cultural forms work against the violent effacements that produce the fictions of purity that lie at the heart of dominant nationalist and diasporic ideologies."[59] In literally rewriting history through graffiti, alternative documentation, and multimedia storytelling, the characters of *The Seine Was Red* engage in such a praxis. Louis's filming of the subversive memorializing actions left by Amel and Omer becomes another such queer diasporic cultural practice. Indeed, this particular genre of documentary film is especially adept at expressing the voices and traces of those who find themselves otherwise omitted or misrecognized. Given the fact that documentary filmmaking can also be done without access to inflated budgets and large film studios, the medium, by its very nature, becomes more accessible and egalitarian. Amateur filmmaking and countermonuments sprayed in red graffiti become tools for the disenfranchised—as queer diasporic cultural forms, they "bring into the present those pasts that are deliberately forgotten within conventional nationalist or diasporic scripts."[60] In uniquely responding to "official history" by including a multitude of voices, they also function as subversive political and cultural tools of memorialization that evidence submerged histories of racism and colonialism.

Although they are but a single surface, the palimpsests left by Sebbar's protagonists widen our understanding of history, memory, and the metropole. The city itself becomes a more racialized space inhabited by French and North Africans, perpetrators and victims, but also by ghosts—murdered Algerians who were not named and certainly not memorialized. However, the palimpsests that they create do not construct dueling versions of history. In leaving the other memorial legible, Omer and Amel open up a third space, giving room to interpretation—not unlike Provencher's theorization of transfiliation, in which procreation occurs through representation. These palimpsests are transgressive acts that queer the historical record. In this way, I interpret their palimpsestic actions as performing a sort of cultural memory similar to Gopinath's concept of queer diasporic cultural forms by actively engaging in the reiterative and recursive process of rethinking temporality and the relationship between past, present, and future.

Often used as shorthand to describe a layering of texts, events, or memories, palimpsests are particularly useful because they are both literal and metaphorical. They preserve and deconstruct while showing the cross contamination of one text by another. A palimpsestuous approach suggests a certain openness and helps to expose the overlapping, competing, and sometimes contradictory nature of forward-thinking, progress-oriented time. Overlying the official narrative of French colonial history as a story of civilization and liberation with the traces of barbarism and dispossession that characterize the French-Algerian War, the palimpsest gives way to a queering of memory. In the queer memory project, Ana Dragojlovic writes, "narratives are multiple, open ended, verbal and embodied, personal and collective, emanating as affective intensities generated by diasporic histories of violence and marginalization."[61] The characters of *The Seine Was Red* queer the palimpsest of memory itself, crafting an archive that is neither fixed nor linear and teleological. In constructing a history replete with blanks and incompleteness, the novel reflects the complexity of memory that is also, to a certain degree, utopic in that it imagines a different past, present, and future—perhaps one that will never exist. As will also be explored in the next chapter, this queer approach to memory disrupts systems and structures (including space and time) that do not otherwise adequately address the lives of those who surpass the limits of categories implied by terms related to race, nationality, or gender that attempt to fix or reify identities.

Leïla Sebbar's pedagogical novel calls us to reconceive the nature and function of memory. The text is itself a palimpsest, writing over generic conventions and literary standards. As the first literary text to take October 17 as its prime site of investigation, its plurality and multivocality do not necessarily counter but instead supplement and complement the existing historical record, which itself is woefully incomplete and distorted. Equally, however, Sebbar trucks with incompleteness, pointing to the always inescapable, nonlinear character of remembering and forgetting. The text itself is replete with empty spaces, ellipses, unfinished sentences, and half-told stories, thereby leaving open the possibility for further palimpsestic and palimpsestuous interventions. *The Seine Was Red*, through these pervasive blanks on the page and charged silences in dialogue, allows other voices to emerge. Perhaps, like Amel and Omer, we might add our own stories, writing over a history that, instead of remembering, often forgets.

5 Queering Identity, Embracing In-Betweenness: Disidentification and Re-membering in Nina Bouraoui's *Tomboy*

> There is something compelling about being both male and female, about having an entry into both worlds. Contrary to some psychiatric tenets, half and halfs are not suffering from confusion about sexual identity, or even from a confusion of gender. What we are suffering from is an absolute despot duality that says we are able to be only one or the other.
>
> —Gloria Anzaldúa, *Borderlands / La Frontera*

In *On the Postcolony*, Achille Mbembe writes that subjects in the postcolony must "have marked ability to manage not just a single identity, but several—flexible enough to negotiate as and when necessary."[1] While not explicitly treating gender and sexuality, Mbembe reminds us that the postcolonial subject learns to adapt, to negotiate, and— most importantly—to remake disciplinary norms, power relations, and categorical binary-based paradigms. Reading postcoloniality in this way, one cannot help but see resonances with queerness, itself a programmatic for destabilizing binary-based thinking and a modality of upending norms. Drawing on Mbembe's formulation, Ayo A. Coly further elaborates: "The postcolony is a theatrical metaparody where all disciplinary norms and signifying practices are eventually fair game for poaching, including relations of power whose convivial logic effects a systemic breakdown of binaries and a porosity of categories. This is queerness at work."[2]

Although this sort of negotiation and flexibility is shared by many figures that I analyze in this book, it is especially salient in *Garçon manqué* (*Tomboy*, 2000), written by the award-winning French Algerian writer Nina Bouraoui. Like Bouraoui's other novels, *Tomboy* engages with the broad themes of identity, desire, violence, memory, and exile while embodying in both form and content both the possibilities and the vulnerabilities of gender fluidity. *Tomboy* lays bare the ambiguity felt by many postcolonial subjects who engage in the identity-maneuvering work that Mbembe describes, and in pointing to the mutability of gender and race, it also uncovers how they both serve as regulatory norms that materialize bodies and make them intelligible. *Tomboy* furthermore exposes how these various vectors of subjectivity and power rely on one another for their own articulation. In this chapter, I take Bouraoui's text as an exemplar of the ways in which the intersection of gender, sexuality, and nationality continues to be haunted by the trauma of the French-Algerian War and how the anxieties of its protracted aftermath also aid in the creation of new modes of thinking about memory, identity, and embodiment that radically question identity and value more redemptive potentialities of in-betweenness.

Bouraoui's novel tells the story of Nina, a young child growing up in Algiers in the wake of the war. Born to an Algerian father and a French mother, Nina moves between identities, never feeling fully at home, neither as French or Algerian nor as girl or boy. Content mirrors style and form, as Bouraoui's text itself resists categorization in its straddling of multiple genres—a mix of novel, memoir, and autobiography, it is all and none. In *Tomboy*, the first-person narrator attempts to find a way to express both queer desire and a certain masculinity, despite a changing female body that seems to betray this gender identity. Queerness and postcoloniality are bridged through the novel's investment in embracing the in-betweenness felt by many postwar subjects, the interstitial space of not quite fitting normative categories. In this context, queerness is realized by orienting the self toward the moments of discomfort and unresolved feelings and memories that have arisen in the temporality of the extended post-decolonization moment that shattered so many subjectivities. In *Tomboy*, the fracturing of identity leads to multiplicity; that is, the novel and the protagonist enact new forms of difference that question the borders of gender and the boundaries of national identity, a process that not only couples but also deconstructs these two essentialist categories.[3] This chapter will explore how, in its articulation of these experiences of coming to terms with nonnormative gender and sexuality, the text can be interpreted as a complex negotiation of identity in the face of fractured embodiment, as well as gender and national hybridity. I undertake this analysis by examining how Bouraoui's writing style—in defying traditional narrative structures—mirrors the hybrid anxieties of the protagonist, whose gender fluidity and queer desire could be said to occupy a space of what Johanna Garvey terms "queer (un)belonging"—one that has the power to reshape relations to community, time, and place.[4] The text decenters the modernist "I" through narrative techniques and disidentificatory strategies, thereby deconstructing preconceptions related to nationality, race, and gender identity, and in doing so, it performs a mode of doing and thinking identity differently. This process simultaneously allows for productive resistance strategies that map onto José Esteban Muñoz's concept of disidentification. Nina's performative enactments of different forms of masculinity through a collection of alter egos can best be understood as a (queer) practice or form of (dis)identification that simultaneously necessitates a queer reading methodology that looks to the shadows, silences, and ruptures while simultaneously keeping embodied histories and gendered experiences at the forefront.

As a tool to resist a conception of power as a fixed discourse, disidentification becomes a survival strategy for the minority subject who does not fit the characteristics of normative citizenship. However, as Muñoz acknowledges, subjectivities are nonetheless formed in relation and response to these exclusionary mechanisms. Identity making is thus "a process that takes place at the point of collision of perspectives that some critics and theorists have understood as essentialist and constructivist. This collision is precisely the moment of negotiation when hybrid, racially predicated, and deviantly gendered identities arrive at representation. In doing so, a representational contract is broken; the queer and the colored come into perception and the social order receives a jolt that may reverberate loudly and widely, or in less dramatic, yet locally indispensable ways."[5] It is precisely this approach to identity formation and disidentification that I read into *Tomboy*. Nina deessentializes being, gender, race, and nationality by disidentifying with fixed identity categories, thus questioning their very foundations.

Despite being born after Algerian independence, Nina is forged and formed by the French-Algerian War. Carrying the conflict and its memories with her, she is made to feel out of place in both countries and cultures.[6] "I am forged by the war," she writes. "I come from a controversial marriage. I bear the suffering of my Algerian family. I remember the rejection of my French kin. I carry these transmissions. Violence no longer leaves me. It inhabits me. It comes from me."[7] Being French Algerian means never escaping the violent past, the traces of which are passed on to the next generation, the children of those individuals and communities who most directly experienced the atrocities of the war. A representative of this often misunderstood, postindependence generation, Nina articulates the pain caused by this marginality in a series of escalating questions: "Who will understand about the children of the 1970s? Who will understand the marriages that took place after Algerian independence? Who will understand about the insane desire to be loved? Two countries. Two solitudes. Who will read about this violence?"[8] The repetition of the rhetorical phrase "Who will understand?" encapsulates the violence of being overlooked and ignored not only by history but also by her two nations. Nina, like so many other biracial French Algerian children of the 1970s, experiences the absence of a true homeland as loneliness, with the two countries becoming "two solitudes."

Resisting any clear-cut categorization in terms of nationality, ethnicity, or gender, Nina embodies both the potential and the difficulty of hybrid identities. Muñoz conceptualizes hybridity as something that captures the fragmentary subject formation of those whose identities cross different and multiple races, sexualities, and genders; queer and mixed-race are, as Muñoz argues, defiant toward any notion of uniform identity.[9] *Tomboy*'s narrator embodies this sort of fragmentary subject formation, highlighting the negotiation of multiplicity and movement—the passing and crossing from one name and identity to another. For Nina, this creates a sense of ambivalence, reminding us that as a culturally constructed phenomenon, hybridity is complex and contradictory, particularly in this historical and geopolitical context: "It's an asset and a liability. Not choosing makes me a nomad. My Algerian face. My French voice. Both light and dark, an internal conflict. I am made up of two warring elements, two jealousies that devour each other."[10] But Nina also refers to a capacity to adapt and adjust to this hybridity and in-betweenness: "I do not dwell in regrets. I adjust to everything quickly. My ability to adjust is maddening, creating several parallel lives and a multitude of small betrayals."[11] While Nina had earlier on referred to this "adaptability" as a liability, I also read it as a survival strategy. This is, in Muñoz's terms, a queer act of disidentification at work.

As Anzaldúa's epigraph evokes, conflict related to hybridity does not necessarily come from a personal crisis of identity but rather from a structure of discrimination, that "absolute despot duality that says we are able to be only one or the other."[12] In "Cultural Identity and Diaspora," Stuart Hall refers to "a conception of 'identity' which lives with and through, not despite difference; by hybridity."[13] Reading this theorization of hybridity through *Tomboy* instantiates a rethinking of alterity and difference. Difference is not the antonym of or a counterpoint to sameness, as Trinh T. Minh-ha reminds us: "Many of us still hold on to the concept of difference not as a tool of creativity to question multiple forms of repression and dominance, but as a tool of segregation, to exert power on the basis of racial and sexual essences. The apartheid type of difference." Trinh elaborates that in many feminist and non-Western contexts, difference is understood differently, so to speak: "Difference, in other words, does not necessarily give rise to separatism. There are differences as well as similarities within the concept of difference."[14] This conceptualization of difference could allow us to reimagine what is indexed by categories such as "masculinity" and "femininity" or "Frenchness" and "Algerianness." It is this project that *Tomboy* engages in—a task also referenced by Trinh through her proposal to affirm difference as a creative tool that could interrogate and subvert structures of domination. In this sense, redefining difference also signifies, enacts, and performs new ways of relating—new relationalities—that have the capacity to reconfigure and queer kinship structures.

While I attempt to provide an outline of a novel that resists summary, my analysis is woven among a collage of scenes and episodes that—true to the queer bent of the argument I put forth—are not presented in a structured sequence. This reading is particularly attuned to the confluence of national identity (as wholly inextricable from race) and gender identity as productive on its own terms and demonstrative of how a decentering of identity can deconstruct the ways in which specific nationalities, sexualities, and genders can be inhabited. Reading Bouraoui's narrative from a queer perspective means reading it as neither metaphor nor pathology—an approach that counters earlier analyses of the novel and is indebted to queer and feminist scholarship that has argued against pathologization and has instead advocated for the embracing of discomfort, unease, and failure precisely because these affects may open up creative possibilities.[15] Resisting normative and linear definitions of gender, nationality, and memory, I show how gender fluidity can be transformative and can offer strategies for coping with exclusion. I specifically outline how this approach resists previous analyses, most of which have understood the main character, Nina, as either a stand-in for the author or a girl with an identity crisis who thinks she wants to be a man. Foregrounding the intersectional entanglements between nationality, race, and gender, my analysis also touches upon the text's unconventional narrative style and use of interpellation in order to reveal how it decenters identity categories and decouples masculinity from men. The text unites memory and embodiment to further establish the entangled and critical relation between trauma and masculinity, transforming the remembering/forgetting binary into a process of "re-membering."

The Violence of Silence

Bouraoui's *Tomboy*, like Leïla Sebbar's *The Seine Was Red*, is situated within a now flourishing literary and cinematic push to represent the French-Algerian War and its twenty-first-century aftermath, including trauma, violence, and memory. Bouraoui's novel takes the body as a point of departure, showing how corporeality cannot be separated from memory and culture. This theme is well articulated by Nina: "Algeria does not flourish on my tongue; it takes root in my body. Algeria does not shape my words. Algeria surfaces in what devours me. Algeria is in my body."[16] Through a constant return to the body, the text specifically highlights Nina's multiple hybrid experiences of growing up shortly after Algeria gained independence from France. The child of a French mother and Algerian father, she is made to feel an outsider throughout her adolescent life in Algiers. Her annual summers spent in France are equally marked by exclusion: she constantly feels that her French maternal grandparents (and her surroundings more broadly) view her as a foreigner whose darker skin marks her as not quite "French." This perpetual exclusion illustrates Elisa Camiscioli's argument that, historically, immigration discourse has articulated that it was impossible for people of color and colonized subjects who were coded as biologically distinct to assimilate into "French" (read: white) culture.[17]

This narrative of biological inferiority is illustrated when, while Nina is in France, her grandparents take her to the doctor out of fear that something is wrong with her Algerian body (the reasons for which remain unknown). There, Nina witnesses the intense institutional violence inflicted on brown bodies such as hers—not least in the way that the doctors attempt to identify some invisible malignancy. By virtue of being Algerian, she is assumed to be suffering from an as-yet-unknown illness that can be identified by the French doctors: "The French health system takes over, appropriating and searching our bodies; it penetrates from head to toe. . . . Tomorrow they will examine me although I am completely healthy."[18] With each doctor's visit, her body is poked, prodded, and pathologized. Nina identifies these sorts of micro- and macroaggressions as evidence that "the war in Algeria has never stopped; it has hardly changed. The war simply has moved to another place and continues its course."[19]

This structural marginalization and violence are further perpetuated through a systematic inability to confront the war itself. Indeed, Nina reveals the "disease" not to be living within her Algerian body but to be omnipresent in French society. This pathology is silence, specifically, silence about the French-Algerian War: "Silence will take over. Silence about the massacres, the suffering in Algeria, and our new life. A silence that spreads contagiously, a real disease, a plague, an epidemic. Silence on every mouth. The silence of France. The silence of the whole world. Silence about Algeria, burned bodies, dismembered bodies, disemboweled bodies, this incredible puzzle of ripped open flesh. Absolute silence about this human disorder, silence about man's future. Silence about his true nature."[20] After reading the word "silence" ten times in this short excerpt, we cannot help but see its pervasiveness and intense violence. Rather than passive, it actively creeps in, like a disease, a contagious epidemic.[21] The way Nina's body is treated is contrasted with the "real disease" through the medicalized vocabulary used to describe the subtle yet omnipresent void surrounding French treatment of Algerian bodies. In *Tomboy*, this is exemplified by Nina's grandfather, who remains "silent on the ever so difficult Algerian life, the future of Algerians, their suffering, the shortages, the scarcity, and the instigation of violence. He says nothing at all."[22] Indeed, the text repeatedly signals the pathological obfuscation that continues to haunt postcolonial France.

Tomboy also demonstrates the ways in which location impacts identification, including gender. Place-names—particularly the names of beaches, streets, and neighborhoods—structure *Tomboy*, with three of the text's four sections corresponding to specific geographical locations: Algiers, Rennes, Tivoli. Through its constant movement between outside public spaces (most specifically the sea) and inside private homes (Nina's home, that of her grandparents, and that of her friend Amine), the text is marked by an interplay between inside and outside. This shifting from interior to exterior and vice versa maps onto the book's exposure of the fluctuating insider/outsider status of not only Nina but also the other children of the war who live in two seemingly disparate cultural and geographic worlds—one Algerian, one French.

Masculinity without Men

Although Nina repeatedly crosses national borders (Algeria, France, and eventually Italy), the most significant boundary crossing in which she engages is that of gendered categories. Nina succinctly summarizes the existential crisis that lies at the root of this dual (and dueling) identity, both national and sexual: "Every morning I scrutinize myself. I have four problems. Am I French or Algerian? Am I a girl or a boy?"[23] Gender is in apposition to nationality; that is, they are positioned close to one another, and, referentially speaking, they overlap. Moreover, in articulating this as four problems rather than two, Nina signals that it is not the choice between two options that is the problem but rather that all four categories are equally inadequate.

Nina's initial movement to masculinity is provoked by memory—even if it is only a memory that has been passed down from previous generations—for she attempts to embody Ahmed, her father's brother who was murdered during the war. This haunted masculinity (see also chapter 1) illustrates María del Pilar Blanco and Esther Pereen's point that "categories of subjectification like gender, sexuality, and race can themselves be conceived as spectral."[24] Like the creatively constituted memories of *The Seine Was Red*'s protagonists, discussed in chapter 4, Nina's transformation into Ahmed could be described as a manifestation partially provoked by "postmemory." In Marianne Hirsch's theorization of postmemory, she details how living with inherited trauma impacts how stories are told in a postwar era in which language and generic storytelling conventions fail. That is, the memories that are passed down "defy narrative reconstruction and exceed comprehension."[25] In this process, Nina fades in and out of the narrative: by taking on and off identities, the book rethinks the nature of the modernist myth of identity itself.[26] While not without risks, this profound desire to remain unclassifiable is also combined with a strong affirmation of thinking subjectivity differently (much like Pierre Guyotat's proposal engaged with in chapter 3). In living contradictions—both/and, neither/nor—Nina imagines and enacts different ways of being. Within this wider narrative, gender becomes subject to rearrangement: "I make myself disappear and assimilate into the world of men."[27] This fading in and out of the narrative allows for transfilial and ancestral voices to emerge, including that of Ahmed, the uncle she never knew, but also of Algerian women massacred during the final year of the war who lived—and died—in her own childhood home.

In addition to Ahmed, Nina takes on a variety of masculine personas throughout the book, including Brio and eventually Amine, and with them new wardrobes, haircuts, and gaits. This transformation allows Nina to negotiate the frustration and anger of not fitting in to embrace a queer (un)belonging that "undo[es] belonging while not leading to the destructive erasure of not-belonging," thus creating new ways of coping with a colonial past that has formed the conditions under which those hybrid bodies both exist *and* no longer fit.[28] As a precondition for postcolonial French Algerian subjects to exist, French colonialism simultaneously denies them a viable place in discourse and in society—in much the same way that, for Foucault, power constitutes that which it governs. It is in response to this dynamic that Nina and all aliases carve out spaces for themselves to thrive.

In Nina's embracing of masculinity, the narrative also offers a profound commentary on what it means to be a man in postindependence Algeria, which Nina explains as follows:

> I will be on the side of power. Algeria is a man; it is a forest of men.... Here, men are alone by dint of being together. Here, men are violent from their unfulfilled desire.... Here, men are sad.... They hope, but they no longer sing. They invent departures and imagine arrivals. They will do better than others and experience the French dream. Their gaze is a weapon, their hands burning embers, their desire a conflict. They hurt themselves, alone. They are fragile. I like them because of it.[29]

Dominant masculinities (particularly like those detailed in chapters 1 and 2) reveal male masculinity "as a hermeneutic, as a counterexample to the kinds of masculinity that seem most informative about gender relations and most generative of social change," Jack Halberstam writes.[30] Queer theory—and Halberstam's work in particular—has offered critical tools with which to uncouple the male body from definitions of masculinity and to question the assumption that masculinity is solely defined by the bodily practices of boys and men. Masculinity is not a homogeneous category inherent to maleness but rather a configuration of practices and discourses that all genders may embody in different ways and to differing degrees. For Nina, this means constructing a form of masculinity that counters dominant French masculinity by valuing fragility and sadness and expressing a desire to become invisible (no longer as an object of desire but as a desiring subject). In what could be seen as a move to disidentify with Frenchness, being "on the side of power" in this case means embodying and desiring masculinity *and* Algerianness.³¹ In being drawn to the fragility of Algerian men, Nina crafts a fluid gender in response to the cultural logics of heteronormativity and hegemonic masculinity—cultural logics that, as Muñoz suggests, work to undergird state power.³²

Queering Genre, Queering Gender

In French there is no distinction between the words "gender" and "genre," with *genre* referring to both literary categorization and gender. *Tomboy* performs this multivalence of "genre," highlighting how they are two sides of the same coin and can be similarly subverted. The text also circumvents any attempt at classification, forcing the reader to ask: Is this a testimony? A memoir? A novel? An autobiographical novel? In its decentering incoherency, the book's genre-bending form both captures the denaturalization of sex and mirrors the effects of the war. Bouraoui's meandering text is often repetitive and unclear, instigating a feeling of struggle (perhaps not dissimilar from chapter 1's analysis of *Muriel* and chapter 3's examination of *Eden, Eden, Eden*). Here, Donna McCormack's astute reflections on the ability of queer postcolonial narratives to draw the reader in can be applied to *Tomboy* in that the text depends on "the willingness of listeners to take on the responsibility for an endless narrative that they must translate from embodied exchanges into a comprehensible language that is still largely incoherent in form."³³ There is a certain instability contained in the narrative form, and its elusive and elliptical structure creates a vulnerability between the reader and the text. Although we feel like we are given only pieces of an unfinished story, the style itself speaks to the experiences of in-betweenness and exile from identity categories.

As evidenced by some of the excerpts cited above, the short sentences, constant repetitions, and poetic and lyrical style read almost as a prose poem. Within this staccato form, a longer sentence with multiple clauses will occasionally appear, and it is often this that jolts the reader. Through the use of indirect discourse and free indirect discourse, the borders between thought and speech are blurred, as are all other boundaries both inside and outside of the text. Quotations, thoughts, and narrative flow together, and the minimal dialogue suggests that much of this text's musings occur in the mind of the narrator. The style mimics and enacts a decentering of narrative structure. Yet in this way it also captures the fleeting and ungraspable nature of memory and speaks to the ways in which subsequent generations would re-member the war—that is, embody the war and attempt to piece it together—all the while acknowledging that its memories can never be coherently arranged or understood.

Both Jarrod Hayes and Donna McCormack have remarked that in the broad field of postcolonial literary scholarship, dominant approaches to analyzing queer and transgender subjectivities tend to reduce such characters to symbols or allegories of the decentering effects of colonialism or of the hybridity proliferating in postcolonial diasporas.[34] While an allegorical approach may have its merits for particular case studies, it also runs the risk of stripping subjects of their agency and pathologizing queerness. The limited scholarship that currently exists on *Tomboy* seems to continue down this same road, reading the protagonist's gender and sexual fluidity as a metaphorical "confusion" caused by the devastating impacts of the French-Algerian War. Such readings point to a broader difficulty in seeing nonnormative, nonbinary, or fluid identities as self-sufficient and standing on their own. I resist an analysis that reads Nina's gender identity and expression as resulting from a "dismayed mindset caused by her lack of identity" or as simply *travestissement* (cross-dressing) or *déguisement* (disguise).[35] Although Ching Selao reads the protagonist's movements of subjectification and desubjectification as a consequence of the narrator's *identité métisse* (mixed identity), which forms her as a subject at the same time as it denies her this subjectivity, I see this movement and its simultaneous subjectification and denial thereof as better understood through the concept of disidentification.[36] And while Helen Vassallo reads the text as fleeing "the confines of a stereotypical feminine model only to embrace a stereotypically masculine one," I regard the narrator's movement between genders as antiessentialist, that is, deconstructing the fixity of preconceived notions of what it means to be a "man" or a "woman" (or neither or both) and reconfiguring dominant masculinity to embrace fragility and sadness, for instance.[37] Nina's movements between various gender identities are profoundly impactful, as they allow for a constant undoing and remaking of subjectivity, pointing to the mutability of gender itself.

Another trend in the existing scholarship on *Tomboy* has been to classify the text as autobiography. For example, after summarizing the primary autobiographical details of Bouraoui's life, Maurice Simo Djom writes: "These are the broad identity traits of *Tomboy*'s author. What about the narrator? Is there a similarity between the author and the narrator? If yes, how far does it go?"[38] Djom then goes on to point out several overlaps and shared biographical details between the author and the narrator. Particularly since *Tomboy* escapes comprehension, I understand the persuasiveness of reading the novel as a memoir of Bouraoui's life. However, instead of answering questions about what this text *is*, this sort of analysis forecloses possibilities for seeing what such a queer approach *does*—how the mixing and blurring is in itself both an aim and a strategy to achieve this aim.

Moreover, interpreting *Tomboy* as a trajectory in line with Bouraoui's life and other literary production has also led to a reading that culminates in a Western-imbued phenomenon of "coming out," a reading that Bouraoui has refuted: "To say that one is homosexual is to be cataloged by one's sexuality, and that bothers me deeply. Homosexuality is not an identity. . . . In regards to my latest book [*Poupée Bella*], people talked about *coming out*. That's not it at all! I am not a provocateur. I am an activist in my own way: I write. To write is an act of resistance. Inside me, there is a real struggle within writing: it's a war!"[39] In addition to eschewing the classification of autofiction and autobiography and countering the idea that her texts are "coming out" narratives, Bouraoui contests the fiction of sexuality as identity and taxonomy (much like Guyotat and Foucault did in chapter 3). Bouraoui's use of writing as activism and resistance, in combination with an anti-identitarian stance, points toward a form of political agency without "the subject," an approach that is also a hallmark of queer theory.

Even as I want to counter hasty interpretations of the text as *merely* autobiographical, neither do I entirely dispose of the idea that Bouraoui is (re)making the self through the novel and its writing. Here, I understand the self as disidentificatory, "whose relation to the social is not overdetermined by universalizing theories of selfhood."[40] In his analysis of James Baldwin's *Just Above My Head*, Muñoz invokes the idea of fiction as a technology of the self: "The 'real self' who comes into being through fiction is not the self who produces fiction, but is instead produced by fiction. Binaries finally begin to falter and fiction becomes the real; which is to say that the truth effect of ideological grids is broken down through Baldwin's disidentification with the notion of fiction—and it does not stop here: fiction then becomes a contested field of self-production."[41] Instead of reading the text as autobiographical, a queer approach means looking to the doubly inflected relationship between self and fiction and to the ways in which fiction is a horizon of self-creation. Through writing, Bouraoui is making a self that is making a self through writing, and in "becoming other to the self the parameters of selfhood are undone. This is the possibility of an ethical response, of listening without knowing what lies ahead and without already knowing how the story goes."[42] Indeed, as Bouraoui suggests above, writing is a survival strategy, a tool of disidentification with which to resist the violence of categorization, just as it is for her protagonist, Nina: "I don't want to be Algerian. I don't want to be French. . . . I am non-descript. . . . I become unclassifiable. I'm not ethnic enough: 'You are not an Arab like other Arabs.' I am too ethnic: 'You are not French.' I am not afraid of myself. My strength defies hatred. My silence is a battle. I will also write because of this. My writing will be in French, while my last name remains Arab. It will be a desertion. But which camp should I choose? Which part of me should I burn?"[43]

In distancing my analysis from previous readings of the novel, I privilege the queerness of subjectivity and embodiment. At the same time, I acknowledge that the text mirrors a broader cultural crisis around gender and nationality. Nina's nonnormative gender must be considered in conjunction with geopolitical histories of normativity and resistance and as such must be read in light of a particular moment during which decolonization was experienced as a liberatory yet violent process that left traumas and memories in and on bodies. This is a text that lays bare how the French-Algerian War instigated an upending of normative representations. In this sense, reading the novel queerly can begin to account for the overlaps and mutual co-constitutions—

both visible and invisible—that shape subjectivity at and beyond this historical moment.

The Void of Identity

While *Tomboy* ultimately evidences the instability of identity, the text opens with an emphasis on the first-person "I" in motion: "I'm running on Chenoua Beach, running with my friend Amine. I follow the foam-filled waves, white explosions. I'm running with the sea that rises and falls beneath the Roman ruins, running in the still-warm winter light. I fall on the sand. I hear the sea advancing, the sound of freighters leaving Africa. I belong to the sand, the sea, and the wind. I am in Algeria. France is far away, behind the huge and dangerous waves."[44] In this passage, the repetition of "I" over and over again mimics the continuous flow of the surrounding water and waves, never stopping, only sometimes slightly shorter or longer than at other times. The proper names cited in this opening phrase, Chenoua and Amine, communicate to the French- or English-language reader that this scene is located in a geographically and culturally different context. While the overuse of the verb "to run" signals movement and flight—that spaces are to be traversed and transgressed—the succinct phrase "I fall on the sand" suggests futility and resignation, indicating that the narrator's desire for movement will meet obstacles. Nearly every sentence (nine in the original, seven in the translation) of the novel's first full paragraph begins with "I" (*je*), with two notable exceptions being those sentences that begin with "France" or its pronoun, "it." In the original French, the repetition of the soft [ʒ] sound of *Alger* and *je* draws on similar sounds, showing the imbrication and overlap of the physical place with the narrator's first-person pronoun. The word "white" (denoted as feminine in the French adjective *blanche*)—the only color named—will be repeated a few lines later, drawing out the literal and metaphoric significance of whiteness, which itself will become a critical trope in the protagonist's negotiation of racial and ethnic in-betweenness.

The sea (both Algerian and French, even as it is the same Mediterranean Sea that they share) also becomes a recurrent theme and one that is marked by ambiguity in its embodiment of contradictions: freedom and constraint, pleasure and danger.[45] The sea also separates the narrator's two lands—France and Algeria—and is described as sustaining, infinite, and engulfing but also violent, suffocating, and isolating.[46] This juxtaposition returns in the lines that geographically situate the text: "I am in Algeria. France is far away, behind the huge and dangerous waves." It is followed by a subtle yet powerful reflection of this physical separation: "It is invisible and imagined. Amine and I fall together. I hold his hand. We are alone, and we are foreigners."[47] Only a punctuation mark separates the two locations ("I am in Algeria. France is far away"), but this full stop highlights their impossibility of ever being united. It is this separation and conflict that will shape the narrator's and her friend Amine's solitude and foreignness.

The arrival of four men at the beach punctuates and interrupts the childhood play of the narrator and Amine: "Men emerge from the dunes, four of them. They are in a hurry. They walk hastily toward the sea: a meeting. They sketch grand gestures with their arms. They are speaking Arabic. Their voices carry across the beach, echoing in the waves and the wind. I feel mesmerized. . . . They brush against our bodies and continue walking past us, their arms reaching toward the horizon."[48] The masculinity that these men embody and that mesmerizes Nina is imposing and forceful. After motioning toward what is on the other side of the sea (France), the men then leave the beach without looking at the narrator and Amine: "We don't exist."[49] Despite its mere three words, this charged sentence holds tremendous weight. Only a few lines later, we learn that it is precisely because they are of mixed Algerian and French descent that they are invisible: "Here, we are nothing. Born of French mothers. Born of Algerian fathers. Our bodies alone reunite the conflicting lands."[50] Highlighting the text's investment in corporeality, it is their bodies that evidence their hybridity, or *métissage*. The outsider/insider tension resides within their existence and will reverberate throughout the text, as Nina repeatedly makes comments such as "I am a foreigner here; I am nothing. France forgets me while Algeria doesn't know who I am. Here, identity is molded. It is dual and broken."[51] Neither Nina nor Amine will ever be able to achieve ethnic or racial "purity": "We will never be real Algerians. Despite our will and longing. Despite the clothing. Despite the land that surrounds us."[52] Again invoking their racial and ethnic ancestry, Nina repeats: "Born of French mothers. Born of Algerian fathers. Two orphans facing the void."[53] They embody difference—a very specific difference formed out of the French-Algerian War—and they will always be seen as "two imposters."[54]

Naming and Becoming

Despite the excessive use of the first-person pronoun in the novel's opening pages, *Tomboy* decenters this "I" specifically through the use of generic reimagination. To draw upon feminist performance studies scholar Elin Diamond, the "I" in the novel could be understood as lacking any "interior secure ego or core identity," in effect meaning that the "I" must always enunciate itself.[55] The "I" comes into being through interpellation—by being named and called. This discursive constitution happens prior to and in excess of the enunciation of the first-person subject. This "I," as Judith Butler suggests in her essay "Critically Queer," "is the historically revisable possibility of a name that precedes and exceeds me, but without which I cannot speak."[56] While "I" is traditionally read as deictic—a self-referential index—the "I" of *Tomboy* is, however, constantly referring to different personas. Incapable of staying intact, it is linked to a process of undoing identity that is already highlighted in the opening scene discussed above: "I become a non-descript, a body without language, without nationality."[57] To fill this void, Nina will take on a variety of masculine personas and will become constantly engaged in a process of becoming, undoing, and remaking—a practice I read as analogous to Halberstam's concept of female masculinity in that it explores how queerness and hybridity can challenge dominant models of gender conformity.[58]

Halberstam's groundbreaking *Female Masculinity* has demonstrated the extent to which alternative masculinities reveal something about gender itself. Rather than an imitation of maleness, "female masculinity actually affords us a glimpse of how masculinity is constructed as masculinity. In other words, female masculinities are framed as the rejected scraps of dominant masculinity in order that male masculinity may appear to be the real thing."[59] Halberstam's study opens with an analysis of Carson McCullers's *The Member of the Wedding* and a reflection on the inadequacy of gendered categories. In both the novel and film versions, tomboy Frankie Addams attempts to change or add to her name, believing that "naming represents the power of definition, and name changing confers the power to reimagine identity, place, relation, and even gender."[60] In countering the attendant futility often associated with the tomboy narrative, Halberstam reads this example as pointing to, first, the inadequacy of the categories available for racial, gendered, and sexual identification and, second, to language as a structure that keeps individuals and objects in place. In *Tomboy*, Bouraoui uncovers the ambivalence of names: they are both liberating and constraining, a trap between longing and belonging. This can also be extended to labels and categories, which equally serve a disciplining function: they limit subjectivity in that they pin down and set strict constraints for what is acceptable and proper for each body. Gender, sexuality, and language are the most regimented forms of social conformity—but they also are subject to rearrangement, and in *Tomboy* this means recognizing differently and multiply gendered bodies and subjectivities.

In thinking Halberstam together with *Tomboy*, I want to ask how names recruit individuals and consequently discipline them along binary gender lines. Subject formation is directly linked to the power of being given a name and being called out: we become subjects through interpellation, by being hailed, as Louis Althusser and Judith Butler have amply theorized.[61] In Althusserian theory, this phenomenon of interpellation has most often been illustrated by the phrase "Hey, you there!," which, when directed at us, pulls us in and makes us into subjects. Meanwhile, Butler draws out the gendered aspects of interpellation and performative utterances in her well-cited examples of "It's a boy!" and "It's a girl!," which are generally conferred at the moment a baby is born.[62] Interpellation also incorporates an ideological element, as we are constantly hailed by various apparatuses that compose state power and control. Labels and names are similarly intertwined with modalities of power and have been used as tools of exclusion.

Constantly met with this interpellation, *Tomboy*'s protagonist, however, attempts to subvert the process whereby names reify gendered and racial identities. For Nina, naming is ambivalent in that it attempts to reify a certain subjectivity: "I go from Yasmina to Nina. From Nina to Ahmed. From Ahmed to Brio. . . . I don't know who I am. One and multiple. Lying and truthful. Strong and weak. Girl and boy."[63] Instead of going by the given name Yasmina, the protagonist becomes Nina. In Althusserian terms, Yasmina is both "recruited" and "transformed" into a proper French subject through the name Nina, even if she will never be fully accepted as such. Mimicking her perception in France as a foreigner, Nina ventriloquizes those around her: "And you, what are you in fact? French or Algerian? We prefer to call you Nina instead of Yasmina. Nina is convenient; it sounds Spanish or Italian. This way we don't have to justify our choice of friends."[64] Moving from Yasmina to Nina is an adjustment, an identity shift that is demanded because the name Yasmina is "too Algerian." Yet to go from Nina to Ahmed, from Ahmed to Brio, the protagonist turns the tables by subverting this name-based transformation and embracing this power to accumulate new names and subjectivities. In morphing into these personas, Nina uncovers that identity and selfhood are processes of invention that leave traces behind.[65]

Subjectification, Disidentification, and Decentering Identity

In *Bodies That Matter*, Butler shifts attention away from constructivist approaches that read social forces as shaping the irreducible materiality of bodies by instead looking to matter itself. She presents a genealogy of the materiality of the body that interrogates how bodies come to matter (in the dual meaning of "matter"—as materiality and as value). Butler argues that constructivist approaches presume a framework of social agency (gender) that acts upon the fixed and passive matter of sexed bodies. In her reflections on subjectification and language, Butler reminds us that in reiterating hegemonic power, space for subversion is created: "There is no subject prior to its constructions, and neither is the subject determined by those constructions; it is always the nexus, the non-space of cultural collision, in which the demand to resignify or repeat the very terms which constitute the 'we' cannot be summarily refused, but neither can they be followed in strict obedience. It is the space of this ambivalence which opens up the possibility of a reworking of the very terms by which subjectivation proceeds—and fails to proceed."⁶⁶ Shifting to a theory of "materialization" enables us to rethink materiality and the matter of bodies as an effect of power. For Butler, it is about recognizing what has been done with bodies, matter, and sex and to use them to do something else.

Butler argues that performativity (a term that she would increasingly replace with the concept of citationality) should not be understood as a deliberate act undertaken by a preexisting subject but rather "as the reiterative and citational practice by which discourse produces the effects that it names." Butler also emphasizes its derivative character and the "reiterative power of discourse to produce the phenomena that it regulates and constrains."⁶⁷ *Tomboy* enacts Butler's aims of dislodging matter from its irreducible status and locating the materiality of sex as a product of regulatory norms and discourses, even as it attempts to undo this naturalization of belonging to categories of binary gender. *Tomboy* effectively decouples sex from gender, the biological from the cultural, and rejects biological sex as determinative of gender. In performing masculinity, the narrator uncovers the tenuous nature of gender.

However, the book takes this a step further in its simultaneous denaturalization of race. As the narrator emphasizes, sex and gender cannot be separated from nationality (coded as race and ethnicity), as exemplified by the previously cited quote: "Every morning I scrutinize myself. I have four problems. Am I French or Algerian? Am I a girl or a boy?"⁶⁸ Nor is Nina's culture and nationality determinative or originary. She is between nationalities, "forever split between this one and that one, enduring a fractured identity, seeing myself as divided."⁶⁹ Butler reminds us that "the failure of identification, is itself the point of departure for a more democratizing affirmation of internal difference."⁷⁰ The protagonist rejects biological sex as the origin or basis of gender, just as she rejects nationality and race as determinative of culture, subjectivity, and opportunity.

By disidentifying with categories like "woman," "French," and "Algerian," the protagonist exemplifies how "power inheres within different forms of refusal."⁷¹ Yet this is not mere rejection—a closing down or shutting off. Instead, Nina enacts a disidentification with the destiny associated with body, physical appearance, and phenotype.

Disidentification is a way of dealing with dominant ideology that is neither identificatory nor counteridentificatory, neither assimilational nor oppositional. In this third space exists a strategy of working on and against that attempts to transform cultural logics from within. Nina embodies both poles of a number of binaries—one/multiple, lying/truthful, strong/weak, girl/boy—and it is this ability to hold multiple and contradicting positions that creates instability and confusion in a "system" that is not built for this. As a hermeneutical process or performance, disidentification rethinks meaning, allowing minority subjects to "decode" cultural fields in which they do not have a voice. Muñoz elaborates that disidentification is "a step further than cracking open the code of the majority; it proceeds to use this code as raw material for representing a disempowered politics or positionality that has been rendered unthinkable by the dominant culture."[72] Nina fully engages in such a process. For example, in responding to the four aforementioned "problems" ("Am I French or Algerian? Am I a girl or a boy?"), Nina distorts the "binary code" and moves between categories without ever fully inhabiting any and, in the process, remakes all of them.

I turn now to two particularly poignant passages from the text that evidence this everyday sort of disidentificatory strategy. In the first scene, we witness Nina negotiating an inability to fit into predetermined categories of nationality and citizenship. Although categories of identity are shown to lack substance—and are even fictional to a certain degree—this does not mean that they do not have effects: "Who will I be in France? Where will I go? How will the French see me? To be French means being without my father, without his strength, his eyes, his guiding hands. To be Algerian means being without my mother, without her face, her voice, her protective hands. Who am I? . . . I am both horribly free and restrained. 'You're not French.' 'You're not Algerian.' I am everything. I am nothing."[73] Here, Nina enacts Sara Ahmed's view of disidentification as a "desire to give up proximity" to such categories, embodying a freedom from identity-based definitions.[74] In problematizing identity and identification, *Tomboy* reveals a process by which "the queer and the colored come into perception and the social order receives a jolt."[75] Disidentification allows the minority subject to resist modes and patterns of identification, not necessarily by abandoning social pressures and proscriptions, but by expanding and problematizing identity and identification, a process Nina summarizes through the proclamation "I am everything. I am nothing."

The second scene that evidences a deployment of disidentification occurs quite early in the novel when Nina is first labeled a tomboy: "Open your eyes. See her ways on the street, hear the comments from waiters and salesgirls. When her cousins are dressed in white, she wears red and green. These are the words of my French grandmother. Her gaze says: 'You're a tomboy.' *No*. My audience is proud of me. *I exist*."[76] Here, the idea of a "lacking boy" (a literal translation of *garçon manqué*, the novel's title) also references a "failed girl." The look of her French grandmother is a look that many gender-nonconforming individuals might recognize, the scrutinizing stares that police our genders, that tell us we have stepped out, or those curious glares that indicate the looker is just trying to figure out: What are you? In response to such stares and comments, Nina disidentifies with all gender labels. The "*No*" is not a "no" of counteridentification; instead, it indicates a resistance to the assuming of any gender category. "*I exist*." Not as a boy, not as a girl. Neither as a tomboy nor as a lacking boy or a failed girl. I exist as I am.

Re-membering

Tomboy also evidences how "becoming" bodies can claim memory in new and transformative ways. Diffracted through a shattered "I" that is no longer self-referential, memory is transformed into a less linear concept in *Tomboy*. The concept of re-membering here functions as a counterhegemonic practice that simultaneously addresses the subject-forming capacities of memory and embraces the vulnerability of the fractured or (dis)membered body. In "Troubling Time/s and Ecologies of Nothingness: Re-turning, Re-membering, and Facing the Incalculable," feminist theorist Karen Barad explains that a critical aspect of the corporeal practice of re-membering, which is "a bodily activity of re-turning," involves "the material reconfiguring of spacetimemattering in ways that attempt to do justice to account for the devastation wrought as well as to produce openings, new possible histories by which time-beings might find ways to endure."[77] In *Tomboy*, re-membering gets at the active and descriptive aspects that inhere within Nina's perpetual becomings: it is both a verb (the gerund "re-membering," which itself suggests incompleteness) *and* an adjective ("re-membering bodies," for instance, could describe bodies that are re-membered or put back together, as well as bodies that hold memories). Nina uncovers how re-membering can allow for claiming gender (and later sexuality) in new and transformative ways. For example, by "re-membering" herself/himself as a man, the narrator becomes someone else, allowing for a different inhabitation of the trauma of forever becoming French Algerian, with neither Frenchness nor Algerianness ever actually occupied.

To help illustrate the queer potential of re-membering, I want to return (or, as Barad would have it, re-turn) to the scene in which the narrator utters the aforementioned quote: "I go from Yasmina to Nina. From Nina to Ahmed. From Ahmed to Brio."[78] What follows from this quote is key, as the passage develops in a way that lays bare the co-constitution of gender, postwar memories, and intergenerational hauntings:

> I don't know who I am. One and multiple. Lying and truthful. Strong and weak. Girl and boy. My body will betray me one day. It will develop into a female body and turn against me. It will resist. I will hold onto Nina forcefully like a wild animal. We find champagne glasses wrapped in newspaper from 1962. My sister is born at the time of the crime: the year of the massacre of the Algerian women from La Résidence, the year of the OAS massacre. It was their last massacre. Their revenge. The curse is everywhere. In my room, all over the apartment walls, on the tile floor, and in the laundry room. We find their weapons under the bathroom plumbing. This madness is the way the men of the OAS celebrated.... This haunted place marked by its noises, shadows, and apparitions. The wind blows constantly: it's the complaint of the Algerian women massacred by the OAS men.[79]

There is no break between Nina's self-reflection on discomfort with gender assignations and the historical trauma she has inherited, which is emphasized by "1962" (repeated three times in the full passage), the final year of the war and the year of Algerian independence. In the days following independence, the OAS—the French right-wing terrorist group that attempted to stifle decolonization—carried out murderous acts across Algeria. This massacre, which took place at La Résidence, Nina's home, has been erased from the historical record, like so many other instances of small- and large-scale violence during the war. Haunted by the OAS violence of 1962, La Résidence retains the memories of the women killed there decades earlier.

The text goes on to elaborate on Nina's feelings of living among this historical and emotional detritus, which causes her to become distraught and even violent. However, instead of turning away from the past, Nina works through intergenerational trauma: "Like a melancholic subject holding onto a lost object, a disidentifying subject works to hold on to this object and invest it with new life."[80] Nina realizes this process even further by inhabiting the ghost of Ahmed, the uncle she never knew. This strategy of working on and against becomes a powerful tool with which to re-member and to queer memory—that is, to inhabit it in transformational ways that subvert its assumed power.

There is, however, yet another curious move, as the passage quickly shifts to desire and sexuality. In grappling with the violent hauntings contained within her home, Nina eventually seeks refuge in Amine's house. Once arriving in his room, she tries to get close to him, to touch him, but he refuses: "You desire me in secret. Your mother wants to separate us. She compulsively repeats her obsession: 'I don't want my son to become a homosexual.' She says the word first. She says my word."[81] Amine's mother feels that under the influence of "this fake girl," as she refers to Nina, Amine will become homosexual.[82] While queer desire is subtly alluded to earlier in the novel (e.g., when Nina meets an older woman named Paola, who takes an interest in her), this is the first explicit mention of homosexuality, which itself is framed as threatening but perhaps also as empowering through its emphasis placed on "my word." The following paragraph then links the narrator's masculinity to the Algerian struggle and to vengeance, interspersing it with sexually suggestive language: "For you [Amine], I invent myself with other eyes and other gestures. For you, I have the hands of a man, strong and clenched in fists. This is how I experience our Algerian history, in combat.... I penetrate you and I dance like a man.... You, me, you, me. I am inside you, Amine. You are invaded."[83] The narrator proceeds to subvert the structures of gender and reverses their assumed roles still further: "I love you like a man. I love you as if you were a girl."[84] This is no longer homosexual desire, for Amine becomes a girl. I also identify this as the moment when Amine takes on another status: Nina's alter ego. Amine has become part of the "I," another masculine persona adopted by the narrator: "You lend me your favorite pants, Amine.... I keep them for a long time. I take them hostage. I refuse to return them. Your mother protests. I live in your clothes, precisely where you hold your hidden sex. Isn't it at this very moment, by this gesture, by this theft, that homosexuality takes hold?"[85]

While some readings of the novel have suggested that Amine is purely fictional—a figment of Nina's imagination—I argue that the reader should not be too hasty to assume that Amine is only constituted by Nina as her double and that he must therefore not exist. In my reading, Amine is an actual person, her childhood friend, but one who eventually takes on an imaginary status when the narrator takes on his persona. A queer approach—one that reads the text and its characters as radically open—allows me to argue that Amine is simultaneously real and fictional, both Nina's friend and alter ego. Yasmina—Nina—Amine. All three names contain the same sounds and vibrations, the *n*'s and *a*'s and *i*'s. Yasmina becomes Nina, Nina becomes Amine. Difference with a sonic twist. Embedded in history, Nina's body carries—indeed, re-members—the history of this conflict. By decentering the definition of the body as inhabited by a single "I"—through both intergenerational trauma and a more agential decentering of gender and sexuality by taking on multiple masculine personas—the possibility to inhabit spaces and traumas in new and transformative ways is created.

Third Space as Queer Potentiality

While *Tomboy* exemplifies the juxtaposition between personal and collective crises stemming from the French-Algerian War and the violent legacy of decolonization, it also suggests something else, some possibility for hope. In the novel's conclusion, Nina embodies re-membering and does the work of re-turning to herself: "It took place in Tivoli that incredible summer. I did not go to Saint-Malo [France] that year but went to Rome instead.... It took place in the Tivoli gardens during this auspicious season—the season of visible bodies. It took place amidst the humid trees, drenched alleys, and flowing waterfalls.... She and I stayed at the Grand Hôtel."[86] While it is never clear what the repeated phrase "It took place" references, nor is the "she" named, I interpret this passage as Nina finding freedom and discovering desire. Rome becomes a third space that dissolves identities, be they racial, gendered, or sexual: "Walking among these men and women, I was no longer afraid of anything. I was no longer French. I was no longer Algerian. I was not even my mother's daughter anymore."[87] Nina embraces the taboo of nonnormative desire that has hovered over the text and allows herself to forget and embrace her being and becoming. Indeed, the text concludes by emphasizing "a new force haunting my body: my desire."[88] It is desire itself that awakens a further deconstruction of the strictures of identity labels and categories: "My body was breaking free. It no longer had French traits. It no longer had Algerian traits."[89]

Barad writes that blurring categories can "serve to demonize, dehumanize, and demoralize. It can also be a source of political agency. It can empower and radicalize."[90] Not only does *Tomboy* blur the categories of gender and race, but it also blurs the generic borders between history and autobiography and between novel and memoir. Through the subversion of generic structures, Bouraoui engages in a queer praxis that allows for new possibilities of meaning, including a renaming of gendered and sexual subjectivities. *Tomboy* thereby decenters identity and reconceptualizes memory as a psychic and embodied process of re-membering. In decoupling masculinity from men, the narrator diminishes the coherence of borders by constantly moving back and forth, by simultaneously occupying multiple spaces, names, or genders, and by revealing the porosity of the borders themselves.

I want to conclude with a more anecdotal take on hybridity. In a blog entry, activist and writer Lauren Jade Martin proposes a theory on living between the lines that echoes the experiences of *Tomboy*'s Nina: "Almost every person I know of mixed-race background is queer. I don't think that is a random coincidence.... There is something in living an interstitial existence—a life between lines—that creates a certain freedom and fluidity. We are anomalies among anomalies, able to enter multiple worlds at multiple times, as both insiders and outsiders."[91] *Tomboy* asks us to start thinking differently about the confluence of queerness and race as embodying an interstitial life between categorical identities. Even as it means constantly suffering from that "absolute despot quality" that Gloria Anzaldúa identified at the outset of this chapter in dictating that "we are able to be only one or the other," having entry into both worlds—living between the lines—holds potential for imagining, enacting, and embodying the force of hybridity and in-betweenness.[92] This offers the possibility to reconfigure identity, including memory and masculinity, and may allow for a proliferation of worlds and voices. As *Tomboy*'s Nina summarizes, "The sea is cradled by two continents. I remain between these two countries. I am between two identities. My equilibrium lies in my solitude, a unifying force. I invent another world, without a voice, without judgment."[93]

Conclusion

Queer Postcolonial Entanglements

To conclude *Hybrid Anxieties*, I want to turn to two more examples that unite the queer and the postcolonial and mingle past, present, and future temporalities. Despite the fact that the French-Algerian War undoubtedly had deleterious effects and its remnants are by no means of the past, at the core of this book is the question of what happens if we look to the "queerer" aspects of the war's legacies—those moments when things don't line up or look different from what they might appear at first glance—in order to recover or identify alternatives: different genders and sexualities that exceed the binary, different ways of embodying memory, different modes of storytelling. If we adjust our focus by a few degrees, other perspectives that take into account the creative and conflictual elements of living in the wake of war take on a new valence.

Award-winning Algerian director Merzak Allouache's comedy *Chouchou* (2003) enjoyed massive box-office success. Not easily categorizable, Allouache's films (eighteen to date) include dramas, comedies, and documentaries. As with other migrant directors working in France, he is, as Will Higbee has pointed out, "clearly grounded in a particular postcolonial 'moment': reinterpreting 'official' versions of France's and Algeria's colonial past, while also challenging reductive stereotypes of France's North African immigrant population found in the nation's postcolonial present."[1] In addition to emphasizing the long-lasting effects of the French-Algerian War, Allouache has also been credited with the emergence of a new wave of Algerian cinema dealing specifically with questions of gender and sexuality.[2]

Grossing more than 33 million euros to date, Allouache's eleventh feature film, *Chouchou*, is a comedy about the experiences of an undocumented transfeminine Algerian immigrant named Choukri (played by well-known actor Gad Elmaleh and based on a comic character created and performed by Elmaleh) who arrives in France presenting as male and soon after begins to present and identify as a woman named Chouchou.[3] While the French-Algerian War is not named, it is implicitly referenced via the film's focus on postcolonial migration from the former colony to the metropole. Like Nina Bouraoui's *Tomboy*, analyzed in chapter 5, Allouache's film similarly paints a portrait of movement between genders and national identities, but this time under the guise of a slapstick comedy. The humor begins straight away, as Chouchou has come disguised as a Chilean asylum seeker fleeing Augusto Pinochet's regime (anachronistic as that is, given the temporal lag between that historical moment and the film's contemporary moment). Indeed, we can imagine there are reasons why this Algerian immigrant would fear revealing her true nationality in France and would instead feel safer pretending to be a Latin American refugee. Attempting to find a place to stay, Chouchou is eventually taken in by two Catholic priests who, although doubting her story, say that they do not need to know exactly why she has ended up in the small Parisian suburb they call home. Soon after, Chouchou secures a job as the assistant to a psychoanalyst, and we quickly learn of Chouchou's gender identity when she opens up to her boss. "I never had problems with homosexuality, but my real dream is to become a woman," she states, upon which the therapist insists that from now on Chouchou should come to work presenting as a woman and will be treated as such in the therapist's office. Despite embracing this womanhood, the film can nevertheless also be interpreted as offering a commentary on the limitations of rigid identity categories. *Chouchou* encourages us to resist any quick move to label its protagonist as homosexual or "crossdressing," even though the viewer may ache to read this character as neatly fitting into existing categories (a tendency that is also partially reflected in the limited scholarship on the film).

Later in the film, Chouchou has a chance encounter with some friends from Algeria who have also migrated to France, and they introduce her to the Apocalypse, a nightclub primarily populated by drag queens, trans women, and gay men. There, Chouchou meets the wealthy Stanislas, with whom she falls in love. There appear to be no obstacles to their relationship—that is, until Inspector Grégoire, a police officer and former patient of Chouchou's employer, creates problems, for he holds Chouchou responsible for blocking him from seeing his therapist and her boss. His behavior toward Chouchou is violent and aggressive (yet comic), although significantly, his harassment is not directed toward her perceived transgender identity or sexual orientation; instead, he targets Chouchou's migration status, threatening to deport her and thus separate her from Stanislas. Running counter to a long history of North African migrants being racially profiled by law enforcement in France, Grégoire's superiors put a stop to the harassment when they realize she is being targeted. Ironically, in saving Chouchou from deportation, law enforcement actually opens up queer kinship possibilities, for now Chouchou is free to be with her lover. The film ends with Chouchou and Stanislas's wedding, where locals of different ages, genders, races, and classes commingle to celebrate the marriage of this unlikely pair. While this may appear unrealistic, I argue that it is precisely this utopian vision of a France embracing all forms of diversity that—despite its over-the-top portrayal—makes the film worthy of serious attention.

While the comedy can be interpreted as a critique of French multiculturalism, most cinemagoers almost certainly did not view it as such.[4] Yet why did this film, which relies so heavily on the themes of migration and transgender subjectivity, garner such ticket sales? As opposed to a latent acceptance, the film's box-office success could instead evidence a working-through of anxieties, with the genre of physical comedy offering a release of pent-up angst regarding the nation's future and its demographic. Given that gender-nonconforming behaviors and identities are often the subject of ridicule in mainstream cinema, it is possible to read the pairing of comedy and gender nonconformity as problematic in the context of *Chouchou*. Allouache's film is thus not immune to critique. Notwithstanding these concerns, which I also share, I read the film as simultaneously exposing significant colonial aftereffects. Indeed, it offers a prescient commentary that prefigures a much larger social debate, revealing a contradiction between an increased acceptance of gender and sexual minorities, on the one hand, and growing hostility toward migrants, on the other.

While at the moment in which the film was released the ending was preposterous—a marriage between an undocumented trans woman and a rich French cisgender man would not have been sanctioned by either the law or the church—it was simultaneously forward-facing in its presaging of a more vociferous social, political, and cultural debate. Indeed, only a few years later, the *mariage pour tous* (marriage for all) movement would grab public attention throughout France and internationally.[5] While often celebrated as a step forward for equal rights, the ways in which this debate reveals the entanglement of colonial aftershocks with anxieties about sexuality and race have received less attention and inquiry. Given that Chouchou self-identifies as a woman, it would be a mistake to read this final scene as referencing gay marriage; nonetheless, juxtaposing the film's finale with contemporary debates on marriage equality (as in the right to marry regardless of gender or sexuality) is revelatory of the continued imbrication of gender, sexuality, and postcoloniality.

Taubira, Racist Anxieties, and Marriage Equality

Law 2013-404, the legislation that would eventually allow for marriage equality, has become more commonly referred to as the Loi Taubira (Taubira Law), named after France's then minister of justice, Christiane Taubira. After introducing the law—which had also been an electoral promise made by François Hollande when he was running for president in 2012—Taubira unwittingly became both the public face of the marriage debate and the target of conservative attacks. A black woman originally from former colony French Guiana, Taubira seemed to embody extreme alterity and a threat to "French culture" for many social and political conservatives. An outspoken critic of injustice and inequality, Taubira had, some years earlier, also gained attention for her work on a 2001 law that recognized the Atlantic slave trade as a crime against humanity. More recently, in 2013 she lent her support to proposals for land reforms as a form of compensation for slavery in France's Caribbean territories.[6]

Although marriage for same-sex couples was legalized on May 18, 2013, the legislation experienced a far-from-smooth passage onto the French statute books. Severe resistance from conservative groups resulted in a racist and homophobic campaign that bitterly divided the French public. One image circulated by the conservative anti-marriage equality La Manif Pour Tous (Demonstration for All) campaign featured a racist, cartoon-like rendering of Taubira spanking a child with a book (the civil code) and the caption "Sauvons les enfants" (Save the children). The small print at the bottom of the image reads "Tous nés d'un homme et d'une femme!" (Everyone is born of a man and a woman!).[7] Other arresting images used in La Manif Pour Tous's marketing campaign utilized traditional French tropes, several even appropriating images from some of the most iconic posters from the May 1968 movement, albeit drastically contradicting the sentiments most associated with the period (e.g., civil rights and sexual liberation). In one such poster, the campaign transformed the original "Mai 68, début d'une lutte prolongée" (May 68, beginning of a long struggle) into "On veut du boulot, pas du mariage homo" (We want jobs, not gay marriage).

In the run-up to the law's passage, Taubira had repeatedly been subjected to racist and sexist slurs, including an attack on the cover of the Far Right magazine *Minute*, in which she was compared to a monkey. One member of the FN was also forced to withdraw her candidacy in a municipal race over a Facebook photo of Taubira alongside a baby monkey, with the caption under the monkey stating "At 18 months" and the other under Taubira's photograph reading "Now."[8] In a 2013 interview with the French newspaper *Libération*, Taubira detailed other racist attacks, which included being taunted with a banana by a child during a protest against same-sex marriage.[9] In that same interview, she stated: "There has been a long slide, in which we have constructed an internal enemy.... Those who are *unable to imagine a future* spend their time telling the French people that they are being invaded, under siege, in danger."[10] As Taubira's words suggest, the marriage equality debate ignited a broader conversation that exposed deep anxieties

7. Protest by La Manif Pour Tous. Courtesy of Audrey Cerdan.

regarding national identity and the future of the French Republic. In *Queer Theory: The French Response*, Bruno Perreau elaborates on this invocation of the threat many saw Taubira as seemingly embodying: "Demonstrators against gay marriage played simultaneously on fear of the enemy within . . . and on racism (by placing sexual minorities in the same category as uncivilized foreigners)."[11] As a symbol of France's colonial past—one that speaks back and demands reparations—Taubira was viciously targeted. Indeed, intense resistance to same-sex marriage seemed to coalesce with racist and xenophobic sentiments, with both conflicts evidencing a deep concern over Frenchness.

According to Vinay Swamy, "France's thrust to maintain a robust national self-identification . . . can be found at the root of many debates about non-normative sexual orientations."[12] While national identity has long been shaped and reshaped in conjunction with social and cultural changes, novel articulations of Frenchness (and Europeanness) have taken on a new valence in the wake of a "borderless" European Union that simultaneously works hard to protect "Fortress Europe." In this context, tensions between hospitality and hostility, which have become even more pronounced, have crystallized around the figure of the migrant or the racialized other.[13] This has also provoked a new set of anxieties about difference not only vis-à-vis race and nationality but also regarding gender and sexuality.

It is the confluence of gender, sexuality, and colonialism that appears in *Chouchou* and the Taubira debate, both of which engage with and question a present postcolonial moment marked by evolving understandings of gender and sexuality. Both the film's conclusion and Law 2013-404's passage might suggest respect and recognition for gender and sexual minorities, yet they also link anxieties about gender and sexual alterity with a fear of migrants and racialized others—as seen in both Inspector Grégoire's targeting of Chouchou and in public attacks on Taubira. Although alternative genders and sexualities might in fact be powerful challenges to patriarchal nationalism, as Gayatri Gopinath has argued, assimilation into the fabric of the state does not necessarily signal a progress-oriented vision that moves us one step closer to reaching acceptance.[14] Here, it is worth heeding Mehammed Amadeus Mack's warning that "certain encouragements to queer can be incorporated within a nationalist agenda that finds in (distorted) queering a useful weapon against a minority or Muslim assertions of identity politics."[15] Such a "top-down" approach masquerades as queering but actually borders on homonationalist practices or romanticizes what is figured as "transgressiveness" in Islamic cultures. These brief snapshots included above serve as lessons: despite the enactment of laws that may, on the surface, signal equal opportunity, we must remain aware of how minority populations are co-opted and how racist and colonial discourses continue to be wielded.[16]

Forward-Dawning Horizons

Throughout this book I have proposed bringing queer theory and postcolonial theory into closer dialogue in order to better analyze and deconstruct the intertwined and compound nature of identities and textual forms in the wake of the French-Algerian War. *Hybrid Anxieties* has specifically sought to lay bare entanglements of race, nationality, and gender as vectors that have shaped—and continue to shape—French and Algerian colonial legacies. My aim has been not only to expose the violence inherent to these entanglements but also to frame their productive potential to reconfigure social engagement. Subjectivity and identity were radically interrogated by and through the destructive impacts of the eight-year war; meanwhile, the underlying anxieties that flooded the post-decolonization era and its extended aftermath have, as I have attempted to show, also been reflected in the consistent undoing of traditional literary and cinematic classifications. Indeed, the texts and films analyzed in the previous five chapters cross many genres, but they never quite fit any single category. Form mirrors content in these texts that contend with the fragmentary and fracturing impacts that the French-Algerian War has had and continues to have on gender, sexuality, and memory.

In *Cruising Utopia: The Then and There of Queer Futurity*, José Esteban Muñoz—whose work has profoundly shaped this book's theorization of identity, transformation, and the cultural logics of domination—acknowledges that a queer utopian hermeneutic must remain open and seek out queer relational formations within the social: "Such a hermeneutic would then be epistemologically and ontologically humble in that it would not claim the epistemological certitude of queerness that we simply 'know' but, instead, strain to activate the no-longer-conscious and to extend a glance toward that which is forward-dawning, anticipatory illuminations of the not-yet-conscious. The purpose of such temporal maneuvers is to wrest ourselves from the present's stultifying hold, to know our queerness as a belonging in particularity that is not dictated or organized around the spirit of political impasse that characterizes the present."[17] While Muñoz's notion of "anticipatory illuminations of the not-yet-conscious" overlaps with the workings of anxiety explored throughout this book—also anticipatory in nature—we must nonetheless maintain a "forward-dawning" approach that breaks the standstill or gridlock marked by the present and embrace the indefiniteness and ambiguity of hybridity. In studying a selection of literary and cinematic texts that queer genre, I hope to have demonstrated that acknowledging, contesting, resisting, and reframing the continued aftermath of colonial events like the French-Algerian War are clearly ongoing projects. Even the most cursory look at current events, both inside and outside France, confirms that our contemporary era continues to be deeply shaped by imperialism in all its forms. And while it is the destructive impacts of war that are most often emphasized in the historical record, I have asked what queer resonances might also be uncovered, cultivated, and nurtured. Indeed, as a conflict over identity, the French-Algerian War allowed for a fundamental and radical deconstruction of subjectivity itself. In gesturing toward examples that radically reconfigure their outlook toward gender, sexuality, and memory by undoing a teleological understanding of time, *Hybrid Anxieties* has also suggested that postcolonial subjects may occupy multiple and conflicting identities, modes of becoming that explode any coherent or static being. Uniting postcoloniality and queerness—both conceptually and methodologically—allows for contradictions to emerge, thus signaling possibilities in the form of simultaneous critique and openness. Identifying the impossible and embracing the contradictory allow us to imagine otherwise. New pasts, presents, and futures emerge that break the chains of memory and envision different ways of inhabiting gender and sexuality.

NOTES

Introduction

1. These lines are excerpted and translated from the poem "Ordre II" (Order II). Sénac, *Selected Poems*, 216. Please note that throughout this book all translations from French are my own unless otherwise indicated.
2. Katia Sainson also identifies a number of metaphors related to cross-gender identification and drag in Sénac's autobiographical writing. Sainson, "'Entre deux feux,'" 40–41.
3. The terms that encapsulate the conflict itself ("French," "Algerian," "war") are not without controversy, as none of these words fully or truly capture either the actors or the lands involved. Even as I refer to the conflict as the "French-Algerian War," I am well aware of the risks of repeating a dichotomy my work aims to deconstruct. I use this term to mark an approach that questions the distinctness of identities, even as it invokes these very terms. Queer theory is caught in a similar bind, as in order to contest binary thinking, it must also reiterate it by using the terms it argues must be undone. I have also chosen to use the term "French-Algerian War" rather than "Algerian War," "Algerian War of Independence," or "Algerian Revolution" for the same reason that James Le Sueur cites. The term "Algerian War" is Franco-centric, as "Algeria has fought many wars without France. Hence, leaving aside the question of whether an undeclared colonial war can be called anything other than a civil war, I have settled on the more specific and neutral name French-Algerian War." Le Sueur, *Uncivil War*, 328.
4. Péroncel-Hugoz, "Assassinat d'un poète," 35, cited in Sainson, "'Entre deux feux,'" 45–46.
5. See, for example, Témime and Tuccelli, *Jean Sénac, l'Algérien*; Sainson, "Jacob's Wound"; Hayes, "Queer Resistance." More generally, Assia Djebar drew attention to Sénac's poetic work, beginning her book

Algerian White (*Le blanc de l'Algérie*) by identifying him as the first poet killed between Algeria's war of independence and the subsequent civil war. Rachid Boudjedra called Sénac "plus Algérien que n'importe quel autre" (more Algerian than any other), stating that his assassination was fueled by hatred of the other. Boudjedra, *Lettres algériennes*, 71, cited in Marx-Scouras, "The Specter of Jean Sénac," 46.

6. Barthes, "Reflections on a Manual," 74.
7. Freeman, *Time Binds*, xvi–xvii.
8. Said, *Culture and Imperialism*, 332.
9. See Lennard Davis's "Constructing Normalcy" for an astute analysis of this process of norm formation and how norms are configurations that arise from particular historical moments.
10. Rosello, *France and the Maghreb*, 1–2.
11. McLeod, *Postcolonial London*, 14.
12. See, for example, Halberstam, *The Queer Art of Failure*; and Coyote and Spoon, *Gender Failure*.
13. For a selection of some of the important work on memory in the context of the French-Algerian War, see Greene, *Landscapes of Loss*; Hubbell, *Remembering French Algeria*; Lorcin, *Algeria & France*; McCormack, *Collective Memory*; Rothberg, *Multidirectional Memory*; Stora, *La gangrène et l'oubli*.
14. See Jakobsen, "Queer Is? Queer Does?"
15. Sedgwick, *Tendencies*, viii.
16. Eng, Halberstam, and Muñoz, "What's Queer," 4.
17. For important critiques into how queer studies has taken whiteness for granted and as the norm, see, among others, Cohen, "Punks, Bulldaggers, and Welfare Queens"; and Johnson, "'Quare' Studies." As a methodological approach, queer of color critique has been particularly influential in recognizing intersections of race, gender, sexuality, class, and nation. For some of the most recent exciting scholarship to emerge in this field, see, for example, Chen, *Animacies*; Ferguson, *Aberrations in Black*; Holland, *The Erotic Life of Racism*; Reddy, *Freedom with Violence*; Rodríguez, *Sexual Futures*; Snorton, *Black on Both Sides*. Additionally, a growing body of work that has put queer studies and critical disability studies in dialogue has also demonstrated queer's mosaic-like character. See, for example, Clare, *Brilliant Imperfection*; McCormack, *Queer Postcolonial Narratives*; McRuer, *Crip Theory*; Puar, *The Right to Maim*; Shildrick, *Dangerous Discourses*.
18. Bérubé, "How Gay Stays White."

19. Hayes, *Queer Nations*, 20.
20. Warner, introduction, xvii.
21. McCormack, *Queer Postcolonial Narratives*, 10–11.
22. Muñoz, *Disidentifications*, 29.
23. Le Sueur, *Uncivil War*, 6.
24. Prior to Ottoman rule and French colonization, "Algeria" was not a country but separate and distinct regions composed of tribes (including Berber, Kabyle, Chaouia, Mzab, and Tuareg). A variety of different languages and dialects were spoken, and customs between these native groups were disparate. In this sense, "Algeria" was an arbitrary construction.
25. The indigenous population had initially been referred to as Français musulmans d'Algérie (French Muslims of Algeria). In 1958 this was changed to Français de souche nord-africaine (French of North African origin) in contrast to Français de souche européenne (French of European origin). Naming and categorization practices became critical at this juncture and profoundly shaped interactions and power structures between "colonizer" and "colonized."
26. The exact number of casualties has been vigorously debated, with French officials claiming approximately 400,000 Algerian deaths and Algerian sources alleging 1.5 million.
27. Quinan, "Technocrats and Tortured Bodies"; and Quinan, "Uses and Abuses."
28. Cited in Cohen, "The Algerian War," 236.
29. Said, *Culture and Imperialism*, 282.
30. Rather than using terms such as "postindependence" and "postwar," Todd Shepard finds the category of "post-decolonization" useful because it avoids regarding 1962 as a breaking point that signified a before-and-after colonial occupation. For this reason, it is a term I also adopt throughout this book. Shepard, *Sex, France, and Arab Men*, 3.
31. An abundance of scholarship has been helpful in showing how shifting geopolitics and new forms of global power (re)shape hegemony and hegemonic masculinities. See, for instance, Connell, *Masculinities*; Mack, *Sexagon*; Nagel, "Masculinity and Nationalism."
32. Curiously, this was the same year that France instituted the Civil Solidarity Pact (Pacte Civil de Solidarité, abbreviated as PaCS), which legally recognized various forms of domestic partnership, including same-sex unions. This confluence of sexuality and colonialism will appear later in this introduction and in the book's conclusion.

33. MacMaster, "Torture," 4–5. Toby Beauchamp has also drawn links between the French-Algerian War and the War on Terror, particularly with respect to the question of "gender transgression." Only three days after the US Department of Homeland Security issued an advisory that male terrorists "may dress as females in order to discourage scrutiny," a *New York Times* article noted that the Pentagon had recently screened the classic 1965 film *The Battle of Algiers*. Beauchamp writes: "The *Times* article suggests that the Pentagon screening was in part to gain tactical insight into the current U.S. war in Iraq. *Algiers* is a film filled with depictions of guerrilla warfare tactics, including those that rely on the links between gender and national identities: Algerian women pass as French to deliver bombs into French civilian settings, while Algerian men attempt to pass as women in hijabs, their disguises broken when French soldiers spy their combat boots. Though neither the DHS Advisory nor the Pentagon's study of the film explicitly reference transgender populations, both nevertheless invoke the ties between gender presentation, national identity and bodies marked as dangerously deceptive." "Artful Concealment," 359.

34. In the context of France, LGBT support organization SOS Homophobie documented in its 2017 report that physical attacks against sexual and gender minorities increased by 20 percent in 2016. SOS Homophobie, "Rapport sur la homophobie," 7. A few years earlier, the National Commission for Human Rights (CNCDH) also noted a fivefold increase in racist, Islamophobic, and anti-Semitic acts over the past twenty years. Alexander Stille, "The Justice Minister and the Banana," *New Yorker*, November 14, 2013, https://www.newyorker.com/news/daily-comment/the-justice-minister-and-the-banana-how-racist-is-france.

35. Bouraoui, *Tomboy*, 33–34. "Je passe de Yasmina à Nina. De Nina à Ahmed. D'Ahmed à Brio. . . . Je ne sais pas qui je suis. Une et multiple. Menteuse et vraie. Forte et fragile. Fille et garçon." Bouraoui, *Garçon manqué*, 62.

36. Bouraoui, *Tomboy*, 98. "Tous les matins je vérifie mon identité. J'ai quatre problèmes. Française? Algérienne? Fille? Garçon?" Bouraoui, *Garçon manqué*, 163.

37. Young, *Colonial Desire*, 4.

38. Bhabha, *The Location of Culture*, 277. Young makes a comparable link between anxieties about racial difference in the nineteenth-century context, writing that "at the heart of racial theory, in its most sinister, offensive move, hybridity also maps out its most anxious, vulnerable

site: a fulcrum at its edge and centre where its dialectics of injustice, hatred and oppression can find themselves effaced and expunged." *Colonial Desire*, 19.
39. Bhabha, *The Location of Culture*, 162.
40. Ahmed, *Queer Phenomenology*, 144.
41. Bhabha, *Nation and Narration*, 211.
42. Lionnet, *Postcolonial Representations*, 12.
43. Young, *Colonial Desire*, 25–26.
44. Freccero, "Queer Times," 485, emphasis in original.
45. See Perreau, *Queer Theory*, 80. Others have argued that the word has sixteenth-century German roots in the word *quer*, meaning "oblique" or "perverse."
46. *Oxford English Dictionary*, s.v. "hybrid."
47. Muñoz, *Disidentifications*, 31–32.
48. *Oxford English Dictionary*, s.v. "anxiety."
49. *Oxford English Dictionary*, s.v. "anxiety," emphasis in original.
50. Shildrick, *Dangerous Discourses*, 94.
51. This tension between repressive and liberatory impulses will be more fully elaborated in my analysis of Pierre Guyotat's *Eden, Eden, Eden*, presented in chapter 3.
52. "Que l'Homme en moi se fasse, pour ma Patrie algérienne." Sénac, *Carnets inédits*, 848, cited in Sainson, "'Entre deux feux,'" 32.
53. Fanon, *The Wretched of the Earth*, 35. "La décolonisation est très simplement le remplacement d'une 'espèce' d'hommes par une autre 'espèce' d'hommes." Fanon, *Les damnés de la terre*, 39.
54. Fanon, *The Wretched of the Earth*, 36. "La décolonisation est véritablement création d'hommes nouveaux." Fanon, *Les damnés de la terre*, 40. We could most certainly critique the universalist "men" of Fanon's phrasing (just as we could criticize his heteronormative biases) and possibly substitute it with a more inclusive term. As John Murungi states in his critique of Fanon, "The word 'men' can no longer be used or understood in the traditional way—a way that rendered women invisible." *African Philosophical Currents*, 105. However, it is crucial to acknowledge that Fanon was in fact interested in the effects that decolonization had on *men* (a word he equated with male bodies).
55. Coly, "*Carmen* Goes Postcolonial," 404.
56. Shepard, *The Invention of Decolonization*, 272, emphasis in original.
57. Shepard, *The Invention of Decolonization*, 2.
58. Swamy, *Interpreting the Republic*, 118.

59. See Scott, *Only Paradoxes to Offer*.
60. Camiscioli, *Reproducing the French Race*, 6.
61. One could certainly argue that homosexuality was always a divisive issue in France. While France was the first European country to abolish laws forbidding consensual sodomy (i.e., acts), it has also been documented that France, more vociferously than its neighbors, policed and criminalized same-sex sexualities (i.e., identities). See Peniston, *Pederasts and Others*. This relationship between acts and identities will be explored in greater detail in chapter 3, but for now I want to underscore that sexuality—and necessarily gender—was a battleground, one that collided with the French colonial project.
62. See Shepard, *Sex, France, and Arab Men*, 137.
63. See Perreau, *Queer Theory*, 10.
64. Navarro-Ayala, *Queering Transcultural Encounters*, 2.
65. Roditi, *De l'homosexualité*, 110, cited in Shepard, *Sex, France, and Arab Men*, 138.
66. Shepard, *The Invention of Decolonization*, 199.
67. Shepard, *Sex, France, and Arab Men*, 29. In this book, Shepard goes on to argue that the French-Algerian War and the so-called sexual revolution (including the events of 1968) are enmeshed and that to adequately understand them, they must be analyzed together.
68. See Butler, *Bodies That Matter*.
69. Ahmed, *Queer Phenomenology*, 198n18.
70. Hayes, *Queer Roots for the Diaspora*, 35; Green, "Queer Theory and Sociology," 27.
71. Seidman, "Identity and Politics," 132.
72. Ashcroft, Griffiths, and Tiffin, *The Empire Writes Back*, 12.
73. See, for example, Boone, *The Homoerotics of Orientalism*; El-Tayeb, *European Others*; Gopinath, *Impossible Desires*; Gopinath, *Unruly Visions*; Hawley, *Postcolonial, Queer*; Hayes, *Queer Nations*; Hayes, *Queer Roots*; Massad, *Desiring Arabs*; McCormack, *Queer Postcolonial Narratives*; Navarro-Ayala, *Queering Transcultural Encounters*; Puar, *Terrorist Assemblages*.
74. See Lugones, "The Coloniality of Gender"; and Lugones, "Heterosexualism."
75. For an insightful analysis of French resistances to queer theory, see Perreau, *Queer Theory*.
76. Conservative group La Manif Pour Tous (Demonstration for All), which heads this movement in France, clearly positions gender and queer theory as incommensurate with French values and as originating in a

non-French context in their (woefully inaccurate) description: "Gender theory was born in the US at the end of the 80s. It posits the superiority of 'gender,' a social construct freely accepted or refused by the subjects, over sex, fruit of an always arbitrary biology. Far from being simply a tool of analysis, gender ideology is a true system, where reality must become asexual, a system which would confine us in stable roles—determinisms—so as to make room for the freedom of choosing and recombining gender." See http://www.lamanifpourtous.fr/c13-comprendre/the-heart-of-the-matter/. It is important to note that this movement is, however, not confined simply to the French context and has been active in other European countries, including Poland, Hungary, and Italy. In Hungary, for example, this led to the 2018 governmental deaccreditation of all gender studies programs.

77. Freccero, *Queer/Early/Modern*, 18-19.
78. Young, *White Mythologies*, 32. Pal Ahluwalia, in "Out of Africa," similarly argues that poststructuralism and deconstruction must be read as emerging from a colonial epoch.
79. Aly, *Becoming Arab in London*, 1.
80. Aly, *Becoming Arab in London*, 6.
81. On the topic of roots from a queer perspective, it is here worth signaling Jarrod Hayes's *Queer Roots for the Diaspora*.
82. Derrida, *Specters of Marx*, xvii, emphasis in the original.
83. Fisher, *Ghosts of My Life*, 72, 19. See also Ayo A. Coly's analysis of hauntology in the context of African women's literature and visual and performance arts, where she argues that although hauntology is a tragedy, it also "ferments new visions, imaginaries, and possibilities." *Postcolonial Hauntologies*, 5.
84. Hayes, *Queer Roots*, 27.
85. Freccero, *Queer/Early/Modern*, 18-19.
86. Amin, *Disturbing Attachments*, 108.
87. Bhabha, *The Location of Culture*, 220.
88. Provencher, *Queer Maghrebi French*, 34. See also Eribon, "Haunted Lives."
89. Rothberg, *Multidirectional Memory*, 3, 11.
90. Many of the figures central to these two conflicts are also the same, including Charles de Gaulle and Maurice Papon, among others.
91. Derderian, "Algeria as a *lieu de mémoire*," 29. For an important recent study of memory in the French-Algerian context, see Hubbell, *Remembering French Algeria*, which adds a new angle by focusing on the *pied-noir*

population after the war. In the tradition of scholars such as Benjamin Stora who have demonstrated the pernicious effects of collective amnesia, Hubbell looks to what she calls "return narratives" in order to show how they can deconstruct attachment to the past and foster different versions of Algeria and the war.

92. Stora, *La gangrène et l'oubli*, 8.
93. Brun and Shepard, "Guerre des sexes."
94. Fisher, "The Metaphysics of Crackle," 53.
95. Stoler, *Along the Archival Grain*, 20.
96. Renan, "What Is a Nation?," 11. "L'oubli, et je dirai meme l'erreur historique, sont un facteur essentiel de la création d'une nation." Renan, *Qu'est-ce qu'une nation?*, 89.
97. Blanco and Pereen, "Introduction," 13.
98. Halberstam, *In a Queer Time and Place*, 70–71.
99. Barad, "Transmaterialities," 407.
100. Barad, "Transmaterialities," 406–7.
101. Gordon, *Ghostly Matters*, 8.
102. Bennett, *Empathic Vision*, 36.
103. For more on intra-action, see Barad, *Meeting the Universe Halfway*; and Barad, "Diffracting Diffraction." I am also inspired by Barad's diffractive reading methodology, which is "attuned to the entanglement of the apparatuses of production, one that enables genealogical analyses of how boundaries are produced rather than presuming sets of well-worn binaries in advance." *Meeting the Universe Halfway*, 30.
104. On women, see, for example, Khanna, *Algeria Cuts*; Lazreg, *The Eloquence of Silence*; Vince, *Our Fighting Sisters*. There are some notable exceptions that have begun to fill this void in the area of masculinity. See, for example, Amine, *Postcolonial Paris*; Shepard, *Mâle décolonisation*, which has also appeared in English as *Sex, France, and Arab Men*; and Brun and Shepard, *Guerre d'Algérie*, which contains an entire section devoted to the theme of masculinities during the war.

1. Haunted Masculinity and Wounds of War

1. Roumette, "Interview with Alain Resnais," 12.
2. Dine, *Images of the Algerian War*, 223; Milne, "The Festivals," 178.
3. Sontag, "Review of *Muriel*," 26. As a side note, it is worth mentioning that these same words could have been used to describe Pierre Guyotat's *Eden, Eden, Eden*, analyzed in chapter 3—in my opinion, a technical masterpiece, almost beyond full comprehension.

4. Whether because of the strict censorship regulations or a lack of interest in portraying the effects of the war on any population other than that of the French *hexagone*, Resnais's choice not to include any visual representation of Muriel was heavily critiqued. For more on this argument, see Boudjedra, *Naissance du cinéma algérien*; and Gauch, "Muriel."
5. Confirmation that the French government did indeed sanction the use of torture would finally come from General Paul Aussaresses in 2001. In his book *Services spéciaux* and in an interview with *Le Monde*, Aussaresses confessed to his own involvement in torture under the orders of Prime Minister Guy Mollet. He defended its use and stated that it was a necessary evil in the war. He would also advocate for the use of torture in the more recent global "War on Terror," particularly in the fight against Al-Qaeda. Florence Beaugé, "'Je me suis resolu à la torture . . . J'ai moi-même procédé à des éxecutions sommaires . . . ,'" *Le Monde*, November 23, 2000, https://www.lemonde.fr/afrique/article/2000/11/23/je-me-suis-resolu-a-la-torture-j-ai-moi-meme-procede-a-des-executions-sommaires_1671136_3212.html. See also Cole, "Intimate Acts," for a discussion of the renewed torture debate instigated by Aussaresses's confession, as well as Louisette Ighilariz's testimony of undergoing torture at the hands of the French military, published in 2001 as *Algérienne*.
6. Sartre, "A Victory," xxix. "Dans la torture, cet étrange match . . . c'est pour le titre d'homme que le tortionnaire se mesure avec le torturé et tout se passe comme s'ils ne pouvaient appartenir ensemble à l'espèce humaine." Sartre and Alleg, *La question*, 116.
7. Lazreg, *Torture*, 255. Similarly, in his analysis of Henri Alleg's epic testimony of torture, *The Question*, Ross Chambers gestures toward the ways in which torture calls up traditional notions of masculinity. He writes that Alleg's testimony "underscores its significance as an up-to-date version of an age-old, hyper-masculine ordeal of pain. Structured as a version of the ancient initiatory topos of the descent into hell as a close encounter with death, his narrative explores the practice of modern torture as an unholy alliance of industrial rationality and ancient trial by ordeal, a man-to-man encounter mediated by pain." "Ordeals of Pain," 209. As a counterpoint to both Sartre's and Chambers's figurations, we might also interpret torture as in stark contrast to "how a man should act." This argument, also suggested by Shepard, highlights how successful "anticolonial critics had been in positioning the 'revolutionary' or heroic Algerian man as the embodiment of (universal or true)

manliness, a figure who had confronted the overwhelming force—and *the sadistic unmanly tactics*, notably torture—of France, and freed his nation and family from colonial oppression." *Sex, France, and Arab Men*, 11, emphasis added. For more on the relationship between torture and masculinity, see also Rejali, "Torture Makes the Man."
8. Showalter, *The Female Malady*, 172.
9. "Cette histoire doit se passer dans une ville reconstruite. Il ne reste plus que quelques îlots de ruines, de vieilles ruines qui ont mal vieilli. Bloc de ciment perle. Maisons ouvertes sur des pieces indéfinissables, pleines de paille, de débris, jardins de bois mort. Mais ces petits domaines d'une ancienne guerre ne peuvent être découverts que par hasard. . . . Tout le reste de la ville est neuf, bêtement neuf. Rues droites, se coupant perpendiculairement, lampadaires distribuant une lueur orangée, avenues comme prêtes pour une prochaine guerre de façon que les chars d'assaut puissent passer plus facilement. Magasins vides, à louer. Parcs de stationnement. Cinémas dont la sonnerie ne s'arrête pas. Murs blancs. Beaucoup d'antennes de télévision . . ." Cayrol and Resnais, *Muriel*, 11.
10. On the spatial aspects of the film, Leo Bersani and Ulysse Dutoit write: "*Muriel* is a wholly centrifugal film. . . . *Muriel* is constantly rushing away from a narrative center never firmly established in the first place. . . . [W]hat would it mean to be in the center no matter where we are? What is the narrative center of *Muriel*?" *Arts of Impoverishment*, 190–91.
11. Ross, *Fast Cars, Clean Bodies*.
12. As a brief side note, it is worth mentioning that screenwriter Jean Cayrol, as a camp survivor, has admitted to being obsessed with the memory and recounting of World War II. It is interesting to think that *Muriel* may have been more about World War II than about Algeria for him, while Resnais has stated that his celebrated documentary *Night and Fog* (also written by Jean Cayrol), which takes the Holocaust as its subject, was actually about Algeria. This parallel further highlights how deeply intertwined these two historical periods were for the writer-filmmaker duo and for the contemporary viewing public.
13. Unlike the other characters of the film, Françoise is described as having "pas de passé ou si peu" (no past or very little). Cayrol and Resnais, *Muriel*, 19. Cayrol also describes her as "l'élément le plus stable" (the most stable element) of the film, which prompts the hypothesis that it is her lack of a past that allows her to be so grounded. Cayrol and Resnais, *Muriel*, 19.
14. Deleuze, *Cinema 2*, 118.

15. See chapter 4, in which I further explore this notion of state commemoration (or lack thereof) in my analysis of Leïla Sebbar's novel *The Seine Was Red*.
16. Roumette, "Interview with Alain Resnais," 13.
17. Lazreg, *Torture*, 112, emphasis in the original.
18. Bernard: "Je vais faire un tour, voir Muriel." Hélène: "Mais tu rentreras pour dîner j'espère? . . . Tu ne m'as jamais dit où tu avais rencontré ton amie, elle n'a pas un nom d'ici." Bernard: "Elle est malade en ce moment." Hélène: "Ah!" Bernard: "Non, elle n'est pas malade." Two other Muriels are mentioned in the film: a young girl in the street called by her mother ("Muriel, come here!") and a newspaper headline about a woman named Muriel who was tortured for thirty hours. All quotations from *Muriel* are my own transcription of the film.
19. Freeman, *Time Binds*, xv.
20. Kuby, "From the Torture Chamber."
21. Lazreg, *Torture*, 133–34. Here it is also worth signaling Raphaëlle Branche's path-breaking study *La torture et l'armée pendant la Guerre d'Algérie*, particularly its interrogation into the complex meaning of torture during the French-Algerian War.
22. This moment occurs at nearly the exact middle of the film. For a discussion of various scholars' false remembrance of the temporal location of this scene in the film, see Wilson, *Alain Resnais*, 91. Given that misremembering is a centerpiece of Resnais's film, it is ironic that arguably the most important scene would be incorrectly referenced. It does, however, also speak to the role that our own affective memory plays in viewing practices and (mis)remembering strategies.
23. "Personne n'avait connu cette femme avant. . . . On y voyait encore. Le hangar était au fond, avec les munitions. D'abord, je ne l'ai pas vue. C'est en m'approchant de la table que j'ai buté sur elle. Elle avait l'air endormie, mais elle tremblait de partout. On me dit qu'elle s'appelle Muriel. Je ne sais pas pourquoi, mais ça ne devait pas être son vrai nom. On était bien cinq autour d'elle. On discutait. Il fallait qu'elle parle avant la nuit. Robert s'est baissé et l'a retournée. Muriel a gémi. Elle avait mis son bras sur ses yeux. On la lâche, elle retombe comme un paquet. C'est alors que ça recommence. On la tire par les chevilles au milieu du hangar pour mieux la voir. Robert lui donne des coups de pied. Il prend une lampe-torche, la braque sur elle. Les lèvres sont gonflées, pleines d'écume. On lui arrache ses vêtements. On essaie de l'asseoir sur une chaise, elle retombe; un bras est comme tordu. Il faut en finir.

Même si elle avait voulu parler, elle n'aurait pas pu. Je m'y suis mis aussi. Muriel geignait en recevant les gifles. La paume de mes mains me brûlait. Muriel avait les cheveux tout mouillés. Robert allume une cigarette. Il s'approche d'elle. Elle hurle. Alors son regard m'a fixé. Pourquoi moi? Elle a fermé les yeux, puis elle s'est mise à vomir. . . . La nuit je suis revenu la voir. J'ai soulevé la bâche. Comme si elle avait séjourné longtemps dans l'eau . . . comme un sac de pommes de terre éventré. Avec du sang sur tout le corps, dans les cheveux . . . des brûlures sur la poitrine. Les yeux de Muriel n'étaient pas fermés. Ça ne me faisait presque rien, peut-être même que cela ne me faisait rien du tout."

24. Postcards took on a particular valence in this context. In *The Colonial Harem*, Malek Alloula reveals how postcard images of North African women that were produced and sent by French colonists, settlers, and tourists in the early twentieth century reinforced Orientalist ideas about Algerian women.

25. ". . . fosse très vite. J'ai déroulé la bâche, et je ne sais pourquoi les yeux de Muriel n'étaient pas ferm . . . C'est avec Muriel que tout a commencé vraiment, que j'ai compris. C'est depuis Muriel que je ne vis plus vraiment. . . . Je suis fichu. Je crois que j'ai envie de mourir, en tout cas je n'en ai plus peur . . ."

26. Levinas, "The Transcendance of Words," 147.

27. See Branche, "La torture dans *Muriel*."

28. *The Little Soldier* provides a notable counterpoint to *Muriel*. In Godard's film, torture was shown, although Algeria was not named. In Resnais's film, Algeria is named, but torture is not shown.

29. Sellier, *Masculine Singular*, 112.

30. Wilson, *Alain Resnais*, 99.

31. Foucault, *Discipline and Punish*.

32. Bernard: "Curieux de te voir ici." Hélène: "Tu me montres quelque chose?" Bernard: "Je n'ai pas envie de faire du cinema. J'accumule des preuves, c'est tout." Hélène: "Des preuves? Contre qui?" Bernard: "Tu ne comprendrais pas."

33. "Il y plus de huit mois que tu es rentré, penses-y."

34. Bernard: "Muriel n'est pas là, tu sais. Tu peux me prêter trois mille francs?" Hélène: "Je ne m'intéresse à Muriel qu'à cause de toi."

35. Khanna, *Algeria Cuts*, 104.

36. Fanon, "Algeria Unveiled," 37–38. For Shepard, supposed concern for Algerian women's well-being also became an evasion tactic: "By showing that women and their liberation were the targets of French

efforts in Algeria, the government could avoid responding to the FLN or engaging a debate on the question of colonialism." *The Invention of Decolonization*, 187.
37. Said, *Orientalism*, 3.
38. Ponzanesi and Waller, introduction, 2.
39. Following Hema Chari, I take "colonial masculinity" to refer not to "a single pattern of control but to specific practices of male domination." "Colonial Fantasies," 282.
40. Gordon, *Ghostly Matters*, 8.
41. Deleuze, *Cinema 2*, 207–8.
42. Wilson, *Alain Resnais*, 96.
43. Gauch, "Muriel," 55.
44. Kaprièlian, "'La guerre d'Algérie n'est pas finie,'" 39. "La guerre d'Algérie n'est pas finie. Le Front national, c'est la guerre d'Algérie. Les propos qu'on entend aujourd'hui, cette espèce de racisme progressiste, l'idée qu'un Français ne peut pas être algérien—et donc qu'un Algérien ne peut pas être français—, c'est vraiment la question de départ de la guerre d'Algérie. Et on voit bien comment en France aujourd'hui cette question n'est pas réglée."
45. Kaprièlian, "'La guerre d'Algérie n'est pas finie,'" 39. "Il m'a fallu des années pour me dire que, peut-être, le fait d'avoir participé à cette guerre et d'avoir vu ces choses avait contribué à son suicide. Il y est resté vingt-huit mois, ça n'est pas rien. J'ai entendu aussi l'histoire de types qui devenaient fous. Ça ressemble à un cliché, mais ça m'a aussi intéressé de trouver le moyen, techniquement, de dire ces clichés."
46. Quoted in the front matter of the novel's translation.
47. Mauvignier, *The Wound*, 197. "Parce que, c'est, de faire ce qu'ils ont fait, je crois pas qu'on peut le dire, qu'on puisse imaginer le dire, c'est tellement loin de tout, faire ça, et pourtant ils on fait ça, des hommes, des hommes ont fait ça, sans pitié, sans rien d'humain, des hommes ont tué à coup de hache ils ont mutilé le père, les bras, ils ont arraché les bras, et ils ont ouvert le ventre de la mere et—." Mauvignier, *Des hommes*, 244.
48. Mauvignier, *The Wound*, 162. "Quels sont les hommes qui peuvent faire ça. Pas des hommes qui peuvent faire ça. Et pourtant. Des hommes." Mauvignier, *Des hommes*, 201.
49. Houston, "Resnais' *Muriel*," 36.
50. The word *harki* was the generic term used to refer to Muslim Algerian soldiers who fought with the French during the war.

51. Mauvignier, *The Wound*, 28–29. "On ne peut pas savoir. On sait déjà. On sait depuis tout le temps. Depuis, je veux dire, depuis—c'est autre chose, ce temps-là. Une chose comme ça, que je pense, qui vient se glisser et brouiller ce moment de notre histoire où tout à coup elle est là, comme un compte à régler vieux de quarante ans, un âge d'homme pour nous regarder et nous dire non, ce n'est pas fini, on croyait que c'était fini mais ce n'était pas fini." Mauvignier, *Des hommes*, 42.

52. Mauvignier, *The Wound*, 101. "Il perçoit un coup plus long et plus fort il lui semble, jusqu'au fond de son être, jusqu'à en avoir les mains moites et pour une fois croiser le regard livide d'un autre appelé qui, comme lui, comme eux, sait que dès cet instant toute sa vie sera perforée de ce coup de sirène qui annonce le départ." Mauvignier, *Des hommes*, 129.

53. Mauvignier, *The Wound*, 77. "[Bernard] avait osé les encadrer, les mettre au mur et les montrer, là, et ne pas en parler, ne rien dire, comme si c'était des photos de vacances, et ne rien m'en direr, à moi, moi qui l'avais pourtant vu si souvent là-bas et avec qui il avait partagé le—" Mauvignier, *Des hommes*, 100.

54. Hirsch, "The Generation of Postmemory," 117.

55. Mauvignier, *The Wound*, 209. "J'ai pensé qu'en Algérie j'avais porté l'appareil photo devant mes yeux seulement pour m'empêcher de voir, ou seulement pour me dire que je faisais quelque chose de—peut-être, disons—utile. Après, je n'ai plus jamais fait de photographie." Mauvignier, *Des hommes*, 258.

56. Mauvignier, *The Wound*, 105. "Pour se donner du courage et pour faire peur." Mauvignier, *Des hommes*, 133.

57. Mauvignier, *The Wound*, 113. "Comme un noyau qu'on recrache après l'avoir fait rouler dans sa bouche très longtemps." Mauvignier, *Des hommes*, 142.

58. "Une litanie, un défilé d'horreurs, une sorte de cauchemar perpétuel." Czarny, "Ecrire la guerre," n.p.

59. Mauvignier, *The Wound*, 113. "Alors on continuera jusqu'au village d'après." Mauvignier, *Des hommes*, 142.

60. Mauvignier, *The Wound*, 204. "En se réveillant et en se levant ni l'angoisse ni les images se passent plus." Mauvignier, *Des hommes*, 253.

61. Mauvignier, *The Wound*, 228. "Je voudrais voir si l'Algérie existe et si moi aussi je n'ai pas laissé autre chose que ma jeunesse, là-bas. Je voudrais voir, je ne sais pas. Je voudrais voir si l'air est aussi bleu que dans me souvenirs. . . . Je voudrais voir quelque chose qui n'existe pas et qu'on laisse vivre en soi, comme un rêve, un monde qui résonne et palpite, je

voudrais, je ne sais pas, je n'ai jamais su, ce que je voulais, là, dans la voiture, seulement ne plus entendre le bruit des canons ni les cris, ne plus savoir l'odeur d'un corps calciné ni l'odeur de la mort—je voudrais savoir si l'on peut commencer à vivre quand on sait que c'est trop tard." Mauvignier, *Des hommes*, 281.
62. Gordon, *Ghostly Matters*, 3, 4, 5. For a brilliant analysis of haunting in a different postwar context (that of the Korean War, often termed the "forgotten war"), see Grace Cho's *Haunting the Korean Diaspora*.
63. Gordon, *Ghostly Matters*, xvi.
64. See Blanco and Pereen, "Introduction," 2, 13-14.

2. "You'll Never Give Me a Bad Conscience!"

1. House and MacMaster, *Paris 1961*, 1.
2. Halbwachs, *On Collective Memory*, 38.
3. See Arendt, *The Origins of Totalitarianism* and *Essays in Understanding*.
4. Maslan, "The Anti-human," 362.
5. Arendt, *The Origins of Totalitarianism*, 296.
6. This dehumanization was not necessarily unique to this particular moment, as persistent use of racialized language up to the present day has regularly been deployed in immigration discourse. For more detail on racialization and racism as a feature of the French Republican landscape, see Camiscioli, *Reproducing the French Race*, 158-59. See also Navarro-Ayala, *Queering Transnational Encounters*, 86-89.
7. Cited in Ross, *May '68 and Its Afterlives*, 43.
8. For testimonies from people who saw protesters being thrown into the Seine River, see Einaudi, *La bataille de Paris*, 172-74, 192-94.
9. House and MacMaster, *Paris 1961*.
10. "Ray Charles pourra chanter ce soir. Après le passage des services de désinfection, le Palais des sports a retrouvé son aspect habituel." Cited in Tristan, *Le silence du fleuve*, 91.
11. "Des noyades d'Algériens? Ça n'a jamais existé.... Quand on poursuivait les meneurs du FLN sur les quais de Paris, il arrivait que ceux-ci se lancent à la Seine en tentant de fuir." Tristan, *Le silence du fleuve*, 101.
12. Sebbar, *The Seine Was Red*, 92.
13. Crewe, "Recalling Adamastor," 75.
14. The phrase is found on the DVD back cover of the American edition. Also included are the following quotes: "Like Hitchcock, only creepier" and "Suspense has a new master."
15. Porton, "Collective Guilt," 50.

16. All quotations from *Caché* are my own transcription of the film.
17. Ford, "From Otherness 'Over There,'" 63.
18. Max Silverman has made a similar point: "What returns to haunt Georges are his, and his country's, stereotyped fears and fantasies of the Algerian buried deep within the French national psyche whose most profoundly repressed moment is 17 October 1961, when these fears spilled over into naked aggression by French forces of law and order on the streets of Paris." "The Empire Looks Back," 246.
19. Shildrick, *Dangerous Discourses*, 92.
20. Gilroy, "Shooting Crabs," 234.
21. Bourdieu, *Pascalian Meditations*, 170–71.
22. Rothberg, *Multidirectional Memory*, 358.
23. See, for example, Macallan and Plain, "*Hidden*'s Disinherited Children."
24. Of course, this issue is not unique to France. As Haneke has pointed out, with only minor adjustments, this story could have taken place anywhere, as every nation has its secrets: "I don't want my film to be seen as specifically about a French problem. It seems to me that, in every country, there are dark corners—dark stains where questions of collective guilt become important." Haneke cited in Porton, "Collective Guilt," 50.
25. Ahmed, *Queer Phenomenology*, 129.
26. Ahmed, *The Cultural Politics*, 67.
27. Ahmed, *The Cultural Politics*, 67, emphasis in original.
28. Ahmed, *Queer Phenomenology*, 135. For an excellent study of the navigation of racialized bodies and spatial logics, specifically what happens when bodies who do not fit somatic norms are made to feel out of place, see also Nirmal Puwar's *Space Invaders*.
29. For more on the connections between education, class, and cultural capital, see Bourdieu, "The School as a Conservative Force" and "Cultural Reproduction and Social Reproduction."
30. Camiscioli, *Reproducing the French Race*, 157.
31. See Mbembe, "Necropolitics."
32. Ahmed, *The Cultural Politics*, 65.
33. Foucault, *The History of Sexuality*, 138–39. See also Tierney, "The Governmentality of Suicide" for a careful analysis of the relationship between Foucault's concept of biopower and suicide.
34. In fact, the title is doubly "hidden" from a US-based, non-French-speaking audience, since the film was marketed using the French title

and not its English translation: "hidden." (In the United Kingdom and Australia, it was, however, marketed as *Hidden*.)

35. For a sustained discussion of the film's conclusion, see Grossvogel, "Haneke"; and Penney, "'You Never Look at Me.'"
36. Fassin, "In the Name of the Republic," 6–7.
37. Patricia Tourancheau, "C'est écrit que c'est bien de mourir en martyr," *Libération*, January 8, 2015, http://www.liberation.fr/societe/2015/01/08/c-est-ecrit-que-c-est-bien-de-mourir-en-martyr_1176518.
38. See, for example, Robert Fisk, "Charlie Hebdo: Paris Attack Brothers' Campaign of Terror Can Be Traced Back to Algeria in 1954: Algeria Is the Post-colonial Wound That Still Bleeds in France," *The Independent*, January 9, 2015, http://www.independent.co.uk/voices/comment/charlie-hebdo-paris-attack-brothers-campaign-of-terror-can-be-traced-back-to-algeria-in-1954-9969184.html.
39. Mark LeVine, "Why Charlie Hebdo Attack Is Not about Radical Islam," *Al Jazeera*, January 10, 2015, http://www.aljazeera.com/indepth/opinion/2015/01/charlie-hebdo-islam-cartoon-terr-20151106726681265.html.
40. For a more thorough tracing of this colonial legacy, see Jonathan Laurence, "The Algerian Legacy: How France Should Confront Its Past," *Foreign Affairs*, January 16, 2015, http://www.foreignaffairs.com/articles/142782/jonathan-laurence/the-algerian-legacy. Here, Laurence also discusses two recent predecessors to the Kouachi brothers, Khaled Kelkal and Mohammed Merah, also French citizens of Algerian origin who committed terrorist acts in 1995 and 2012, respectively.
41. Andrew Higgins and Maia de la Baume, "Two Brothers Suspected in Killings Were Known to French Intelligence Services," *New York Times*, January 8, 2015, http://www.nytimes.com/2015/01/08/world/two-brothers-suspected-in-killings-were-known-to-french-intelligence-services.html.
42. Amnesty International, "France Faces 'Litmus Test' for Freedom of Expression as Dozens Arrested in Wake of Attacks," January 16, 2015, https://www.amnesty.org/en/latest/news/2015/01/france-faces-litmus-test-freedom-expression-dozens-arrested-wake-attacks/.
43. See Boyer and Wallace, "U.S. Portrayals."

3. Eros and Eden

1. Rubin, "Thinking Sex," 4.
2. Foucault, "Sex, Power," 163.

3. See Shepard, "'Something Notably Erotic,'" for an extended analysis of how such discourses and widespread references to sex, deviance, and normalcy—which he calls "sex talk"—worked to discipline and control in 1960s and 1970s France. In "From the Torture Chamber to the Bedchamber," Emma Kuby also makes an important point about the use of the language of sexual deviancy, which she argues was deployed by French antiwar activists to condemn the practice of torture by the French military.
4. On the link between sex and politics in his work, see Guyotat, *Littérature interdite*, 54.
5. In this way, the work can be regarded as responding to his concern that "décolonisation est 'déséroticisation'" (decolonization is "de-eroticization"). Guyotat, *Carnets de bord*, 200.
6. See, for example, Amin, *Disturbing Attachments*; Brun and Shepard, *Guerre d'Algérie*; Mak, *Sexagon*; Provencher, *Queer Maghrebi French*; Shepard, *Sex, France, and Arab Men*.
7. Kellner, "Marcuse," 3.
8. Jay, "Anamnestic Totalization," 9.
9. Marcuse, "Progress and Freud's Theory of Instincts," 41, cited in Jay, "Anamnestic Totalization," 9.
10. Benhabib, translator's introduction, xxxiii. As signaled in the introduction, this notion is also a mark of both queer and postcolonial approaches to memory.
11. Marcuse, *Eros and Civilization*, 207–8.
12. Altman, *Homosexual Oppression and Liberation*, 61.
13. Drucker, "Conceptions of Sexual Freedom," 35.
14. Foucault also wrote a preface, but it arrived too late to be included in the final printing. However, he composed a theoretically evocative article entitled "Il y aura scandale, mais . . ." (There will be scandal, but . . .), to which I will turn later in the chapter.
15. Barthes, "What Happens to the Signifier," n.p. "Cependant, quelles qu'en soient les péripéties institutionnelles, la publication de ce texte est importante: tout le travail critique, théorique, en sera avancés, sans que le texte cesse jamais d'être séducteur: à la fois inclassable et indubitable, repère nouveau et départ d'écriture." Barthes, "Ce qu'il advient au signifiant," 276.
16. It is also worth noting that Guyotat's text appeared soon after the rise of the new novel, or *nouveau roman*, in the 1960s, a literary style that experimented with form and problematized traditional novelistic struc-

tures as a way to complicate subjectivity. It is within—or perhaps in response to—this tradition that *Eden, Eden, Eden* appears, and while there may be similarities in the revolution that the new novelists and Guyotat triggered by shattering traditional structure and language, Guyotat most certainly "accepts and rejects, or radicalizes, both subjectivity and objectivity in a far more complex way than did the new novel." Kendall, "Eden and Atrocity," 14.

17. The online review portal Goodreads is full of people experiencing dizziness and nausea while reading *Eden, Eden, Eden*, as well as Guyotat's previous novel *Tomb for 500,000 Soldiers*, further emphasizing the ways in which his literary production pushes the reader to the limits of consciousness.
18. See Eribon, *Dictionnaire*, 234; Woods, *A History of Gay Literature*, 354; Heathcoate, "Autobiography, Sexuality, and Identity," 48.
19. Guyotat cited in Roger Clarke, "Three Cheers for Pornography," *Independent*, April 28, 1995, https://www.independent.co.uk/arts-entertainment/three-cheers-for-pornography-1617394.html.
20. Guyotat, *Littérature interdite*, 112.
21. Jean Cayrol (screenwriter of *Muriel*, which I analyzed in chapter 1) is widely credited as launching Guyotat's career. He published one of Guyotat's first novellas in his journal *Écrire 10* and served as a mentor to the young writer in the 1960s.
22. Kendall, "Eden and Atrocity," 11.
23. By one calculation, 14 percent of publications devoted to the war were censored (Stora, *Le livre*, 77), including some of the best-known literature and cinema of the period. By means of a few examples: Jean-Luc Godard's film *The Little Soldier* and Henri Alleg's autobiography of torture, *The Question*, were both banned, as were select issues of Jean-Paul Sartre's journal *Les Temps Modernes*. Jean Genet's play *The Screens* (1961) could not be staged until 1966 for reasons of censorship. Alain Resnais also faced censorship challenges when making *Muriel* (see chapter 1). See Anne Simonin's "La littérature saisie par l'histoire" for a more complete analysis of censored literature both during and after the war.
24. Noël, "The Outrage against Words," 15.
25. This detail is mentioned by Atlas Press, the publisher of the book's English translation.
26. As an anecdotal aside, the relationship between Genet and Guyotat was complex in its own right, with Genet purportedly trying to seduce Guyotat while he was on military leave in Marseille. Brun, *Pierre Guyotat*,

99. *Tout!*, 7, cited in Amin, *Disturbing Attachments*, 77. "Peut-être que si je n'étais jamais allé au lit avec des algériens [*sic*], je n'aurais jamais pu approuver le F.L.N. J'aurais probablement été de leurs bord, de toute façon, mais c'est l'homosexualité qui m'a fait réaliser que les algériens [*sic*] n'étaient pas différents des autres hommes." *Tout!*, 7, cited in Amin, *Disturbing Attachments*, 208n3.

27. Amin, *Disturbing Attachments*, 79.
28. Amin, *Disturbing Attachments*, 77.
29. "Pierre est venu à la cause algérienne; il n'en est pas parti." Brun, *Pierre Guyotat*, 101.
30. Brun, *Pierre Guyotat*, 101.
31. "S'il y a violence dans ce texte, elle est donc *violence de classe*, du premier au dernier mot—et cette violence de classe est souvent signifiée par les termes d'une violence *d'espèce à espèce*." Guyotat, *Littérature interdite*, 32, emphasis in original.
32. "La guerre d'Algérie n'est pas seulement une guerre: elle est aussi 'un moment de [sa] jeunesse,' autant de dire de sa formation d'homme." Brun, *Pierre Guyotat*, 93.
33. Guyotat, *Littérature interdite*, 108.
34. "Toute cette période algérienne constitue un bloc semi-conscient, mais capital: il est possible aussi que cette 'arrivée' de mes contradictions sur un lieu extrême . . . ait provoqué leur élucidation et leur *intégration au politique*. Mais il faut attendre la redaction de *Tombeau pour cinq cent mille soldats* pour lire les effets de ce choc: du plus loin que je me souvienne, la pulsion sexuelle a toujours, pour moi, recouvert en fait, la pulsion vers le proletariat." Guyotat, *Littérature interdite*, 109–10, emphasis in original.
35. Guyotat, *Carnets de bord*, 566, cited in Kendall, "Eden and Atrocity," 16.
36. "À mesure que j'avance dans ce temps d'Algérie, dans ce pays et ces hommes d'Algérie, je comprends ce qu'est la 'responsabilité collective.' . . . Le cauchemar persiste. J'ai roulé dans des paysages de guerre et de meurtre où l'on ne peut imaginer autre chose que du bétail égorgé, d'autres hommes que ~~des esclaves~~ des otages, où chaque arbre restant debout semble porter des traces de balles ou de sang, où chaque ruine noircie porte des inscriptions telles que 'La France est forte, la France reste,' etc. des paysages auxquels on pense après coup comme à certains 'mauvais' rêves." Guyotat cited in Brun, *Pierre Guyotat*, 99.
37. "Directement produite par un fait biographique—non pas hasard, mais contrainte historique: conscription et guerre d'Algérie. . . .

[Q]uand le texte est écrit... je retourne vers ces zones sub-désertiques et désertiques. Ces zones, je les ai traversées d'une part comme semi-esclave (deuxième classe soumis au bon vouloir des officiers, jusqu'à l'interrogatoire et l'emprisonnement); d'autre part comme 'nomade' non-citoyen.... Ces deux conditions d'irresponsabilité relative, constituent le lieu mental à partir duquel a pu être osé un discours inouï: l'acte sexuel est, ici, écrit, traité, cela dit, à un niveau moins immédiat, il est certain qu' 'une écriture qui prend immédiatement tous ses risques,' n'a pu être produite qu'à partir d'un terrain lui-même risqué—Il est à noter que *Eden, Eden, Eden* s'achève, s'interrompt, se dissout en un lieu de géographie générale." Guyotat, *Littérature interdite*, 29.
38. Kendall, "Eden and Atrocity," 18.
39. Guyotat himself commented on this aspect, writing that the text must be read "as reestablishing in fact the scientific notion of genesis, mask, distorted for centuries under the myth of 'Adam and Eve.'" "Comme rétablissant dans les faits la notion scientifique de genèse, masque, déformée depuis des siècles sous le mythe d' 'Adam et Ève.'" Guyotat, *Littérature interdite*, 56.
40. In his preface to the novel, Roland Barthes would also reference this notion of freedom: "*Eden, Eden, Eden* is a free text, free of all subjects, of all objects, of all symbols." Barthes, "What Happens to the Signifier," n.p. "*Éden, Éden, Éden* est un texte libre: libre de tout sujet, de tout objet, de tout symbole." Barthes, "Ce qu'il advient au signifiant," 275.
41. Brun, *Pierre Guyotat*, 202.
42. Kendall, "Eden and Atrocity," 12.
43. Guyotat, *Eden, Eden, Eden*, 1. "/ Les soldats, casqués, jambes ouvertes, foulent, muscles retenus, les nouveau-nés emmaillotés dans les châles écarlates, violets: les bébés roulent hors des bras des femmes accroupies sur les tôles mitraillés des G.M.C.; le chauffeur repousse avec son poing libre un chèvre projetée dans la cabine; / au col Ferkous, une section du RIMA traverse la piste; les soldats sautent hors des camions; ceux du RIMA se couchant sur la caillasse, la tête appuyée contre les pneus criblés de silex, d'épines, dénudent le haut de leur corps ombragé par le garde-boue; les femmes bercent les bébés contre leurs siens: le movement de bercée remue renforcés par la sueur de l'incendie les parfums dont leurs haillons, leurs poils, leurs chairs sont imprégnés: huile, girofle, henné, beurre, indigo, soufre d'antimoine—au bas du Ferkous, sous l'éperon chargé de cèdres calcinés, orge, blé, ruchers, tombes, buvette, école, gaddous, figuiers, mechtas, murets tapissés d'écoulements de

cervelles, vergers rubescents, palmier, dilates par le feu, éclatent: fleurs, pollen, épis, brins, papiers, étoffes macules de lait, de merde, de sang, écorces, plumes, soulevés, ondulent, rejetés de brasier à brasier par le vent qui arrache le feu, de terre;" Guyotat, *Éden, Éden, Éden*, 15–16.

44. Guyotat, *Eden, Eden, Eden*, 1–2. "[L]e soldat, sa poitrine écrasant le bébé accollé au sein, écarte le cheveux que la femme a répandus sur ses yeux, caresse le front de la femme avec ses doigts poudrés de poussière d'onyx; l'orgasme fait jaillir de sa bouche un jet de salive qui mouille le crane beurré du bébé; le sexe ressorti repose en s'amollissant sur les châles dont il prend la teinture;" Guyotat, *Éden, Éden, Éden*, 16.

45. For a careful analysis of how certain scenes and locations in Guyotat's narrative map onto specific geographical locations and memories, see Brun, *Pierre Guyotat*, 193–94.

46. Guyotat, *Littérature interdite*, 34.

47. "En niant le déchirement (mâle/femelle, humain/animal), la division bipolaire, la nature hybride des prostitués impose, avec la logique du 'deux à la fois,' un troisième terme, ni mixte, ni neutre, à la fois mixte et neutre, excentré, irreductible, et 'hors la loi.'" Brun, *Pierre Guyotat*, 207.

48. Guyotat, *Carnets de bord*, 525, cited in Kendall, "Eden and Atrocity," 12n8.

49. Hester, "Revisiting," 34.

50. This stylistic syncope was mirrored by the other sort of syncope experienced by the author: his aforementioned two-week coma caused by loss of consciousness resulting from insufficient blood flow to the brain.

51. Edelman, *No Future*.

52. Muñoz, *Cruising Utopia*, 27.

53. See, in particular, Deleuze and Guattari, *Anti-Oedipus* and *A Thousand Plateaus*. See also Guattari, "A Liberation of Desire."

54. Shildrick, *Dangerous Discourses*, 132.

55. Shildrick, *Dangerous Discourses*, 134–35.

56. Brun, *Pierre Guyotat*, 211, cited in Hester, "Revisiting," 42.

57. Guyotat, *Carnets de bord*, 485, cited in Kendall, "Eden and Atrocity," 18, emphasis in original.

58. "Il n'y a pas, ici, 'désir.' . . . [L]e mouvement est exclusivement économique; il n'y a pas 'amour.'" Guyotat, *Littérature interdite*, 31. Elsewhere, Guyotat described it in these terms: "Eden is the product of a permanent sexual craving, made even more acute as the text accumulates . . . according to a cyclical, indestructible process." "Eden est le produit d'une envie sexuelle permanente, rendue encore plus aiguë

au fur et à mesure de l'accumulation textuelle . . . selon un processus cyclique, indestructible." *Littérature interdite*, 68.
59. Foucault, "The Gay Science," 389.
60. Davidson, *The Emergence of Sexuality*, 212–13.
61. Davidson, *The Emergence of Sexuality*, 212.
62. See Foucault, *The History of Sexuality*, 1–35.
63. Foucault, *The History of Sexuality*, 34.
64. Foucault, *The History of Sexuality*, 157.
65. Foucault mentions colonialism only glancingly in *Security, Territory, Population* (see 89, 292). Foucault did, however, compose a significant portion of *The Archaeology of Knowledge*—perhaps his most celebrated work—during a self-imposed exile in postindependence Tunisia (1966–68). According to Pal Ahluwalia, the text, which marks a major paradigm shift in Foucault's thinking, was shaped by his exposure to the impacts of French imperialism. Ahluwalia, "Post-structuralism's Colonial Roots," 598–99.
66. Macey, *The Lives of Michel Foucault*, 83. Alexander Weheliye has taken Foucault to task for ignoring racism (even as he acknowledged biopolitical forms of racial injustice). *Habeas Viscus*, 53–73. See also Stoler, who asks of Foucault: "Why have we been so willing to accept his history of a nineteenth-century sexual order that systematically excludes and/or subsumes the fact of colonialism within it?" *Race*, 5–6. Nonetheless, it is important to acknowledge that in the field of postcolonial studies, the discursive approach that Edward Said developed in his field-defining *Orientalism* drew heavily upon Foucault's conceptualizations of power and knowledge.
67. "Il y manque ce bruit de guerre qui avait permis à votre premier roman d'être entendu." Foucault, "Il y aura scandale," 74.
68. "C'est d'en deçà du corps que votre texte nous arrive: surfaces, éclatements, ouvertures-blessures, vêtements et peaux qui se retournent et s'inversant, liquids blancs et rouges, 'ruissellement du dehors éternel.'" Foucault, "Il y aura scandale," 75.
69. "Une élégance—matérialiste—pour sauver le sujet, le moi, l'âme." Foucault, "Il y aura scandale," 74.
70. "J'ai l'impression que vous rejoignez par là ce qu'on sait de la sexualité depuis longtemps, mais qu'on tient soigneusement à l'écart pour mieux protéger le primat du suject, l'unité de l'individu et l'abstraction du 'sexe,' qu'elle n'est point à la limite du corps quelque chose comme le 'sexe,' qu'elle n'est pas non plus, de l'un de l'autre, un moyen de com-

munication, qu'elle n'est pas même le désir fundamental ni primitive de l'individu, mais la trame même de ses processus lui est largement antérieure; et l'individu, lui, n'en est qu'un prolongement précaire, provisoire, vite efface; il n'est, en fin de compte, qu'une forme pale qui surgit pour quelques instants d'une grande souche obstinée, repetitive. Les individus, des pseudopodes vite rétractés de la sexualité. Si nous voulions savoir ce que nous savons, il faudrait renoncer à ce que nous imaginons de notre individualité, de notre moi, de notre position de sujet. Dans votre texte, c'est peut-être la première fois que les rapports de l'individu et de la sexualité sont franchement et décidément renversés: ce ne sont plus les personnages qui s'effacent au profit des éléments, des structures, des pronoms personnels, mais la sexualité qui passe de l'autre côté de l'individu et cesse d'être 'assujettie.'" Foucault, "Il y aura scandale," 75.

71. Kendall, "Eden and Atrocity," 17.
72. For an extended analysis of Foucault's dismissal of the "repressive hypothesis" and his implicit critique of Marcuse, see Renaud, "Rethinking."
73. Foucault did, however, generally write favorably of the Frankfurt School. See Foucault, "Adorno, Horkheimer, and Marcuse," 117.
74. Jay, "Anamnestic Totalization," 8–9.
75. See Marcuse, *An Essay on Liberation*.
76. Muñoz, *Cruising Utopia*, 136.
77. Rodríguez, "Queer Sociality," 339.
78. "Ce triple Éden semble proposer une alternative au monde." Brun, *Pierre Guyotat*, 217.
79. "Je n'ai pas d' 'orientation sexuelle' unique, j'ai en moi un double désir, deux sexualités que je n'ai jamais mises sur le même plan.... La pulsion non hétérosexuelle est pour moi une manière d'expulser le plus gros du désir, le plus gros désir, le plus animal, le plus dangereux, pour parvenir à un désir plus doux, plus profond, procréateur." Guyotat cited in Brun, "Conscience du temps," 10.
80. Marcuse, *The Aesthetic Dimension*, 9.
81. Muñoz, *Cruising Utopia*, 1.

4. Queer Palimpsests and October 17, 1961

1. McLeod, *Beginning Postcolonialism*, 252, emphasis in original.
2. Dinshaw et al., "Theorizing Queer Temporalities," 182.
3. Sturken, "Narratives of Recovery," 234.

4. As Joshua Cole points out, the story of October 17, 1961, is particularly challenging to accurately communicate because it is not easy to discern whether it was about "Algerians demanding independence or French people demanding the rights to public space in the city or simply frightened laborers and their families with few options, caught between the fear of punishment by the FLN for not participating and the fear of certain violence from a police force that had been unhinged by attacks on its members." "Entering History," 134.
5. Mauvignier cited in Kaprièlian, "'La guerre d'Algérie,'" 39.
6. Freccero, "Queer Spectrality," 311.
7. Ahmed, *Queer Phenomenology*, 20.
8. McCormack, *Queer Postcolonial Narratives*, 9.
9. Hubbell, *Remembering French Algeria*, 217. In her epistolary exchange with Nancy Huston, Sebbar also writes: "I realize that this *division* from which I could suffer, today I cling to it and want to preserve it" (Je m'aperçois que cette *division* dont j'ai pu souffrir, aujourd'hui j'y tiens et je veux la préserver). *Lettres parisiennes*, 28, cited in Hubbell, *Remembering French Algeria*, 213, emphasis in original. These same concerns around hybridity will return in my analysis of Nina Bouraoui's *Tomboy*, presented in chapter 5.
10. "C'est là et seulement là que je me rassemble corps et âme et que je fais le pont entre les deux rives." Sebbar and Huston, *Lettres parisiennes*, 148, cited in Hubbell, *Remembering French Algeria*, 213.
11. Fulton, "Elsewhere in Paris," 32.
12. A number of novels have mentioned the event in passing: Georges Mattei, *La guerre des gusses*; Didier Daeninckx, *Meurtres pour mémoire* (which was also made into a television movie by Laurent Heynemann); Nacer Kettane, *Le sourire de Brahim*; Jean-François Vilar, *Bastille tango*; Tassadit Imache, *Une fille sans histoire*. William Gardner Smith's *The Stone Face* seems to be the earliest literary treatment of the massacre. Interestingly, it was written by an African American expatriate living in Paris in the early 1960s. A selection of films about the massacre includes Philip Brooks and Alan Hayling, *Drowning by Bullets*; Alain Tasma, *Nuit noire: Le 17 octobre 1961*; Yasmina Adi, *Ici on noie les Algériens: 17 octobre 1961*; and Michael Haneke, *Caché* (see chapter 2 for an extended analysis).
13. *Les porteurs de valises*, or "the suitcase carriers," was the name accorded to French people living in France who were part of a clandestine network that supported Algerian militants in the struggle for independence.
14. Donadey, "Anamnesis and National Reconciliation," 29, 112.

15. "Les programmes de recherche universitaire accordent à l'histoire de la présence française outre-mer, notamment en Afrique du Nord, *la place qu'elle mérite*. Les programmes scolaires reconnaissent en particulier le rôle positif de la présence française outre-mer, notamment en Afrique du Nord, et accordent à l'histoire et aux sacrifices des combattants de l'armée française issus de ces territoires la place éminente à laquelle ils ont droit." Loi no. 2005-158, emphasis added.
16. For more details on the colonial absences in the French curriculum, see also Jo McCormack's informative essay "Memory in History."
17. Sebbar, *The Seine Was Red*, 1. "Sa mère ne lui a rien dit, ni la mère de sa mère. Elles se voient souvent, la mère et la fille, elles bavardent en français, en arabe, et Amel ne comprend pas tout." Sebbar, *La Seine était rouge*, 9.
18. Sebbar, *The Seine Was Red*, 1. "Si elle demandait ce qu'elles se disent dans l'autre langue, 'la langue du pays' dit Lalla, sa grand-mère lui répondrait, comme chaque fois: 'Des secrets, ma fille, des secrets, ce que tu ne dois pas savoir, ce qui doit être caché, ce que tu apprendras, un jour quand il faudra.'" Sebbar, *La Seine était rouge*, 9.
19. Sebbar, *The Seine Was Red*, 1. In the original French, "must be kept hidden" is written as "ce qui doit être caché." Sebbar, *La Seine était rouge*, 9. This phrase makes all the more evident the connection to Haneke's film *Caché* (as discussed in chapter 2), which dealt with the intergenerational effects of the same event. Sebbar, *The Seine Was Red*, 2. "On le voit tous les jours à la télé, on le lit, je le lis dans les livres." Sebbar, *La Seine était rouge*, 10.
20. Sebbar, *The Seine Was Red*, 2. "Dans les livres, à la télé ... C'est pas pareil ce que je te dirai un jour, au jour dit, et ta mère aussi." Sebbar, *La Seine était rouge*, 10.
21. While Hirsch developed the concept of postmemory in the context of the Holocaust, her analysis is equally pertinent to France's postdecolonization era. Hirsch elaborates on the concept of postmemory: "The particular relation to a parental past described, evoked, and analyzed in these works has come to be seen as a 'syndrome' of belatedness or 'post-ness' and has been variously termed 'absent memory' (Fine 1988), 'inherited memory,' 'belated memory,' 'prosthetic memory' (Lury 1998, Landsberg 2004), 'mémoire trouée' (Raczymow 1994), 'mémoire des cendres' (Fresco 1984), 'vicarious witnessing' (Zeitlin 1998), 'received history' (Young 1997), and 'postmemory.'" "The Generation of Postmemory," 105. The mere fact that so many terms

exist for expressing relationship to a parental past suggests not only the importance but also the inability to capture this phenomenon in a single word or phrase. See also Hirsch's book-length study of the same phenomenon, entitled *The Generation of Postmemory*.

22. Hirsch, "The Generation of Postmemory," 107.
23. Silverman, *Palimpsestic Memory*, 3.
24. Provencher, *Queer Maghrebi French*, 44–52.
25. Provencher, *Queer Maghrebi French*, 47, emphasis in original.
26. For an artistic take on this same theme, I direct the reader to Zineb Sedira's brilliant multimedia artwork, in particular *Mother Tongue* (2002), *Mother, Father and I* (2003), and *Gardiennes d'images* (2010). Like Sebbar, she confronts the challenges of intergenerational communication and plays with interstitial spaces, collapsing public and private, France and Algeria, past and present with the seeming goal of deconstructing these binaries.
27. Stora, *La gangrène et l'oubli*, 9. Anne Tristan also mentions the demonstration briefly, although her figures state that 1,000 women and 550 children were arrested. *Le silence du fleuve*, 80.
28. Sebbar, *The Seine Was Red*, 12. "On aura oublié, ce sera flou, approximatif, sans intérêt, je t'assure.... Demande à ton père, tu verras." Sebbar, *La Seine était rouge*, 18.
29. Sebbar, *The Seine Was Red*, 12. "Combien veulent les oublier, les oublient." Sebbar, *La Seine était rouge*, 18.
30. Sebbar, *The Seine Was Red*, 12. "Tu as vraiment besoin de faire ce film? C'est pas ton histoire." Sebbar, *La Seine était rouge*, 18.
31. Sebbar, *The Seine Was Red*, 12. "Justement je veux le faire, je le ferai parce que c'est pas mon histoire. 1954-1962. Le 17 octobre 1961, à Paris et vous dans cette guerre colonial.... [J]e dois savoir, pas tout, mais comprendre un peu." Sebbar, *La Seine était rouge*, 18.
32. Sturken, "Narratives of Recovery," 237.
33. Carrier, *Holocaust Monuments*, 209.
34. Norindr, "Mourning."
35. See Donadey, "Anamnesis and National Reconciliation."
36. See Rothberg, *Multidirectional Memory* and "Between Auschwitz and Algeria."
37. Sebbar, *The Seine Was Red*, 14. "EN CETTE PRISON / LE 11 NOVEMBRE 1940 / FURENT INCARCÉRÉS / DES LYCÉENS ET DES ÉTUDIANTS / QUI À L'APPEL DU GÉNÉRAL DE GAULLE / SE DRESSÈRENT LES PREMIERS / CONTRE L'OCCUPANT." Sebbar, *La Seine était rouge*, 20.

38. Sebbar, *The Seine Was Red*, 15. "1954–1962 / DANS CETTE PRISON / FURENT GUILLOTINÉS / DES RÉSISTANTS ALGÉRIENS / QUI SE DRESSÈRENT / CONTRE L'OCCUPANT FRANÇAIS." Sebbar, *La Seine était rouge*, 21–22.

39. As a side note, it is worth mentioning the response (or lack thereof) of then president de Gaulle to the October 1961 massacre. As historian Michel Winock writes, "Le silence de l'Élysée en ces jours-là est resté comme un meurtrissure" (The silence of the Élysée Palace in those days was bruising), cited in Stora, *La gangrène et l'oubli*, 100. De Gaulle's disappearance from Omer and Amel's edited plaque thus mirrors his own absence at the time.

40. Foucault, "Nietzsche, Genealogy, History," 94, 139, 152.

41. Muñoz, *Cruising Utopia*, 28.

42. *Oxford English Dictionary*, s.v. "palimpsest."

43. De Quincey, "The Palimpsest," 150.

44. Benstock, *Women on the Left Bank*, 350.

45. De Quincey, "The Palimpsest," 107.

46. Philippe Lejeune and Gerard Genette are both credited with the first usages of "palimpsestuous" (*palimpsestueuse*) to describe the complex relationality embodied in the palimpsest. Dillon, "Reinscribing De Quincey's Palimpsest," 260–61.

47. See Genette, *Palimpsestes*.

48. Dillon, "Reinscribing De Quincey's Palimpsest," 254.

49. Sebbar, *The Seine Was Red*, 39. "Une femme géante, debout, comme dressée face à l'ennemi, courageuse. Elle tient un drapeau, l'étendard de la victoire? De la défaite?" Sebbar, *La Seine était rouge*, 42.

50. Sebbar, *The Seine Was Red*, 39. "En sautant des mots, des noms." Sebbar, *La Seine était rouge*, 42.

51. Sebbar, *The Seine Was Red*, 39. "La statue / LA DÉFENSE DE PARIS / inaugurée ... afin de rappeler / le courage des Parisiens / pendant le terrible siège de 1870-1871. / A été réinstallée à son emplacement intial ... / Elle a été inaugurée le 21 septembre 1983." Sebbar, *La Seine était rouge*, 42.

52. Sebbar, *The Seine Was Red*, 65–66. "Sur le quai du métro, des hommes, des Algériens, sont parqués, les mains sur la tête, c'est une rafle, on va les conduire dans des centres de détention, comme mon père au palais des Sports. Jusque devant un hôtel fameux, je l'ai jamais vu, Flora m'a dit son nom, ça ressemble à 'Grillon,' demande-lui, les flics ont raflé les Algériens." Sebbar, *La Seine était rouge*, 65–66.

53. Sebbar, *The Seine Was Red*, 67. "ICI DES ALGÉRIENS ONT ÉTÉ MATRAQUÉS / SAUVAGEMENT / PAR LA POLICE DU PRÉFET PAPON / LE 17 OCTOBRE 1961." Sebbar, *La Seine était rouge*, 68.
54. Sebbar, *The Seine Was Red*, 87. "A LA MÉMOIRE / DES SOLDATS DES FORCES FRANÇAISES / DE L'INTÉRIEUR ET DES HABITANTS DES Ve ET / ARRONDISSEMENTS QUI SUR CES LIEUX / LA MORT EN COMBATTANT." Sebbar, *La Seine était rouge*, 85. The actual full plaque reads: "A la mémoire des soldats des Forces Françaises de l'Intérieur et des habitants des Ve et VIe arrondissements qui, sur ces lieux, trouvèrent la mort en combattant."
55. Sebbar, *The Seine Was Red*, 93. "ICI DES ALGÉRIENS SONT TOMBÉS / POUR L'INDÉPENDANCE / DE L'ALGÉRIE / LE 17 OCTOBRE 1961." Sebbar, *La Seine était rouge*, 90.
56. *Here We Drown Algerians: October 17, 1961* (*Ici on noie les Algériens: 17 octobre 1961*) is also the title of a 2011 documentary directed by Yasmina Adi.
57. Amel and Omer's new memorial also calls to mind a statement made by Pierre Bourdieu soon after the publication of Sebbar's novel. At a conference in Paris in October 2000, Bourdieu spoke directly to many of the issues related to the 1961 massacre and to the subsequent national amnesia, an appropriate call with which I believe Sebbar would concur: "I have often wished that the shame of being the powerless witness of hateful and organized state violence can turn into collective shame. Today I would like that the memory of the monstrous crimes of October 17, 1961, in which are concentrated all the horrors of the Algerian War, be inscribed on a stela, in a high place in every city in France, and alongside the portrait of the President of the Republic on display in all public buildings, town halls, police stations, courthouses, and schools, as a solemn warning against any relapse into racist barbarism" (J'ai maintes fois souhaité que la honte d'avoir été le témoin impuissant d'une violence d'État haineuse et organisée puisse se transformer en honte collective. Je voudrais aujourd'hui que le souvenir des crimes monstrueux du 17 octobre 1961, sorte de concentré de toutes les horreurs de la guerre d'Algérie, soit inscrit sur une stèle, en un haut lieu de toutes les villes de France, et aussi, à côté du portrait du président de la République, dans tous les édifices publics, mairies, commissariats, palais de Justice, écoles, à titre de mise en garde solennelle contre toute rechute dans la barbarie raciste). Bourdieu cited in Le Cour Grandmaison, *Le 17 octobre 1961*, 253.

58. Amine, *Postcolonial Paris*, 164. On October 17, 2019, a new monument was inaugurated by Paris mayor Anne Hidalgo "pour mieux rendre hommage" (in order to better pay homage) to the victims of the 1961 massacre. This commemorative stela portrays the silhouettes of demonstrators against the backdrop of the Seine River. "Paris: une stèle en hommage aux victimes algériennes du 17 octobre 1961," *Le Point*, October 17, 2019, https://www.lepoint.fr/politique/paris-une-stele-en-hommage-aux-victimes-algeriennes-du-17-octobre-1961--17-10-2019-2341964_20.php.
59. Gopinath, *Impossible Desires*, 4.
60. Gopinath, *Impossible Desires*, 4.
61. Dragojlovic, "Politics of Negative Affect," 94.

5. Queering Identity, Embracing In-Betweenness

1. Mbembe, *On the Postcolony*, 104.
2. Coly, "*Carmen* Goes Postcolonial," 394.
3. Spurlin, "Contested Borders," 114.
4. Garvey, "Spaces of Violence," 760.
5. Muñoz, *Disidentifications*, 6.
6. Given our linguistic reliance on gender pronouns, I admit that challenges arise in writing about the protagonist. I attempt to address this by adopting the same gendered language or pronouns that the narrator does, using feminine pronouns to refer to Nina and masculine pronouns when referencing other selves or alter egos.
7. Bouraoui, *Tomboy*, 18. "Je viens de la guerre. Je viens d'un marriage contesté. Je porte la souffrance de ma famille algérienne. Je porte le refus de ma famille française. Je porte ces transmissions-là. La violence ne me quitte plus. Elle m'habite. Elle vient de moi." Bouraoui, *Garçon manqué*, 32.
8. Bouraoui, *Tomboy*, 19. "Qui saura les enfants de 1970? Qui saura les mariages de l'indépendance? Qui saura le désir fou d'être aimé? Deux pays. Deux solitudes. Qui lira cette violence-là?" Bouraoui, *Garçon manqué*, 34.
9. Muñoz, *Disidentifications*, 31–32.
10. Bouraoui, *Tomboy*, 18. "C'est une richesse. C'est une pauvreté. Ne pas choisir c'est d'être dans l'errance. Mon visage algérien. Ma voix française. J'ai l'ombre de ma lumière. Je suis l'une contre l'autre. J'ai deux éléments, agressifs. Deux jalousies qui se dévorent." Bouraoui, *Garçon manqué*, 33.

11. Bouraoui, *Tomboy*, 97. "Moi je ne regrette pas longtemps. Je m'adapte à tout. Très vite. C'est comme une folie, cette faculté d'adaptation. C'est plusieurs vies à la fois. C'est une multitude de petites trahisons." Bouraoui, *Garçon manqué*, 162.
12. Anzaldúa, *Borderlands*, 41.
13. Hall, "Cultural Identity and Diaspora," 245.
14. Trinh, "Not You / Like You," n.p.
15. For a selection of this scholarship on the power of affect and emotions traditionally conceived of as "negative," see, for example, Ahmed, *The Cultural Politics*; Ahmed, *The Promise of Happiness*; Cvetkovich, *An Archive of Feelings*; Cvetkovich, *Depression*; Dragojlovic, "Politics of Negative Affect"; Halberstam, *The Queer Art of Failure*; Love, *Feeling Backward*.
16. Bouraoui, *Tomboy*, 100. "L'Algérie n'est pas dans ma langue. Elle est dans mon corps. L'Algérie n'est pas dans mes mots. Elle est à l'intérieur de moi. . . . Elle est physique." Bouraoui, *Garçon manqué*, 167.
17. Camiscioli, *Reproducing the French Race*, 157.
18. Bouraoui, *Tomboy*, 66–67. "La médicine française sur nous. Cette pénetration. Du crâne aux orteils. . . . Demain, on m'examine. Mais moi je vais très bien." Bouraoui, *Garçon manqué*, 110–11.
19. Bouraoui, *Tomboy*, 61. "La guerre d'Algérie ne s'est jamais arrêtée. Elle s'est transformée. Elle s'est déplacée. Et elle continue." Bouraoui, *Garçon manqué*, 101.
20. Bouraoui, *Tomboy*, 70. "Le silence prendra tout. Silence sur les massacres en Algérie. Sur la douleur. Sur notre nouvelle vie. Un silence qui court. Que se transmet par contagion. Une vraie maladie. Une peste. Une épidémie. Silence sur toutes les lèvres. Silence de la France. Sur le corps brûlés. Sur les corps dépecés. Sur le corps éventrés. Sur cet incroyable puzzle de chairs séparées. Sur ce désordre humain. Sur l'avenir de l'homme. Sur sa veritable nature." Bouraoui, *Garçon manqué*, 115.
21. In his landmark text *La gangrène et l'oubli*, Benjamin Stora describes the repression of memory around the French-Algerian War in similar pathological terms. As Stora demonstrates, however, this gangrene ironically shows itself to erode the very foundations of French society and culture: *liberté, égalité, fraternité*.
22. Bouraoui, *Tomboy*, 63. "Qui ne dit rien sur l'Alger. . . . Sur la vie de plus en plus difficile des Algériens. Sur l'avenir des Algériens. Sur les souffrances des Algériens. Sur le manqué. Sur les pénuries. Sur la violence

naissante. Rien." Bouraoui, *Garçon manqué*, 104. Further reflections on the metaphor of racism as a disease are also articulated later in the novel: "There is no doubt racism is a disease, a vice, a shameful disease that flourishes sometimes in the silence of the hearth.... The hatred of the other means imagining him against one's own body as if possessed, robbed, penetrated. Racism is a fantasy.... Racism is a disease like leprosy or necrosis." Bouraoui, *Tomboy*, 90. "Oui, le racisme est une maladie. Un vice. Une maladie honteuse. Qui se développe parfois dans le silence des maisons.... Haïr l'autre, c'est l'imaginer contre soi. C'est sentire possédé. Volé. Pénétré. Le racisme est un fantasme.... Le racisme est une maladie. Une lèpre. Une nécrose." Bouraoui, *Garçon manqué*, 149.

23. Bouraoui, *Tomboy*, 98. "Tous les matins je vérifie mon identité. J'ai quatre problèmes. Française? Algérienne? Fille? Garçon?" Bouraoui, *Garçon manqué*, 163.
24. Blanco and Pereen, "Spectral Subjectivities," 310.
25. Hirsch, "The Generation of Postmemory," 107.
26. Fernandes, "Confessions d'une enfant du siècle," 68.
27. Bouraoui, *Tomboy*, 8. "Je me fais disparaître. J'intègre le pays des hommes." Bouraoui, *Garçon manqué*, 15.
28. Garvey, "Spaces of Violence," 758.
29. Bouraoui, *Tomboy*, 21. "Je serai dans la force. L'Algérie est un homme. L'Algérie est un forêt d'hommes.... Ici, les hommes sont seuls à force d'être ensemble. Ici, les hommes sont violents à force de désir.... Ici, les hommes sont tristes.... Ils espèrent. Ils ne chantent plus. Ils inventent un depart. Ils inventent une arrivée. Ils feront mieux que les autres. Ils sauront. Le rêve français. Leur regard est une arme. Leur main est une braise. Leur désir est un conflit. Ils se blessent, seuls. Ils sont fragiles. Je les aime pour ça." Bouraoui, *Garçon manqué*, 37–38.
30. Halberstam, *Female Masculinity*, 3.
31. For a different albeit complementary take on "queering Frenchness," see Navarro-Ayala, *Queering Transcultural Encounters*.
32. Muñoz, *Disidentifications*, 5.
33. McCormack, *Queer Postcolonial Narratives*, 36.
34. See Hayes, *Queer Nations*, 69–72; and McCormack, *Queer Postcolonial Narratives*, 6–7.
35. Barthel, "Seeing the Self," 1; Selao, "Porter l'Algérie," 83.
36. Selao, "Porter l'Algérie," 78.
37. Vassallo, "Unsuccessful Alterity?," 43.

38. "Tels sont les grands traits de l'identité de l'auteur de *Garçon manqué*. Qu'en est-il de la narratrice? Existe-t-il une similitude entre l'auteur et la narratrice? Si oui, jusqu'où va-t-elle?" Djom, *L'hybridité*, 56.
39. Emphasis in original. "Dire que l'on est homosexuelle, c'est être catalogué par sa sexualité, et cela me dérange profondément. L'homosexualité, ce n'est pas une identité. . . . À propos de mon dernier livre [*Poupée Bella*] on a parlé de *coming out*. Pas du tout! Je ne suis pas une provocatrice. Je suis militante à ma manière: j'écris. Ecrire, c'est un acte de résistance. À l'intérieur de moi, il se mène un vrai combat dans l'écriture: c'est une guerre!" Dominique Simonnet, "'Écrire, c'est retrouver ses fantomes,'" *L'Express*, May 31, 2004, https://www.lexpress.fr/culture/livre/ecrire-c-est-retrouver-ses-fantomes_819681.html.
40. Muñoz, *Disidentifications*, 20.
41. Muñoz, *Disidentifications*, 20.
42. McCormack, *Queer Postcolonial Narratives*, 35.
43. Bouraoui, *Tomboy*, 18. "Ne pas être algérienne. Ne pas être française. . . . Je suis indéfinie. . . . Je deviens inclassable. Je ne suis pas assez typée. 'Tu n'es pas une Arabe comme les autres.' Je n'ai pas peur de moi. Ma force contre la haine. Mon silence est un combat. J'écrirai aussi pour ça. J'écrirai en français en portant un nom arabe. Ce sera une desertion. Mais quel camp devrais-je choisir? Quelle partie de moi brûler?" Bouraoui, *Garçon manqué*, 33.
44. Bouraoui, *Tomboy*, 3. "Je cours sur la plage du Chenoua. Je cours avec Amine, mon ami. Je longe les vagues charges d'écume, des explosions blanches. Je cours avec la mer qui monte et descend sous les ruines romaines. Je cours dans la lumière d'hiver encore chaude. Je tombe sur le sable. J'entends la mer qui arrive. J'entends les cargos quitter l'Afrique. Je suis au sable, au ciel et au vent. Je suis en Algérie. La France est loin derrière les vagues amples et dangereuses." Bouraoui, *Garçon manqué*, 7.
45. In contrast to the freedom of the beach, the streets of Algiers become a marker of exclusion and violence, as place-names throughout the city silently reference the French-Algerian War. Rue d'Isly, for instance, was a significant site of colonial brutality. On March 26, 1962, just one week after President de Gaulle had called for a cease fire and the Evian Accords had been signed, a demonstration—this time by French citizens and supporters of keeping Algeria French—was held in the city's Bab-el-Oued neighborhood. In response to what they claimed were gunshots, the French military opened fire. With a death toll of eighty and two hundred wounded, most of the victims were French Jews. The

event also partially ignited the mass exodus of the *pied-noir* population from Algeria.

46. As indicated in chapters 2 and 4, water itself was a marker of violence throughout the French-Algerian War, with numerous Algerian protesters being drowned in the Seine River during the massacre of October 17, 1961. Water has also long been an instrument of torture, with waterboarding and "the bathtub" being ubiquitously employed by French forces scrambling to hold on to the North African colonies. Nina invokes this history in her words: "I am not afraid to drown; I know how to struggle with the water and the waves. I am Algerian; I am not afraid of the sea. I almost drowned a thousand times." Bouraoui, *Tomboy*, 88. "Je n'ai pas peur de me noyer. Je sais comment lutter. Avec l'eau. Avec les vagues. Je suis algérienne. Je n'ai pas peur de la mer. J'ai failli me noyer mille fois." Bouraoui, *Garçon manqué*, 146.
47. Bouraoui, *Tomboy*, 3. "Je suis en Algérie. La France est loin derrière les vague amples et dangereuses. Elle est invisible et supposée. Je tombe avec Amine. Je tiens sa main. Nous sommes seuls et étrangers." Bouraoui, *Garçon manqué*, 7.
48. Bouraoui, *Tomboy*, 3. "Des hommes surgissent des dunes. Ils sont quatres et presses. Ils marchent vite en direction de la mer, un rendez-vous. Ils ont des grands gestes. Ils parlent en arabe. Leurs voix traversent la plage. Elles sont avec les vagues. Elles sont avec le vent. C'est une emprise.... Ils passent près de nos corps. Il ne s'arrêtent pas. Ils tendent la main vers l'horizon." Bouraoui, *Garçon manqué*, 7–8.
49. Bouraoui, *Tomboy*, 3. "Nous n'existons pas." Bouraoui, *Garçon manqué*, 8.
50. Bouraoui, *Tomboy*, 4. "Ici nous ne sommes rien. De mère française. De père algérien. Seuls nos corps rassemblent les terres opposées." Bouraoui, *Garçon manqué*, 8.
51. Bouraoui, *Tomboy*, 16. "Ici je suis une étrangère. Ici je ne suis rien. La France m'oublie. L'Algérie ne me reconnaît pas. Ici l'identité se fait. Elle est double et brisée." Bouraoui, *Garçon manqué*, 29.
52. Bouraoui, *Tomboy*, 5. "On ne sera jamais de vrais Algériens. Malgré l'envie et la volonté. Malgré le vêtement. Malgré la terre qui entoure." Bouraoui, *Garçon manqué*, 10.
53. Bouraoui, *Tomboy*, 19. "De mère française. De père algérien. Deux orphelins contre la falaise." Bouraoui, *Garçon manqué*, 35.
54. Bouraoui, *Tomboy*, 5. "Deux imposteurs." Bouraoui, *Garçon manqué*, 11.
55. Diamond, *Performance and Cultural Politics*, 5.
56. Butler, "Critically Queer," 18.

57. Bouraoui, *Tomboy*, 4. "Je deviens un corps sans type, sans langue, sans nationalité." Bouraoui, *Garçon manqué*, 9. Type, language, and nationality are all missing for the narrator. As with Amel, the protagonist of Sebbar's *The Seine Was Red*, discussed in the previous chapter, language is an exclusionary mechanism. Nina does not speak Arabic, and language, words, and sounds exclude her and inflict violence, often in the form of racial slurs.
58. Halberstam, *Female Masculinity*, 9.
59. Halberstam, *Female Masculinity*, 1.
60. Halberstam, *Female Masculinity*, 8.
61. See Butler, *The Psychic Life of Power*, 106–31. As Althusser writes, a name functions in such a way that "it 'recruits' subjects among the individuals (it recruits them all), or 'transforms' the individuals into subjects (it transforms them all)." "Ideology," 162.
62. Butler, *Gender Trouble*, 151.
63. Bouraoui, *Tomboy*, 33–34. "Je passe de Yasmina à Nina. De Nina à Ahmed. D'Ahmed à Brio.... Je ne sais pas qui je suis. Une et multiple. Menteuse et vraie. Forte et fragile. Fille et garçon." Bouraoui, *Garçon manqué*, 62.
64. Bouraoui, *Tomboy*, 74. "Et toi? Qui es-tu vraiment? Française, algérienne? On préfère t'appeler Nina plutôt que Yasmina. Nina ça arrange. Ça fait espagnol ou italien. Comme ça on n'a pas à expliquer nos fréquentations." Bouraoui, *Garçon manqué*, 127.
65. The protagonist also refers to this as a constant process of becoming: "With men, I will become a man, a body without a name, a voice without a face. I will assimilate and become an element, a fragment, one of the shadows among them." Bouraoui, *Tomboy*, 22–23. "Je deviendrai un homme avec les hommes. Je deviendrai un corps sans nom. Je deviendrai une voix sans visage. Je deviendrai une partie. Je deviendrai un élément. Je deviendrai une ombre serrée." Bouraoui, *Garçon manqué*, 40. This focus on "becoming" is in tension with a more elusive "being," which *Tomboy* reveals as unstable and even dangerous for those who do not fit traditional identity categories.
66. Butler, *Bodies That Matter*, 124.
67. Butler, *Bodies That Matter*, 2–3.
68. Bouraoui, *Tomboy*, 98.
69. Bouraoui, *Tomboy*, 10. "Être séparée toujours de l'un et de l'autre. Porter une identité de fracture. Se penser en deux parties." Bouraoui, *Garçon manqué*, 19.
70. Butler, *Bodies That Matter*, 219.

71. Halberstam, *Female Masculinity*, 9.
72. Muñoz, *Disidentifications*, 31.
73. Bouraoui, *Tomboy*, 10–11. "Qui serai-je en France? Où aller? Quels seront leurs regards? Être française, c'est être sans mon père, sans sa force, sans ses yeux, sans sa main qui conduit. Être algérienne, c'est être sans ma mère, sans son visage, sans sa voix, sans ses mains qui protegent. Qui je suis? . . . Moi, je suis terriblement libre et entravée. 'Tu n'es pas française.' 'Tu n'es pas algérienne.' Je suis tout. Je ne suis rien." Bouraoui, *Garçon manqué*, 20.
74. Ahmed, "Mixed Orientations," 145.
75. Muñoz, *Disidentifications*, 6.
76. Bouraoui, *Tomboy*, 36, emphasis added. "Ouvre les yeux. Son allure dans la rue. Les réflexions des gens. Du garçon de café. De la vendeuse. Quand ses cousins sont en blanc, elle porte du rouge et du vert. Voilà les mots de ma grand-mère française. Son regard. Tu es un garçon manqué. Non. Mes spectateurs sont fiers de moi. Je suis." Bouraoui, *Garçon manqué*, 64. At another point in the text, Nina is once again labeled a tomboy: "Nina is a tomboy, a failed girl. Nina, if this keeps up you will grow a weenie or a goatee." Bouraoui, *Tomboy*, 64. "Nina, un garçon manqué. Nina, une fille ratée. Nina, à force, il te poussera un zizi. Ou une barbichette." Bouraoui, *Garçon manqué*, 107.
77. Barad, "Troubling Time/s," 84, 63.
78. Bouraoui, *Tomboy*, 33–34.
79. Bouraoui, *Tomboy*, 34. "Je ne sais pas qui je suis. Une et multiple. Menteuse et vraie. Forte et fragile. Fille et garçon. Mon corps me trahira un jour. Il sera formé. Il sera féminin. Il sera contre moi. Il fera résistance. Je retiendrai Nina, de force, comme un animal sauvage. On retrouve des coupes à champagne enroulées dans du papier journal daté de 1962. On retrouve des couteaux ensanglantés. Dans l'appartement. Du sang de 1962. Ma soeur nait en 1962. Au temps du crime. L'année du massacre des femmes algériennes de la Résidence. L'année du massacre de l'OAS. Le dernier massacre. Leur esprit de vengeance. Dans ma chambre. Contre les murs de l'appartement. Sur le carrelage. Dans la buanderie. Partou. Une malédiction. On retrouve leurs armes sous les tuyaux de la salle de bains. Leur alcool. Cette folie. La fête des hommes de l'OAS. . . . Ce lieu hanté. Marqué. Ses bruits. Ses ombres. Ses apparitions. Le vent permanent: la plainte des femmes algériennes massacrées par les hommes de l'OAS." Bouraoui, *Garçon manqué*, 60–61.
80. Muñoz, *Disidentifications*, 12.

81. Bouraoui, *Tomboy*, 34. "Tu me désires en secret. Ta mère veut nous séparer. Elle dit. Elle répète. Son obsession: Je ne veux pas que mon fils devienne homosexuel. Elle dit le mot en premier. Elle dit mon mot." Bouraoui, *Garçon manqué*, 61.
82. Bouraoui, *Tomboy*, 34. "Cette fausse fille." Bouraoui, *Garçon manqué*, 61.
83. Bouraoui, *Tomboy*, 35. "Pour toi je m'invente. Avec d'autres yeux. Avec d'autres gestes. Pour toi j'ai les mains d'un homme, fortes et serrées en coup-de-poing. C'est ainsi que je vis notre histoire algérienne. En combat. . . . Je te traverse. Et je danse comme un homme. . . . Toi, moi, toi, moi. Je suis en toi, Amine. Tu es pénétré." Bouraoui, *Garçon manqué*, 62.
84. Bouraoui, *Tomboy*, 35. "Je t'aime comme un homme. Je t'aime comme si tu étais une fille." Bouraoui, *Garçon manqué*, 63.
85. Bouraoui, *Tomboy*, 38–39. "Tu me prêtes ton pantalon préféré, Amine. . . . Je le garde longtemps. En otage. Je refuse de le rendre. Ta mère proteste. Je vis dans ton vêtement, là où précisément tu tiens ton sexe caché. N'est-ce pas à cet instant, par ce geste, par ce vol, que prend l'homosexualité?" Bouraoui, *Garçon manqué*, 68.
86. Bouraoui, *Tomboy*, 111. "C'est arrivé à Tivoli. Dans cet été exceptionnel. Je ne suis pas allée à Saint-Malo mais à Rome. . . . C'est arrive là. Dans cette saison propice à ça. Cette saison des corps. C'est arrivé dans les jardins de Tivoli. Avec ces arbres humides, ces allées trempées, ces cascades. . . . Nous sommes descendues au Grand Hôtel." Bouraoui, *Garçon manqué*, 183.
87. Bouraoui, *Tomboy*, 111. "Parmi ces hommes. Parmi ces femmes. Je n'étais plus française. Je n'étais plus algérienne. Je n'étais même plus la fille de ma mère." Bouraoui, *Garçon manqué*, 184.
88. Bouraoui, *Tomboy*, 112. "La nouveauté qui hantait mon corps: le désir." Bouraoui, *Garçon manqué*, 186.
89. Bouraoui, *Tomboy*, 112. "Mon corps se détachait de tout. Il n'avait plus rien de la France. Plus rien de l'Algérie." Bouraoui, *Garçon manqué*, 185.
90. Barad, "Transmaterialities," 392.
91. Martin cited in Ahmed, *Queer Phenomenology*, 199.
92. Anzaldúa, *Borderlands*, 41.
93. Bouraoui, *Tomboy*, 14. "Je reste entre deux pays. Je reste entre deux identités. Mon équilibre est dans la solitude, une unite. J'invente un autre monde." Bouraoui, *Garçon manqué*, 26.

Conclusion

1. Higbee, "Locating the Postcolonial," 53.

2. See, for example, Khalil, "The Myth of Masculinity"; and Rosello, "Dissident or Conformist Passing."
3. Because Chouchou specifically states, "I have always wanted to be a woman," I use feminine pronouns throughout, even though nearly all other scholarly analyses of the film refer to Chouchou with the pronouns "he," "him," and "his."
4. Similar critiques of French multiculturalism are put forth by Rees-Roberts, *French Queer Cinema*; Rosello, "Dissident or Conformist Passing"; Swamy, *Interpreting the Republic*.
5. It is important to note that France had already put in place the PaCS law, which permitted civil unions of many sorts, even as it put strict limitations on kinship and family structures. Adoption, for example, was not permitted.
6. See Perreau, *Queer Theory*, 11, 36–45, 60.
7. Although I would have liked to have included this image, after contacting La Manif Pour Tous to obtain copyright permission, they expressly stated that I could not reproduce the poster in this book.
8. Josh Vardey, "Black Minister Compared to a Monkey—Again," *France24*, November 13, 2013, https://www.france24.com/en/20131113-france-racism-black-minister-taubira-monkey-banana-magazine-cover.
9. Fabrice Rousselet and Sonya Faure, "Taubira: 'Ces attaques racistes sont une attaque au coeur de la République,'" *Libération*, November 5, 2013, https://www.liberation.fr/societe/2013/11/05/taubira-ces-attaques-racistes-sont-une-attaque-au-coeur-de-la-republique_944839.
10. Alexander Stille, "The Justice Minister and the Banana," *New Yorker*, November 14, 2013, https://www.newyorker.com/news/daily-comment/the-justice-minister-and-the-banana-how-racist-is-france, emphasis added.
11. Perreau, *Queer Theory*, 11.
12. Swamy, *Interpreting the Republic*, 131.
13. For a nuanced exploration of the category of hospitality and its representations in French and North African literature, see Rosello, *Postcolonial Hospitality*.
14. Gopinath, *Impossible Desires*, 9. In her critical genealogy, *Anachronism and Its Others*, Valerie Rohy offers a similar take by bridging queer temporality, race, and sexuality to explore the links between nationalist efforts and gay marriage in a US context.
15. Mack, *Sexagon*, 19.

16. Scholarship on homonationalism has provided us with a helpful framework for analyzing this phenomenon. This is in large part thanks to Jasbir K. Puar's groundbreaking *Terrorist Assemblages*. See also Puar's follow-up article, "Rethinking Homonationalism."
17. Muñoz, *Cruising Utopia*, 28.

BIBLIOGRAPHY

Ahluwalia, Pal. "Out of Africa: Post-structuralism's Colonial Roots." *Postcolonial Studies* 8, no. 2 (2005): 137–54.
———. "Post-structuralism's Colonial Roots: Michel Foucault." *Social Identities* 16, no. 5 (2010): 597–606.
Ahmed, Sara. *The Cultural Politics of Emotion*. Edinburgh: Edinburgh University Press, 2014.
———. "Mixed Orientations." *Subjectivity* 7, no. 1 (2014): 92–109.
———. *The Promise of Happiness*. Durham NC: Duke University Press, 2010.
———. *Queer Phenomenology*. Durham NC: Duke University Press, 2006.
Alleg, Henri. *La question*. Paris: Éditions de Minuit, 1961.
———. *The Question*. Lincoln: University of Nebraska Press, 2006.
Alloula, Malek. *The Colonial Harem*. Minneapolis: University of Minnesota Press, 1986.
Althusser, Louis. "Ideology and Ideological State Apparatuses (Notes towards an Investigation)." In *Lenin and Philosophy and Other Essays*, translated by Ben Brewster, 85–126. New York: Monthly Review Press, 1971.
Altman, Dennis. *Homosexual Oppression and Liberation*. Sydney: Angus and Robertson, 1971.
Aly, Ramy. *Becoming Arab in London: Performativity and the Undoing of Identity*. London: Pluto Press, 2015.
Amin, Kadji. *Disturbing Attachments: Genet, Modern Pederasty, and Queer History*. Durham NC: Duke University Press, 2017.
Amine, Laila. *Postcolonial Paris: Fictions of Intimacy in the City of Light*. Madison: University of Wisconsin Press, 2018.
Anzaldúa, Gloria. *Borderlands / La Frontera: The New Mestiza*. 3rd ed. San Francisco: Aunt Lute Books, 2007.
Arendt, Hannah. *Essays in Understanding, 1930–1954: Formation, Exile, and Totalitarianism*. New York: Schocken Books, 2005.
———. *The Origins of Totalitarianism*. San Diego: Harcourt, 1973.

Ashcroft, Bill, Gareth Griffiths, and Helen Tiffin. *The Empire Writes Back: Theory and Practice in Post-colonial Literatures.* 2nd ed. New York: Routledge, 2003.

Aussaresses, Paul. *Services spéciaux: Algérie, 1955-1957.* Paris: Perrin, 2001.

Barad, Karen. "Diffracting Diffraction: Cutting Together-Apart." *Parallax* 20, no. 3 (2016): 168-87.

———. *Meeting the Universe Halfway: Quantum Physics and the Entanglement of Matter and Meaning.* Durham NC: Duke University Press, 2007.

———. "TransMaterialities Trans*/Matter/Realities and Queer Political Imaginings." *GLQ: A Journal of Lesbian and Gay Studies* 21, no. 2/3 (2015): 387-422.

———. "Troubling Time/s and Ecologies of Nothingness: Re-turning, Remembering, and Facing the Incalculable." *New Formations* 92 (2017): 56-86.

Barthel, Danielle. "Seeing the Self in the Mirror: Shifting Identity in Bouraoui's *Tomboy*." *The Spectrum* 1 (2012): 1-8.

Barthes, Roland. "Ce qu'il advient au signifiant." Preface to *Éden, Éden, Éden*, by Pierre Guyotat, 275-76. Paris: Gallimard, 1985.

———. "Reflections on a Manual." Translated by Sandy Petrey. *PMLA* 112, no. 1 (January 1997): 69-75.

———. "What Happens to the Signifier." Preface to *Eden, Eden, Eden*, by Pierre Guyotat, translated by Graham Fox, v-vi. London: Creation Books, 1995.

Beauchamp, Toby. "Artful Concealment and Strategic Visibility: Transgender Bodies and U.S. State Surveillance after 9/11." *Surveillance & Society* 6, no. 4 (2009): 356-66.

Benhabib, Seyla. Translator's introduction to *Hegel's Ontology and the Theory of Historicity*, by Herbert Marcuse, translated by Seyla Benhabib, ix-xl. Cambridge MA: MIT Press, 1987.

Bennett, Jill. *Empathic Vision: Affect, Trauma, and Contemporary Art.* Stanford CA: Stanford University Press, 2005.

Benstock, Shari. *Women on the Left Bank: Paris, 1900-1940.* Austin: University of Texas Press, 2010.

Bergson, Henri. *Matter and Memory.* Translated by Nancy Margaret Paul and W. Scott Palmer. New York: Dover Philosophical Classics, 2004.

Bersani, Leo, and Ulysse Dutoit. *Arts of Impoverishment: Beckett, Rothko, Resnais.* Cambridge MA: Harvard University Press, 1993.

Bérubé, Allan. "How Gay Stays White and What Kind of White It Stays." In *The Making and Unmaking of Whiteness*, edited by Birgit Brander Rasmussen et al., 234-65. Durham NC: Duke University Press, 2001.

Bhabha, Homi. *The Location of Culture.* London: Routledge, 1994.

———. *Nation and Narration*. New York: Routledge, 1990.

Blanco, María del Pilar, and Esther Pereen. "Introduction: Conceptualizing Spectralities." In *The Spectralities Reader: Ghosts and Haunting in Contemporary Cultural Theory*, edited by María del Pilar Blanco and Esther Pereen, 1–28. New York: Bloomsbury, 2013.

———. "Spectral Subjectivities: Gender, Sexuality, Race / Introduction." In *The Spectralities Reader: Ghosts and Haunting in Contemporary Cultural Theory*, edited by María del Pilar Blanco and Esther Pereen, 309–16. New York: Bloomsbury, 2013.

Boone, Joseph A. *The Homoerotics of Orientalism*. New York: Columbia University Press, 2014.

Boudjedra, Rachid. *Lettres algériennes*. Paris: B. Grasset, 1995.

———. *Naissance du cinéma algérien*. Paris: F. Maspéro, 1971.

Bouraoui, Nina. *Garçon manqué*. Paris: Stock, 2000.

———. *Tomboy*. Translated by Marjorie Attignol Salvodon and Jehanne-Marie Gavarini. Lincoln: University of Nebraska Press, 2007.

Bourdieu, Pierre. "Cultural Reproduction and Social Reproduction." In *Power and Ideology in Education*, edited by Jerome Karabel and A. H. Halsey, 487–511. Oxford: Oxford University Press, 1977.

———. *Pascalian Meditations*. Translated by Richard Nice. Stanford CA: Stanford University Press, 2000.

———. "The School as a Conservative Force: Scholastic and Cultural Inequalities." In *Contemporary Research in the Sociology of Education*, edited by John Eggleston, 32–46. London: Methuen, 1974.

Boyer, Ashley M., and Lacey N. Wallace. "U.S. Portrayals of the 2015 French Surveillance Laws." *French Politics* 15 (2017): 237–53.

Branche, Raphaëlle. "La torture dans *Muriel* d'Alain Resnais, une réflexion cinématographique sur l'indicible et l'inmontrable." *L'Autre* 3, no. 1 (2002): 69–77.

———. *La torture et l'armée pendant la Guerre d'Algérie, 1954–1962*. Paris: Gallimard, 2001.

Brun, Catherine. "Conscience du temps: Entretien avec Pierre Guyotat." *Europe* 961 (May 2009): 9–16.

———. *Pierre Guyotat: Essai biographique*. Paris: Éds. L. Scheer, 2005.

Brun, Catherine, and Todd Shepard. *Guerre d'Algérie: Le sexe outragé*. Paris: CNRS Éditions, 2016.

———. "Guerre des sexes, politiques des genres." In *Guerre d'Algérie: Le sexe outragé*, edited by Catherine Brun and Todd Shepard. Paris: CNRS Éditions, 2016.

Butler, Judith. *Bodies That Matter: On the Discursive Limits of "Sex."* New York: Routledge, 1993.

———. "Critically Queer." GLQ: *A Journal of Lesbian and Gay Studies* 1 (1993): 17–32.

———. *Gender Trouble: Feminism and the Subversion of Identity.* New York: Routledge, 1999.

———. *The Psychic Life of Power: Theories in Subjection.* Stanford CA: Stanford University Press, 1997.

Camiscioli, Elisa. *Reproducing the French Race: Immigration, Intimacy, and Embodiment in the Early Twentieth Century.* Durham NC: Duke University Press, 2009.

Carrier, Peter. *Holocaust Monuments and National Memory Cultures in France and Germany Since 1989: The Origins and Political Function of the Vél' d'Hiv' in Paris and the Holocaust Monument in Berlin.* New York: Berghahn Books, 2005.

Cayrol, Jean, and Alain Resnais. *Muriel.* Paris: Éditions du Seuil, 1963.

Chambers, Ross. "Ordeals of Pain (Concerning Henri Alleg's *La question*)." In *Entre Hommes*, edited by Todd Reeser and Lewis Seifert, 207–23. Newark: University of Delaware Press, 2008.

Chari, Hema. "Colonial Fantasies and Postcolonial Identities: Elaboration of Postcolonial Masculinity and Homoerotic Desire." In *Postcolonial, Queer: Theoretical Intersections*, edited by John C. Hawley, 79–97. Albany: State University of New York Press, 2001.

Chen, Mel Y. *Animacies: Biopolitics, Racial Mattering, and Queer Affect.* Durham NC: Duke University Press, 2012.

Cho, Grace M. *Haunting the Korean Diaspora: Shame, Secrecy, and the Forgotten War.* Minneapolis: University of Minnesota Press, 2008.

Clare, Eli. *Brilliant Imperfection: Grappling with Cure.* Durham NC: Duke University Press, 2017.

Cohen, Cathy. "Punks, Bulldaggers, and Welfare Queens: The Radical Potential of Queer Politics?" GLQ: *A Journal of Gay and Lesbian Studies* 3 (1997): 437–65.

Cohen, William. "The Algerian War and the Revision of France's Overseas Mission." *French Colonial History* 4 (2003): 227–39.

Cole, Joshua. "Entering History: The Memory of Police Violence in Paris, October 1961." In *Algeria and France, 1800–2000: Identity, Memory, Nostalgia*, edited by Patricia M. E. Lorcin, 117–34. Syracuse NY: Syracuse University Press, 2006.

———. "Intimate Acts and Unspeakable Relations: Remembering Torture and the War for Algerian Independence." In *Memory, Empire and Postcolonialism*, edited by Alec Hargreaves, 125–41. Lanham MD: Lexington Books, 2005.

Coly, Ayo A. "*Carmen* Goes Postcolonial, *Carmen* Goes Queer: Thinking the Postcolonial as Queer." *Culture, Theory and Critique* 57, no. 3 (2015): 391–407.

———. *Postcolonial Hauntologies: African Women's Discourses of the Female Body*. Lincoln: University of Nebraska Press, 2019.

Connell, Raewyn. *Masculinities*. Berkeley: University of California Press, 2005.

Coyote, Ivan, and Rae Spoon. *Gender Failure*. Vancouver: Arsenal Pulp Press, 2014.

Crewe, Jonathan. "Recalling Adamastor: Literature as Cultural Memory in 'White' South Africa." In *Acts of Memory: Cultural Recall in the Present*, edited by Mieke Bal, Jonathan Crewe, and Leo Spitzer, 75–86. Hanover NH: University Press of New England, 1999.

Cvetkovich, Ann. *An Archive of Feelings: Trauma, Sexuality, and Lesbian Public Cultures*. Durham NC: Duke University Press, 2003.

———. *Depression: A Public Feeling*. Durham NC: Duke University Press, 2012.

Czarny, Norbert. "Écrire la guerre." *La Quinzaine Littéraire* 998, September 1–15, 2009, https://www.nouvelle-quinzaine-litteraire.fr/mode-lecture/ecrire-la-guerre-1226.

Daeninckx, Didier. *Meurtres pour mémoire*. Paris: Gallimard, 1984.

Davidson, Arnold. *The Emergence of Sexuality: Historical Epistemology and the Formation of Concepts*. Cambridge MA: Harvard University Press, 2001.

Davis, Lennard J. "Constructing Normalcy." In *Disability Studies Reader*, 2nd ed., edited by Lennard J. Davis, 3–16. New York: Routledge, 2006.

Deleuze, Gilles. *Cinema 2: The Time Image*. Minneapolis: University of Minnesota Press, 1989.

Deleuze, Gilles, and Félix Guattari. *Anti-Oedipus: Capitalism and Schizophrenia*. Translated by Robert Hurley, Mark Seem, and Helen R. Lane. Minneapolis: University of Minnesota Press, 1983.

———. *A Thousand Plateaus: Capitalism and Schizophrenia*. Translated by Brian Massumi. Minneapolis: University of Minnesota Press, 1987.

De Quincey, Thomas. "The Palimpsest." In *Confessions of an English Opium Eater and Other Writings*, edited by Barry Milligan, 89–190. New York: Penguin Books, 2003.

Derderian, Richard. "Algeria as a *lieu de mémoire*: Ethnic Minority Memory and National Identity in Contemporary France." *Radical History Review* 83 (Spring 2002): 28–43.

Derrida, Jacques. *Specters of Marx: The State of the Debt, the Work of Mourning, and the New International*. Translated by Peggy Kamuf. New York: Routledge, 1994.

Diamond, Elin. *Performance and Cultural Politics*. New York: Routledge, 1996.

Dillon, Sarah. "Reinscribing De Quincey's Palimpsest: The Significance of the Palimpsest in Contemporary Literary and Cultural Studies." *Textual Practice* 19, no. 3 (2005): 243–63.

Dine, Philip. *Images of the Algerian War: French Fiction and Film, 1954–1992*. Oxford: Clarendon Press, 1994.

Dinshaw, Carolyn, Lee Edelman, Roderick A. Ferguson, Carla Freccero, Elizabeth Freeman, Judith Halberstam, Annamarie Jagose, Christopher S. Nealon, and Tan Hoang Nguyen. "Theorizing Queer Temporalities: A Roundtable Discussion." *GLQ: A Journal of Lesbian and Gay Studies* 13, no. 2/3 (2007): 177–95.

Djebar, Assia. *Algerian White: A Narrative*. New York: Seven Stories Press, 2000.

———. *Le blanc de l'Algérie*. Paris: A. Michel, 1995.

Djom, Maurice Simo. *L'hybridité dans le roman autobiographique francophone contemporain*. Paris: Connaissances et Savoirs, 2017.

Donadey, Anne. "Anamnesis and National Reconciliation: Re-membering October 17, 1961." In *Immigrant Narratives in Contemporary France*, edited by Susan Ireland and Patrice J. Proulx, 47–56. Westport CT: Greenwood Press, 2001.

———. "Between Amnesia and Anamnesis: Re-membering the Fractures of Colonial History." *Studies in 20th Century Literature* 23, no. 1 (Winter 1999): 111–16.

Dragojlovic, Ana. "Politics of Negative Affect: Intergenerational Hauntings, Counter-archival Practices and the Queer Memory Project." *Subjectivity* 11, no. 4 (April 2018): 91–107.

Drucker, Peter. "Conceptions of Sexual Freedom in Marcuse, Foucault and Rubin." *INSEP* 2, no. 2 (2014): 31–38.

Dworkin, Craig. "The Stutter of Form." In *The Sound of Poetry, the Poetry of Sound*, edited by Marjorie Perloff and Craig Dworkin, 166–83. Chicago: University of Chicago Press, 2009.

Edelman, Lee. *No Future: Queer Theory and the Death Drive*. Durham NC: Duke University Press, 2004.

Einaudi, Jean-Luc. *La bataille de Paris, le 17 octobre 1961*. Paris: Seuil, 1991.
El-Tayeb, Fatima. *European Others: Queering Ethnicity in Postnational Europe*. Minneapolis: University of Minnesota Press, 2011.
Eng, David, Judith Halberstam, and José Esteban Muñoz. "What's Queer about Queer Studies Now?" *Social Text* 23, no. 3/4 (2005): 1-17.
Eribon, Didier, ed. *Dictionnaire des cultures gays et lesbiennes*. Paris: Larousse, 2003.
———. "Haunted Lives: AIDS and the Future of Our Present." *Qui Parle* 18, no. 2 (2010): 309-321.
Fanon, Frantz. "Algeria Unveiled." In *A Dying Colonialism*. Translated by Haakon Chevalier, 35-67. New York: Grove Press, 1967.
———. *Les damnés de la terre*. Paris: La Decouverte & Syros, 2002.
———. *The Wretched of the Earth*. New York: Grove Press, 1963.
Fassin, Didier. "In the Name of the Republic: Untimely Meditations on the Aftermath of the *Charlie Hebdo* Attack." *Anthropology Today* 31, no. 2 (2005): 3-7.
Ferguson, Roderick. *Aberrations in Black: Toward a Queer of Color Critique*. Minneapolis: University of Minnesota Press, 2004.
Fernandes, Martine. "Confessions d'une enfant du siècle: Nina Bouraoui ou la 'bâtarde' dans *Garçon manqué* et *La vie heureuse*." *L'Esprit Créateur* 45, no. 1 (Spring 2005): 67-78.
Fisher, Mark. "The Metaphysics of Crackle: Afrofuturism and Hauntology." *Dancecult: Journal of Electronic Dance Music Culture* 5, no. 2 (2013): 42-55.
———. *Ghosts of My Life: Writings on Depression, Hauntology, and Lost Futures*. Winchester UK: Zero Books, 2014.
Ford, Hamish. "From Otherness 'Over There' to Virtual Presence: *Camp de Thiaroye—The Battle of Algiers—Hidden*." In *Postcolonial Cinema Studies*, edited by Sandra Ponzanesi and Marguerite Waller, 63-77. New York: Routledge, 2012.
Foucault, Michel. "Adorno, Horkheimer, and Marcuse: Who Is a 'Negator of History'?" In *Remarks on Marx: Conversations with Duccio Trombadori*, translated by R. James Goldstein and James Cascaito, 115-30. New York: Semiotext(e), 1991.
———. *Discipline and Punish: The Birth of the Prison*. New York: Vintage Books, 1995.
———. "The Gay Science." Translated by Nicolae Morar and Daniel W. Smith. *Critical Inquiry* 37, no. 3 (Spring 2011): 385-403.
———. *The History of Sexuality: Volume 1*. London: Viking, 1986.

———. "Il y aura scandale, mais . . ." In *Dits et écrits: 1954-1988*, edited by Daniel Defert and François Ewald, 74-75. Paris: Gallimard, 1994.

———. "Nietzsche, Genealogy, History." In *Language, Counter-memory, Practice: Selected Essays and Interviews*, translated by Donald F. Bouchard and Sherry Simon, 139-64. Ithaca NY: Cornell University Press, 1996.

———. *Security, Territory, Population: Lectures at the Collège de France, 1977-78*. Edited by Michel Senellart, translated by Graham Burchell. New York: Palgrave Macmillan, 2009.

———. "Sex, Power, and the Politics of Identity." In *Ethics: Subjectivity and Truth*, edited by Paul Rabinow, translated by Robert Hurley et al., 163-73. New York: New Press, 1997.

Freccero, Carla. *Queer/Early/Modern*. Durham NC: Duke University Press, 2006.

———. "Queer Spectrality: Haunting the Past." In *The Spectralities Reader: Ghosts and Haunting in Contemporary Cultural Theory*, edited by María del Pilar Blanco and Esther Pereen, 335-59. New York: Bloomsbury, 2013.

———. "Queer Times." *South Atlantic Quarterly* 106, no. 3 (2007): 485-94.

Freeman, Elizabeth. *Time Binds: Queer Temporalities, Queer Histories*. Durham NC: Duke University Press, 2010.

Fulton, Dawn. "Elsewhere in Paris: Creolised Geographies in Leïla Sebbar's *La Seine était rouge*." *Culture, Theory & Critique* 48, no. 1 (2007): 25-38.

Garvey, Johanna X. K. "Spaces of Violence, Desire, and Queer (Un)belonging: Dionne Brand's Urban Diasporas." *Textual Practice* 25, no. 4 (2011): 757-77.

Gauch, Suzanne. "Muriel, or the Disappearing Text of the Algerian War." *L'Esprit Créateur* 41 (2001): 47-57.

Genette, Gérard. *Palimpsestes: La littérature au second degré*. Paris: Textual Practice Éditions de Seuil, 1982.

Gilroy, Paul. "Shooting Crabs in a Barrel." *Screen* 48, no. 2 (2007): 233-35.

Godard, Jean-Luc. *Le Petit Soldat (The Little Soldier)*. Santa Monica CA: Distributed by Genius Entertainment, 2007.

Gopinath, Gayatri. *Impossible Desires: Queer Diasporas and South Asian Public Cultures*. Durham NC: Duke University Press, 2005.

———. *Unruly Visions: The Aesthetic Practices of Queer Diaspora*. Durham NC: Duke University Press, 2018.

Gordon, Avery. *Ghostly Matters: Haunting and the Sociological Imagination*. Minneapolis: University of Minnesota Press, 2008.

Green, Adam Isaiah. "Queer Theory and Sociology: Locating the Subject and the Self in Sexuality Studies." *Sociological Theory* 25, no. 1 (March 2007): 26-45.

Greene, Naomi. *Landscapes of Loss: The National Past in Postwar French Cinema*. Princeton NJ: Princeton University Press, 1999.

Grossvogel, David I. "Haneke: The Coercing of Vision." *Film Quarterly* 60, no. 4 (2007): 36-43.

Guattari, Félix. "A Liberation of Desire." Translated by George Stambolian. In *Soft Subversions: Texts and Interviews 1977-1985*, edited by Sylvère Lotringer, 141-57. Los Angeles: Semiotext(e), 2009.

Guyotat, Pierre. *Carnets de bord, Volume 1*. Paris: Lignes et Manifeste, 2005.

———. *Éden, Éden, Éden*. Paris: Gallimard, 1985.

———. *Eden, Eden, Eden*. Translated by Graham Fox. London: Creation Books, 1995.

———. *Littérature interdite*. Paris: Gallimard, 1972.

———. *Tombeau pour cinq cent mille soldats*. Paris: Gallimard, 1967.

———. *Tomb for 500,000 Soldiers*. London: Creation Books, 2003.

Halberstam, J. Jack. *Female Masculinity*. Durham NC: Duke University Press, 1998.

———. *In a Queer Time and Place: Transgender Bodies, Subcultural Lives*. New York: NYU Press, 2005.

———. *The Queer Art of Failure*. Durham NC: Duke University Press, 2011.

Halbwachs, Maurice. *On Collective Memory*. Chicago: University of Chicago Press, 1992.

Hall, Stuart. "Cultural Identity and Diaspora." In *Colonial Discourse and Postcolonial Theory*, edited by Patrick Williams and Laura Chrisman, 392-403. New York: Columbia University Press, 1994.

Haneke, Michael. *Caché*. Culver City CA: Sony Pictures Classics, 2005.

Hawley, John C., ed. *Postcolonial, Queer: Theoretical Intersections*. Albany NY: SUNY Press, 2001.

Hayes, Jarrod. *Queer Nations: Marginal Sexualities in the Maghreb*. Chicago: University of Chicago Press, 2000.

———. "Queer Resistance to (Neo-)colonialism in Algeria." In *Post-colonial, Queer: Theoretical Intersections*, edited by John C. Hawley, 79-97. Albany: State University of New York Press, 2001.

———. *Queer Roots for the Diaspora: Ghosts in the Family Tree*. Ann Arbor: University of Michigan Press, 2016.

Heathcoate, Owen. "Autobiography, Sexuality, and Identity in Pierre Guyotat's *Formation* and *Arrière-Fond*." *French Studies Bulletin* 31, no. 116 (October 2010): 46–49.

Hester, Diarmuid. "Revisiting Pierre Guyotat's *Éden, Éden, Éden*: Splanchnology, Writing, Matter, and the Devastation of Ethics." *French Forum* 40, no. 1 (2015): 31–45.

Higbee, Will. "Locating the Postcolonial in Transnational Cinema: The Place of Algerian Émigré Directors in Contemporary French Film." *Modern & Contemporary France* 15, no. 1 (2007): 51–64.

Hirsch, Marianne. "The Generation of Postmemory." *Poetics Today* 29, no. 1 (Spring 2008): 103–28.

———. *The Generation of Postmemory: Writing and Visual Culture after the Holocaust*. New York: Columbia University Press, 2012.

Holland, Sharon Patricia. *The Erotic Life of Racism*. Durham NC: Duke University Press, 2012.

House, Jim, and Neil MacMaster. *Paris 1961: Algerians, State Terror, and Memory*. New York: Oxford University Press, 2006.

Houston, Penelope. "Resnais' *Muriel*." *Sight and Sound* 33, no. 1 (Winter 1963–64): 34–36.

Hubbell, Amy L. *Remembering French Algeria: Pieds-Noirs, Identity, and Exile*. Lincoln: University of Nebraska Press, 2015.

Ighilariz, Louisette. *Algérienne*. Paris: Fayard, 2001.

Imache, Tassadit. *Une fille sans histoire*. Paris: Calmann Lévy, 1989.

Jakobsen, Janet R. "Queer Is? Queer Does? Normativity and the Problem of Resistance." *GLQ: A Journal of Lesbian and Gay Studies* 4, no. 4 (1998): 511–36.

Jay, Martin. "Anamnestic Totalization: Reflections on Marcuse's Theory of Remembrance." *Theory & Society* 11, no. 1 (1982): 1–15.

Johnson, E. Patrick. "'Quare' Studies, or (Almost) Everything I Know about Queer Studies I Learned from My Grandmother." *Text and Performance Quarterly* 21, no. 1 (2001): 1–25.

Kaprièlian, Nelly. "'La guerre d'Algérie n'est pas finie.'" *Les Inrockuptibles*, no. 719 (September 2009): 38–41.

Kellner, Douglas. "Marcuse and the Quest for Radical Subjectivity." *Social Thought & Research* 22, no ½/2 (1999): 1–24.

Kendall, Stuart. "Eden and Atrocity: Pierre Guyotat's Algeria." *Comparative Studies of South Asia, Africa and the Middle East* 28, no. 1 (2008): 11–19.

Kettane, Nacer. *Le sourire de Brahim: Roman*. Paris: Denoël, 1985.

Khalil, Andrea. "The Myth of Masculinity in the Films of Merzak Allouache." *Journal of North African Studies* 12, no. 3 (September 2007): 329–45.

Khanna, Ranjana. *Algeria Cuts: Women and Representation, 1830 to the Present*. Stanford CA: Stanford University Press, 2008.

Kuby, Emma. "From the Torture Chamber to the Bedchamber: French Soldiers, Antiwar Activists, and the Discourse of Sexual Deviancy in the Algerian War (1954–1962)." *Contemporary French Civilization* 38, no. 2 (2013): 131–53.

Lazreg, Marnia. *The Eloquence of Silence: Algerian Women in Question*. New York: Routledge, 1994.

———. *Torture and the Twilight of Empire: From Algiers to Baghdad*. Princeton NJ: Princeton University Press, 2008.

Le Cour Grandmaison, Olivier. *Le 17 octobre 1961: Un crime d'état à Paris*. Paris: Dispute, 2001.

Le Sueur, James D. *Uncivil War: Intellectuals and Identity Politics during the Decolonization of Algeria*. 2nd ed. Lincoln: University of Nebraska Press, 2005.

Levinas, Emmanuel. "The Transcendence of Words." In *The Levinas Reader*, edited by Séan Hand, 144–49. Oxford: Blackwell Publishers, 1997.

Lionnet, Françoise. *Postcolonial Representations: Women, Literature, Identity*. Ithaca NY: Cornell University Press, 1995.

Lorcin, Patricia M. E. *Algeria & France, 1800–2000: Identity, Memory, Nostalgia*. Syracuse NY: Syracuse University Press, 2006.

Love, Heather. *Feeling Backward: Loss and the Politics of Queer History*. Cambridge MA: Harvard University Press, 2007.

Lugones, María. "The Coloniality of Gender." *Worlds & Knowledges Otherwise* 2, no. 2 (2008): 1–17.

———. "Heterosexualism and the Colonial/Modern Gender System." *Hypatia: A Journal of Feminist Philosophy* 22, no. 1 (2007): 186–209.

Macallan, Helen, and Andrew Plain. "*Hidden*'s Disinherited Children." *Senses of Cinema* 42 (2007), http://sensesofcinema.com/2007/cinema-engage/hidden/.

Macey, David. *The Lives of Michel Foucault*. New York: Vintage, 1995.

Mack, Mehammed Amadeus. *Sexagon: Muslims, France, and the Sexualization of National Culture*. New York: Fordham University Press, 2016.

MacMaster, Neil. "Torture: From Algiers to Abu Ghraib." *Race & Class* 46, no. 2 (2004): 1–21.

Marcuse, Herbert. *The Aesthetic Dimension: Toward a Critique of Marxist Aesthetics*. Boston: Beacon, 1978.

———. *Eros and Civilization: A Philosophical Inquiry into Freud*. Boston: Beacon, 1974.

———. *An Essay on Liberation*. Boston: Beacon Press, 1969.

Marx-Scouras, Danielle. "The Specter of Jean Sénac." *L'Esprit Créateur* 43, no. 1 (Spring 2003): 45–57.

Maslan, Susan. "The Anti-human: Man and Citizen before the Declaration of the Rights of Man and of the Citizen." *South Atlantic Quarterly* 103, no. 2/3 (Spring/Summer 2004): 357–74.

Massad, Joseph A. *Desiring Arabs*. Chicago: University of Chicago Press, 2007.

Mattei, Georges. *La guerre des gusses*. Paris: Éditions de l'Aube, 2001.

Mauvignier, Laurent. *Des hommes*. Paris: Éditions de Minuit, 2009.

———. *The Wound*. Translated by David Ball and Nicole Ball. Lincoln: University of Nebraska Press, 2015.

Mbembe, Achille. "Necropolitics." Translated by Libby Meintjes. *Public Culture* 15, no. 1 (Winter 2003): 11–40.

———. *On the Postcolony*. Berkeley: University of California Press, 2001.

McCormack, Donna. *Queer Postcolonial Narratives and the Ethics of Witnessing*. New York: Bloomsbury, 2015.

McCormack, Jo. *Collective Memory: France and the Algerian War (1954–1962)*. Lanham MD: Lexington Books, 2007.

———. "Memory in History, Nation Building, and Identity: Teaching about the Algerian War in France." In *Algeria and France, 1800–2000: Identity, Memory, Nostalgia*, edited by Patricia M. E. Lorcin, 135–49. Syracuse NY: Syracuse University Press, 2006.

McLeod, John. *Beginning Postcolonialism*. Manchester UK: Manchester University Press, 2010.

———. *Postcolonial London: Rewriting the Metropolis*. New York: Routledge, 2004.

McRuer, Robert. *Crip Theory: Cultural Signs of Queerness and Disability*. New York: New York University Press, 2006.

Milne, Tom. "The Festivals: Venice and Trieste." *Sight and Sound* 32, no. 4 (Autumn 1963): 177–79.

Muñoz, José Esteban. *Cruising Utopia: The Then and There of Queer Futurity*. New York: NYU Press, 2009.

———. *Disidentifications: Queers of Color and the Performance of Politics*. Minneapolis: University of Minnesota Press, 1999.

Murungi, John. *African Philosophical Currents*. New York: Routledge, 2018.

Nagel, Joane. "Masculinity and Nationalism: Gender and Sexuality in the Making of Nations." *Ethnic and Racial Studies* 21, no. 2 (March 1998): 242–69.

Navarro-Ayala, Luis. *Queering Transcultural Encounters: Bodies, Images, and Frenchness in Latin America and North Africa*. Cham, Switzerland: Palgrave Macmillan, 2019.

Noël, Bernard. *The Castle of Communion*. Translated by Paul Buck and Glenda George. London: Atlas, 1993.

———. "The Outrage against Words." *ubu Editions*, 2007, http://www.ubu.com/ubu/pdf/noel_outrage.pdf.

Norindr, Panivong. "Mourning, Memorials, and Filmic Traces: Reinscribing the *Corps étrangers* and Unknown Soldiers in Bertrand Tavernier's Films." *Studies in 20th Century Literature* 23, no. 1 (1999): 117–41.

Peniston, William. *Pederasts and Others: Urban Culture and Sexual Identity in Nineteenth-Century Paris*. New York: Routledge, 2004.

Penney, James. "'You Never Look at Me from Where I See You': Postcolonial Guilt in *Caché*." *New Formations* 70 (2011): 77–93.

Perreau, Bruno. *Queer Theory: The French Response*. Stanford CA: Stanford University Press, 2016.

Ponzanesi, Sandra, and Marguerite Waller. Introduction to *Postcolonial Cinema Studies*, edited by Sandra Ponzanesi and Marguerite Waller, 1–16. London: Routledge, 2012.

Porton, Richard. "Collective Guilt and Individual Responsibility: An Interview with Michael Haneke." *Cineaste* 31, no. 1 (2005): 50–51.

Provencher, Denis M. *Queer Maghrebi French: Language, Temporalities, Transfiliations*. Liverpool: Liverpool University Press, 2017.

Puar, Jasbir K. "Rethinking Homonationalism." *International Journal of Middle East Studies* 45, no. 2 (May 2013): 336–39.

———. *The Right to Maim: Debility, Capacity, Disability*. Durham NC: Duke University Press, 2017.

———. *Terrorist Assemblages: Homonationalism in Queer Times*. Durham NC: Duke University Press, 2007.

Puwar, Nirmal. *Space Invaders: Race, Gender, and Bodies out of Place*. New York: Berg, 2004.

Quinan, Christine. "Technocrats and Tortured Bodies: Simone de Beauvoir's *Les Belles Images*." *Women: A Cultural Review* 25, no. 3 (2014): 256–69.

———. "Uses and Abuses of Gender and Nationality: Torture and French-Algerian War." In *Gender, Globalization, and Violence: Postcolonial Conflict Zones*, edited by Sandra Ponzanesi, 111–25. New York: Routledge, 2014.

Reddy, Chandan. *Freedom with Violence: Race, Sexuality, and the US State*. Durham NC: Duke University Press, 2011.

Rees-Roberts, Nick. *French Queer Cinema*. Edinburgh: Edinburgh University Press, 2008.

Rejali, Darius M. "Torture Makes the Man." *South Central Review* 24, no. 1 (2007): 151–69.

Renan, Ernest. *Qu'est-ce qu'une nation? Suivi de Préface aux Discours et conférences; et Préface à Souvenirs d'enfance et de jeunesse*. Marseille: Le Mot et le Reste, 2007.

———. "What Is a Nation?" In *Nation and Narration*, edited by Homi Bhabha, 8–22. New York: Routledge, 1990.

Renaud, Jeffrey. "Rethinking the Repressive Hypothesis: Foucault's Critique of Marcuse." *Symposium* 17, no. 2 (Fall 2013): 77–93.

Resnais, Alain. *Muriel, ou le temps d'un retour: Muriel, or the Time of a Return*. London: Eureka!, 2009.

Rodríguez, Juana María. "Queer Sociality and Other Sexual Fantasies." *GLQ: A Journal of Lesbian and Gay Studies* 17, no. 2/3 (2011): 331–48.

———. *Sexual Futures, Queer Gestures, and Other Latina Longings*. New York: NYU Press, 2015.

Rohy, Valerie. *Anachronism and Its Others: Sexuality, Race, Temporality*. Albany NY: SUNY Press, 2009.

Rosello, Mireille. "Dissident or Conformist Passing: Merzak Allouache's Chouchou." *South Central Review* 28, no. 1 (Spring 2011): 2–17.

———. *France and the Maghreb: Performative Encounters*. Gainesville: University Press of Florida, 2005.

———. *Postcolonial Hospitality: The Immigrant as Guest*. Stanford CA: Stanford University Press, 2002.

Ross, Kristin. *Fast Cars, Clean Bodies: Decolonization and the Reordering of French Culture*. Cambridge MA: MIT Press, 1995.

———. *May '68 and Its Afterlives*. Chicago: University of Chicago Press, 2002.

Rothberg, Michael. "Between Auschwitz and Algeria: Multidirectional Memory and the Counterpublic Witness." *Critical Inquiry* 33, no. 1 (2006): 158–84.

———. *Multidirectional Memory: Remembering the Holocaust in the Age of Decolonization*. Stanford CA: Stanford University Press, 2009.

Roumette, Sylvain. "Interview with Alain Resnais." *Clarté: Mensuel de l'Union des étudiants communistes de France* 33 (February 1961): 12.

Rubin, Gayle S. "Thinking Sex: Notes for a Radical Theory of the Politics of Sexuality." In *The Lesbian and Gay Studies Reader*, edited by Henry Abelove, Michèle Aina Barale, and David M. Halperin, 3–44. New York: Routledge, 1993.

Said, Edward W. *Culture and Imperialism*. New York: Vintage Books, 1994.

———. *Orientalism*. New York: Vintage Books, 1994.

Sainson, Katia. "'Entre deux feux': Jean Sénac's Struggle for Self-Determination." *Research in African Literatures* 42, no. 1 (Spring 2011): 32–48.

———. "Jacob's Wound: Jean Sénac, Albert Camus, and the Question of Algerian Nationalism." *French Review* 83, no. 6 (2010): 1202–15.

Sartre, Jean-Paul. "A Victory." In *The Question*, by Henri Alleg, translated by John Calder, xiii–xxv. Lincoln: University of Nebraska Press, 2006.

Sartre, Jean-Paul, and Henri Alleg. *La question de Henri Alleg: Une victoire de J. P. Sartre*. Paris: Éditions de Minuit, 1958.

Scott, Joan Wallach. *Only Paradoxes to Offer: French Feminists and the Rights of Man*. Cambridge MA: Harvard University Press, 1997.

Sebbar, Leïla. *La Seine était rouge*. Paris: Éditions Thierry Magnier, 1999.

———. *The Seine Was Red: Paris, October 1961*. Translated by Mildred Mortimer. Bloomington: Indiana University Press, 2008.

Sedgwick, Eve Kosofsky. *Tendencies*. Durham NC: Duke University Press, 1993.

Seidman, Steven. "Identity and Politics in a 'Postmodern' Gay Culture: Some Historical and Conceptual Notes." In *Fear of a Queer Planet: Queer Politics and Social Theory*, edited by Michael Warner, 105–42. Minneapolis: University of Minnesota Press, 1993.

Selao, Ching. "Porter l'Algérie: *Garçon manqué* de Nina Bouraoui." *L'Esprit Créateur* 45, no. 3 (Fall 2005): 74–84.

Sellier, Geneviève. *Masculine Singular: French New Wave Cinema*. Durham NC: Duke University Press, 2008.

Sénac, Jean. *Dérisions et vertige: Trouvures*. Paris: Presses Universitaires de France, 1983.

———. *The Selected Poems of Jean Sénac*. Translated by Katia Sainson and David Bergman. Riverdale-on-Hudson NY: Sheep Meadow Press, 2010.

Shepard, Todd. *The Invention of Decolonization: The Algerian War and the Remaking of France*. Ithaca NY: Cornell University Press, 2006.

———. *Mâle décolonisation: "L'homme arabe" et la France, de l'indépendance algérienne à la révolution iranienne (1962–1979)*. Paris: Payot, 2017.

———. *Sex, France, and Arab Men, 1962–1979*. Chicago: University of Chicago Press, 2017.

———. "'Something Notably Erotic': Politics, 'Arab Men,' and Sexual Revolution in Post-decolonization France, 1962–1974." *Journal of Modern History* 84, no. 1 (March 2012): 80–115.

Shildrick, Margrit. *Dangerous Discourses of Disability, Subjectivity and Sexuality*. New York: Palgrave, 2009.

Showalter, Elaine. *The Female Malady: Women, Madness and English Culture, 1830–1980*. London: Penguin, 1987.

Silverman, Max. "The Empire Looks Back." *Screen* 46, no. 2 (2007): 245–49.

———. *Palimpsestic Memory: The Holocaust and Colonialism in French and Francophone Fiction and Film*. New York: Berghahn Books, 2013.

Simonin, Anne. "La littérature saisie par l'histoire: Nouveau roman and guerre d'Algérie aux Éditions de Minuit." *Actes de la Recherche en Sciences Sociales* 111–12 (March 1996): 59–75.

Smith, William Gardner. *The Stone Face: A Novel*. New York: Farrar, Straus, 1963.

Snorton, C. Riley. *Black on Both Sides: A Racial History of Trans Identity*. Minneapolis: University of Minnesota Press, 2017.

Sontag, Susan. "Review of *Muriel*." *Film Quarterly* 17, no. 2 (Winter 1963–64): 22–27.

SOS Homophobie. "Rapport sur la homophobie: Lutte contre la lesbophobie, la gayphobie, la biphobie et la transphobie." Paris, 2017. https://sos-homophobie.org/rapport-annuel-2017.

Spurlin, William J. "Contested Borders: Cultural Translation and Queer Politics in Contemporary Francophone Writing from the Maghreb." *Research in African Literatures* 47, no. 2 (Summer 2016): 104–20.

Stoler, Ann Laura. *Along the Archival Grain: Epistemic Anxieties and Colonial Common Sense*. Princeton NJ: Princeton University Press, 2010.

———. *Race and the Education of Desire: Foucault's History of Sexuality and the Colonial Order of Things*. Durham NC: Duke University Press, 1995.

Stora, Benjamin. *La gangrène et l'oubli: La mémoire de la Guerre d'Algérie*. Paris: La Découverte & Syros, 1998.

———. *Le livre, mémoire de l'histoire: Réflexions sur le livre et la guerre d'Algérie*. Paris: Préau des Collines, 2005.

Sturken, Marita. "Narratives of Recovery: Repressed Memory as Cultural Memory." In *Acts of Memory: Cultural Recall in the Present*, edited by Mieke Bal, Jonathan Crewe, and Leo Spitzer, 231–48. Hanover NH: University Press of New England, 1999.

Swamy, Vinay. *Interpreting the Republic: Marginalization and Belonging in Contemporary French Novels and Films*. Lanham MD: Lexington Books, 2011.

Témime, Émile, and Nicole Tuccelli. *Jean Sénac, l'Algérien: Le poète des deux rives*. Paris: Autrement, 2003.

Tierney, Thomas F. "The Governmentality of Suicide: Peuchet, Marx, Durkheim, and Foucault." *Journal of Classical Sociology* 10, no. 4 (2010): 357–89.
Trinh T. Minh-ha. "Not You / Like You: Post-colonial Women and the Interlocking Question of Identity and Difference." *Inscriptions* 3-4 (1988). https://culturalstudies.ucsc.edu/inscriptions/volume-34/trinh-t-minh-ha/.
Tristan, Anne. *Le silence du fleuve: Ce crime que nous n'avons toujours pas nommé*. Bezons, France: Au Nom de la Mémoire, 1991.
Vassallo, Helen. "Unsuccessful Alterity? The Pursuit of Otherness in Nina Bouraoui's Autobiographical Writing." *International Journal of Francophone Studies* 12, no. 1 (2009): 37–53.
Vilar, Jean-François. *Bastille tango*. Paris: Presses de la Renaissance, 1986.
Vince, Natalya. *Our Fighting Sisters: Nation, Memory and Gender in Algeria, 1954–2012*. Manchester UK: Manchester University Press, 2015.
Warner, Michael. Introduction to *Fear of a Queer Planet: Queer Politics and Social Theory*, edited by Michael Warner, vii–xxxi. Minneapolis: University of Minnesota Press, 1993.
Weheliye, Alexander. *Habeas Viscus: Racializing Assemblages, Biopolitics, and Black Feminist Theories of the Human*. Durham NC: Duke University Press, 2014.
Wilson, Emma. *Alain Resnais*. Manchester UK: Manchester University Press, 2006.
Woods, Gregory. *A History of Gay Literature: The Male Tradition*. New Haven CT: Yale University Press, 1998.
Young, Robert J. C. *Colonial Desire: Hybridity in Theory, Culture and Race*. New York: Routledge, 1995.
———. *White Mythologies: Writing History and the West*. New York: Routledge, 1993.

INDEX

activism, 23, 71, 140, 163, 206n3
The Aesthetic Dimension (Marcuse), 125
aesthetics, 1, 2, 4, 127
affect, 83, 117, 219n15; memory and, 29, 30, 199n22; subjectivity and, 59
agency, 15, 23, 48, 50, 58, 77, 79, 88, 162, 169; political, 163, 176; queer modes of, 5-6
Ahluwalia, Pal, 195n78, 211n65
Ahmed, Sara, 129; analysis of fear, 83, 88; characterization of whiteness, 82, 84; conceptualization of queer, 22; on disidentification, 171; on hybridity, 16
Algeria: colonization of, 9-10; decolonization of, 19-21; masculinity and, 160-61, 174-75; poststructuralism and, 25-26; resistance, 139-41; revolution in, 9, 20, 23; struggle for independence, 2, 10-13, 25, 72-75, 174. *See also* French-Algerian War
Algerian War of Independence. *See* French-Algerian War
Algerian women, 30, 31, 54, 57-58, 200n24, 200n36
Alleg, Henri, 11, 52, 197n7
Allouache, Merzak, 35, 179-82

Alloula, Malek, 200n24
Althusser, Louis, 223n61; interpellation, 168-69
Altman, Dennis, 102
Aly, Ramy, 25
Amin, Kadji, 26, 107
Amine, Laila, 147
amnesia, 27, 32, 39, 136, 139; collective, 44, 72, 137, 195n91. *See also* forgetting; re-membering
Anti-Oedipus (Deleuze and Guattari), 117
anxiety: desire and, 19; fear and, 83-85; about gender and sexuality, 15, 21, 22, 182, 185; hybridity and, 4, 18-19, 23, 113, 153, 186; about masculinity, 22, 31, 57, 61-62, 88; about national identity, 15, 21, 35, 182-83, 185; postcolonial, 43, 78, 124; about racial difference, 15, 21, 182-85, 192n38
Anzaldúa, Gloria, 155, 177
Arendt, Hannah, 73-74
art: as a form of radical subjectivity, 125-26. *See also* literature
Ashcroft, Bill, 23
Aussaresses, Paul, 197n5

Baldwin, James, 164
Barad, Karen, 176, 196n102; re-membering, 29–30, 127–28, 172–73, 176, 196n102
Barthes, Roland, 4, 103, 209n40
Beauchamp, Toby, 192n33
becoming: naming and, 167–69; processes of, 6, 30; *Tomboy* and, 172–73, 176, 223n65
belonging, 8, 29, 168; (queer) un-, 34, 153, 159–60; queerness and, 116, 186
Bennett, Jill, 30
Benstock, Shari, 143
Bergson, Henri, 41
Bérubé, Allan, 8
Bhabha, Homi: hybridity, 15–16; postcolonial time, 26
biopolitics, 124, 211n66
biopower, 119, 204n33. *See also* Foucault, Michel; power
Blanco, María del Pilar, 29, 159
Bodies that Matter (Butler), 169–70
the body: *Caché* and, 79, 88; *Eden, Eden, Eden* and, 33, 98, 107, 108, 113, 114; Foucault's "bodies and pleasures", 118, 120–22, 123; fractured embodiment, 19, 61, 114; as marked by torture, 46–47; materiality of, 169–70; *Muriel* and, 40, 42, 50, 53–55, 57–58, 61–62; racialized, 20, 84, 204n28; *Tomboy* and, 34–35, 152, 156–58, 164, 166–68, 172–73, 175–76;
Boudjedra, Rachid, 189n5
Bouraoui, Nina: life, 163–64; literary production, 163; *Tomboy*, 15, 34–35, 151–77; writing as activism, 163–64; writing style, 153

Bourdieu, Pierre, 80, 217n57
Branche, Raphaëlle, 52, 199n21
Brun, Catherine, 28, 108, 111, 115, 118, 125
Butler, Judith, 167; *Bodies that Matter*, 169–70; constitutive outside, 22; interpellation, 168; performativity, 170

Caché (dir. Haneke), 32, 71–93, 129, 133–34, 136; masculinity, 72, 77, 83, 88, 89; postcolonial haunting, 75–79; representations of women, 86–87; symbolic capital, 82, 84, 88; symbolic violence, 32, 76, 79, 80–85, 88, 93
Camiscioli, Elisa, 20, 85, 157
Carrier, Peter, 139
The Castle of Communion (Noël), 106–7
Cayrol, Jean, 39, 42, 45, 105, 109, 111, 207n21; *Muriel*, 50, 198n13; on World War II, 198n12
censorship: concerning sex and sexuality, 106, 119; *Eden, Eden, Eden* and, 104–7; of publications devoted to the war, 52, 207n23; Resnais's work and, 41, 52–53, 55, 197n4
Chambers, Ross, 197n7
Charlie Hebdo: attacks on, 14, 32, 72, 90–93; "Je suis Charlie" movement, 92. *See also* terrorism
Chouchou (dir. Allouache), 35, 179–82, 185
cinema, 4, 6, 186; Algerian women in, 57–58; Allouache's Algerian, 179–80; about the French-Algerian War, 14–15; Haneke's cinematic strategy, 77, 86; *Nouvelle Vague* movement in, 40; of Resnais, 39–41, 51–53

citizenship: access to French, 85, 89; human rights and, 32; statelessness and, 72–75
Civilization and Its Discontents (Freud), 99–100
Cole, Joshua, 213n4
collective memory, 13; amnesia and, 27, 195n91; *Charlie Hebdo* and, 92; Halbwachs's theory of, 71–72, 75; individual and, 72, 76; Marcuse on, 101. *See also* memory
colonialism: French, 81, 90, 105, 160; as an ideology, 17–18, 24, 57; violence and, 32, 41, 71, 72, 93, 98, 100, 129, 147. *See also* decolonization; postcolonialism
Coly, Ayo A., 19, 151, 195n83
Crewe, Jonathan, 75
Cruising Utopia (Muñoz), 186

Davidson, Arnold, 119
decolonization: French-Algerian War and, 4, 9–12, 19–21; and gender and sexuality, 19–23, 98, 164; in Guyotat's work, 106, 107; origin of the term, 20
"Decolonization of Algiers" (Fonfrède), 20
deconstruction: Algeria and, 25–26; countermonuments as acts of, 144; Derridean, 1, 26; Guyotat and, 109, 118, 124; queer theory and, 9, 18, 23, 25–26; of subjectivity, 102–3, 104, 117–18, 187; *Tomboy* and, 153, 162–63, 176
Deleuze, Gilles: on desire, 117–18; on *Muriel*, 45–46, 59–60
De Quincey, Thomas, 142–43
Derderian, Richard, 27
Derrida, Jacques, 26

desire: Ahmed on, 129; anxiety and, 18–19; Deleuzian, 117–18; Foucault on, 118–19; Guyotat and, 98, 104, 117–18, 125–26; hybridity and, 18; queer, 2, 3, 34, 35, 125, 152, 153, 174; *Tomboy* and, 152, 153, 160, 174–75, 176
desubjectification, 107, 118, 162. *See also* subjectification
Diamond, Elin, 167
Dillon, Sarah, 144
disidentification: Ahmed on, 171; Baldwin and, 164; Muñoz's theorization of, 153–54, 155, 171; *Tomboy* and, 153–55, 162, 164, 169–72
Djebar, Assia, 189–90n5
Donadey, Anne, 131, 139
Dragojlovic, Ana, 149
Drucker, Peter, 102
dystopia, 124. *See also* utopia

Edelman, Lee, 116
Eden, Eden, Eden (Guyotat), 33, 97–126, 147; deformation of language, 103, 110, 113, 114, 115–16, 117; dismantling subjectivity, 104, 106, 109, 112, 114, 115, 117–18, 124, 125, 126; masculinity, 106, 108, 114; portrayals of violence, 98, 99, 104–5, 108–9, 112–13, 114–15, 117, 124, 125; sexuality and revolution, 33, 98, 101, 103, 107, 109, 111, 121, 123, 194n67
Eng, David, 7
Eros and Civilization (Marcuse), 99, 102, 123

Fanon, Frantz: Algerian women, 57; analysis of fear and movement, 83; decolonization, 19–20

Index 249

Fassin, Didier, 90
fear: Ahmed on, 83, 88; and anxiety, 18–19, 83
female masculinity, 167–68
Ferenczi, Sandor, 101
Fisher, Mark, 26, 28
FLN (National Liberation Front): the events of October 17, 1961, 74–75, 130–31; struggle for independence, 10–12, 34
Fonfrède, Henri, 20
Ford, Hamish, 77
forgetting: France's colonial past, 27–28, 93; October 17, 1961, 71–72, 75; remembering and, 28–30, 34–35, 42, 44, 130, 131, 139, 149, 156; *The Seine Was Red* and, 128, 130, 131, 137, 139, 149; as shaping subjectivities and identities, 20, 128, 144; as symbolic violence, 85. *See also* amnesia
Foucault, Michel: attitude toward colonialism, 120; bodies and pleasures, 118, 120–22, 123; characterization of Marcuse, 123; on *Eden, Eden, Eden*, 99, 121, 122; framework of power, 6, 88, 160; genealogical approach, 141–42; *The History of Sexuality*, 104, 118, 123; letter to Guyotat, 120–21; the modern liberal subject, 22; *scientia sexualis*, 119–20; sex, sexuality, and subjectivity, 118–22
Freccero, Carla, 5, 16, 24–25, 26, 129
Freeman, Elizabeth, 5, 48
French-Algerian War: censorship and, 105–6; *Chouchou* and, 179–82, 185; contemporary legacy of, 89–93, 179–87; *Eden, Eden, Eden* and, 111–17, 120–21, 124; masculinity and, 12, 19, 21–22, 30–31, 42, 63–64, 197n7; queer sexuality and, 21, 98, 106–9; as resisting a defined beginning and end, 128; terms that encapsulate the conflict, 13, 189n3; *Tomboy* and, 154, 156–58, 173–75; World War II and, 12, 27–30, 44–46, 106, 121, 138–42, 144–47; *The Wound* and, 65–69
Frenchness: failing, 43–49; novel understandings of, 20, 184; as a "white project", 85
Freud, Sigmund, 99, 100, 101, 123
futurity: contesting traditional lines of, 26–27; queer, 186–87; reproductive, 116, 119, 135. *See also* temporality

Garvey, Johanna, 153
de Gaulle, Charles: response to October 17, 1961, 140, 216n39; return to the French presidency, 12; understanding of French identity, 4, 5; as World War II hero, 12, 140
gender: French republicanism and, 20; performative nature of, 6, 8, 153, 168, 170; postcolonial gender constructs, 86–89; sexuality, decolonization, and, 19–22
gender fluidity, 152–53, 156, 161, 162
gender theory: backlash, 24, 194n76
Genet, Jean, 63, 103, 207n23; homosexuality and the Algerian cause, 107, 114; relationship with Guyotat, 207n26
Genette, Gérard, 144, 216n46
genre: of documentary film, 147–48; *Eden, Eden, Eden* and, 33,

98; gender and, 161; in Sebbar's work, 134–35; *Tomboy* and, 15, 152; in the wake of the French-Algerian War, 3, 4, 8, 186
Ghostly Matters (Gordon), 59, 69–70
Gide, André, 21
Gilroy, Paul, 79
Godard, Jean-Luc, 52, 200n28, 207n23
Gopinath, Gayatri, 147–48, 185
Gordon, Avery, 30, 59, 69–70
Griffiths, Gareth, 23
Guattari, Félix, 117–18
guilt, 50, 61; collective, 204n24; postcolonial, 84, 86
Guyotat, Pierre, 125–26; class relations, 108, 109, 118; *Eden, Eden, Eden*, 33, 97–126, 147; experiences of colonial combat, 107; letter to Jean Cayrol, 109–10, 111; literary techniques, 112–15, 115–16; postwar writings, 108–9; time in Algeria, 107–8; *Tomb for 500,000 Soldiers*, 104, 109, 120, 121, 207n17

Halberstam, J. Jack, 7, 29, 127, 160, 167–68
Halbwachs, Maurice, 71–72, 75
Hall, Stuart, 155
Haneke, Michael: *Caché*, 32, 72–93, 204n24; on hidden national memories, 32, 72; use of mise en abyme, 77, 86
haunting, 26, 30, 32, 43, 69, 203n62; ghosts and, 59, 69–70; intergenerational, 173; postcolonial, 23–26, 75–80
hauntology: Coly's analysis of, 195n83; Derrida's concept of, 26. *See also* haunting

Hayes, Jarrod, 8, 23, 26, 162
Heathcoate, Owen, 104
Hegel, Georg Wilhelm Friedrich, 47, 99
hegemonic masculinity, 83; constructed against (Algerian) femininity, 58; contestation of, 5, 9, 160
Hester, Diarmuid, 115–16
heteronormativity, 25, 49, 161
Higbee, Will, 179
Hirsch, Marianne, 67, 134, 159, 214n21
The History of Sexuality (Foucault), 22, 104, 118, 123
homonationalism, 185, 227n16
homophobia: in 1950s and 1960s politics, 21, 22; *La Manif Pour Tous* ("Demonstration for All"), 183, 184; Sénac's resistance to, 3; SOS Homophobie report, 192n34
homosexuality, 3, 22, 102, 104, 108, 115, 180; "coming out" narratives, 163; as divisive political issue, 20–21, 182–85, 194n61; Homosexual Front of Revolutionary Action (FHAR), 107; ideal citizen defined against, 21; *Tomboy* and, 174–75. *See also* sexuality
House, Jim, 71
Hubbell, Amy, 130, 195n91
hybrid anxieties: concept of, 18–19. *See also* anxiety; hybridity
hybridity, 35, 176–77, 186; concept of, 15–19; *Eden, Eden, Eden* and, 113, 115; Muñoz's theorization of, 154; queerness and, 16–17, 167; *The Seine Was Red* and, 130, 135; *Tomboy* and, 153, 154–55, 166; Young on racial difference and, 192n38

identity, 15, 23, 25, 186; *Eden, Eden, Eden* and, 98, 104, 107, 112, 118, 121, 122, 123, 124; Foucault on the traps of, 97, 119, 122; fragmentation of, 5, 54; Muñoz on the formation of, 154–55, 186; national, 4, 27, 44, 47, 60, 62–63, 89, 133, 144, 184; postcolonial identity-maneuvering work, 151–52; postwar, 27–28, 44; queering, 6, 22, 23, 126; *Tomboy* and, 152–54, 155–56, 158, 159, 162, 163, 165–67, 169–73, 176, 177; the war as a conflict over, 9, 12, 62–63, 187

identity politics: debates around, 98, 137; during the French-Algerian War, 9, 130

immigration, 14, 83, 157, 203n6

in-betweenness: Sénac's embodiment of, 2–3; *Tomboy* and, 34, 152, 155, 161, 165, 177. *See also* hybridity; third space

intergenerationality: hauntings, 173–74; transmission, 132–35, 215n26; trauma and, 29–30, 106, 174, 175

interpellation, 167–69

Islamophobia, 90, 92, 192n34

Jay, Martin, 101, 123

Kellner, Douglas, 100
Kendall, Stuart, 106, 110–11, 122
Khanna, Ranjana, 57
Kuby, Emma, 48, 206n3

Lazreg, Marnia, 47, 48; analysis of torture, 41–42
Le Pen, Jean-Marie, 14

Le Sueur, James, 9, 189n3
Lévinas, Emmanuel, 51
LeVine, Mark, 91
libinality, 98, 99, 101–2, 103, 111, 120, 123, 124
Lionnet, Françoise, 16
literature: "memory boom" in, 6–7, 71; in the post-decolonization period, 4, 6; queering genre and, 4–5, 186; role in rethinking subjectivity, 102–3, 126, 186, 207n16. *See also* genre; writing
The Little Soldier (dir. Godard), 52, 200n28, 207n23

Macey, David, 120
Mack, Mehammed Amadeus, 185
MacMaster, Neil, 13, 71
manliness, 42, 49, 197n7. *See also* masculinity
Marcuse, Herbert, 33, 99–103, 124; Foucault's critique of, 123, 212n73; libidinous revolution, 101, 111, 123; Muñoz's reworking of, 124–25; pleasure principle, 101–2, 111; theorization of time, 116, 123
marriage equality, 35, 182–84
Martin, Lauren Jade, 176–77
Marxist theory, 99, 101, 123
masculinity, 12, 30–33, 35, 89, 93, 98, 136–37; *Caché* and, 72, 77, 83, 88, 89; colonial, 58, 88, 201n39; colonial power and, 57, 62; decolonization and, 19, 21–22; fragmentation of dominant, 77; memory and, 31, 33, 35, 41–42, 54, 60, 61, 136, 177; *Muriel* and, 42–43, 49, 57–58, 60–62, 69; postwar, 42, 114; *Tomboy* and,

34, 152, 153, 155, 156, 158–61, 162, 166, 167, 170, 174, 175, 176, 177; torture and, 41–42, 197n7; war and, 42–43; *The Wound* and, 42–43, 63–64, 69. *See also* hegemonic masculinity
Maslan, Susan, 73
Matter and Memory (Bergson), 41
Mauvignier, Laurent, 7, 63, 128; *The Wound*, 31–32, 42–43, 62–70
Mbembe, Achille, 86, 151, 152
McCormack, Donna, 9, 129, 161, 162
McCormack, Jo, 214n16
McCullers, Carson, 167–68
McLeod, John, 6, 127
The Member of the Wedding (McCullers), 167–68
memorialization, 29, 144. *See also The Seine Was Red*
memory, 15, 19, 27, 75, 86, 139, 190n13; Barad's reconceptualization of, 29–30; and forgetting, 28–29, 42, 128; masculinity and, 31, 32, 33, 35, 42–43, 54, 60, 61, 62, 136, 177; memory-oblivion dichotomy, 30, 156; palimpsestic nature of, 34, 134, 138, 143–44, 149; repression of, 128, 219n21; *The Seine Was Red* and, 129–30, 132, 136, 142, 149; subject-forming capacities of, 35, 172; temporality and, 66, 123, 127; *Tomboy* and, 34–35, 152, 156, 159, 162, 164, 176, 177, 179; *The Wound* and, 63, 66. *See also* palimpsest
métissage, 16, 166. *See also* hybridity
mise en abyme: Haneke's use of, 77–79, 86; Resnais's modernist, 49–53

modernism: refusal of, 124; and subjectivity, 100, 102–3
modernization: and decolonization, 46, 62; post–World War II, 11
multidirectional memory, 27, 139, 142
Muñoz, José Esteban, 7, 142, 161, 164; belonging, 116, 186; disidentification, 9, 153, 155, 171; hybridity, 17, 154; queer time, 116–17, 186; queer utopianism, 124–25, 126
Muriel, or the Time of a Return (*Muriel, ou le temps d'un retour*) (dir. Resnais), 31, 39–70, 198n10, 198n12; bodies as marked by torture, 46–47; compared with *The Wound*, 62, 64, 68; dissonance between the visual and auditory, 51–52; kaleidoscopic filming technique, 53–58; masculinity and memory, 41–42, 54, 60, 61; World War II, 44–46
Murungi, John, 193n54

naming, 167–69, 175, 176; categorization practices and, 17, 191n25; misnaming, 47, 48, 49
nationalism: Algerian, 10, 20; contemporary French, 14, 91–92; Gopinath on patriarchal, 185; Sénac resisting, 3
nationality: French identity and, 5, 9–10, 12, 41, 89, 133, 184–85; *Tomboy* and, 34, 153, 154, 156, 158–59, 164, 167, 170, 171
necropolitics, 86, 124
Noël, Bernard, 106–7
Norindr, Panivong, 139
normalization: anti-, 123; Foucault on discourses of, 119; regimes of, 4, 5, 6, 23; and subjectivity, 100
November 2005 riots, 14, 89, 91

OAS (Secret Armed Organization), 12, 91, 173–74
October 17, 1961: background, 71–75, 213n4; *Caché* and, 75–77, 80; compared with January 7, 2015, 91–92; remembering, 71–72, 128–30, 217n57; *The Seine Was Red* and, 130–42, 145–49
On Collective Memory (Halbwachs), 71–72
Orientalism: Algerian women and, 200n24; perversion and, 21–22; Said's concept of, 57–58, 211n66

palimpsest: as a tool of queer analysis, 28, 129, 143–44. See also *The Seine Was Red*
palimpsestic: in contrast to palimpsestuous, 143–45; nature of memory, 34, 138
palimpsestuous, 216n46; approach, 148, 149; in contrast to palimpsestic, 143–45
Papon, Maurice, 72, 74, 77, 146
pathologization, 156, 157–58, 162; of anxiety, 18; pathological manliness, 49; pleasure as resisting, 119; sexual identities and, 22–23, 97
Pereen, Esther, 29, 159
performativity, 5; Butler's theory of, 168, 170; of gender and sexuality, 6, 8, 153
Perreau, Bruno, 17, 21, 184
polymorphous perversity: Altman's conceptualization of, 102; Marcuse's theoretical framework, 99–103
pleasure: Foucault on bodies and, 118–19, 122, 123; Nietzsche's perpetuity of, 101

pleasure principle, 101–2, 111
Ponzanesi, Sandra, 57–58
populism, 13–14
postcolonialism, 127; and haunting, 75–79. See also colonialism
postcoloniality, 26–27, 151, 152, 187. See also queer postcoloniality
postcolonial temporality, 26–27, 28, 66, 75, 127, 128, 179, 185, 187
the postcolony, 151
post-decolonization: Shepard on the category of, 191n30
postmemory: Hirsch's theorization of, 134, 159, 214n21; mechanisms of, 134
poststructuralism, 195n78; Algeria and, 25; French approach to, 24–25; and Guyotat's approach, 113, 115; queer theory and, 23
power: Butler on, 169, 170; disidentification and, 153; Foucauldian framework of, 6, 54–55, 88, 120, 122, 160, 211n66; Foucault's critique of Marcuse, 123; naming and, 168, 191n25; symbolic, 82
Provencher, Denis M., 26–27, 135, 148
Puar, Jasbir K., 227n16
Puwar, Nirmal, 84

queer, 7–8; Ahmed's conceptualization of, 22; Freeman on, 48; origin of the word, 17; as a reading method, 5, 9, 24, 128, 129–30, 143, 153, 156, 163, 164–65, 175
queer diasporic cultural forms, 33, 147–48
queering, 8, 19, 23, 26, 117, 125, 185; genre and gender, 161–65; of kinship, 8, 49, 106, 111, 135, 155,

181; of memory, 148–49; re-membering and, 30
queerness, 8, 34, 48, 116, 142, 144, 151, 152, 177, 186, 187; hybridity and, 16–18
queer postcoloniality: analytical approach, 5–9, 18, 24, 26, 129–30, 151, 152, 179, 185, 187; McCormack on queer postcolonial narratives, 129, 161
queer temporality, 26–30, 34, 43, 66, 127, 226n14; *Eden, Eden, Eden* and, 116–17; Halberstam on, 127; Muñoz's conceptualization of, 116–17; Provencher on, 26–27
queer theory, 7–9, 22–23, 104, 116, 119, 127, 163, 189n3; critiques of, 8, 24–25, 194n75; decolonialization and, 19; and deconstruction, 23, 25; and Derrida's concept of hauntology, 26; French resistances to, 24, 194n74; on masculinity, 160; postcolonial studies and, 5, 26, 185; on sex and sexuality, 97–98
The Question (Alleg), 52, 197n7, 207n23

race: *Tomboy* and, 152, 153, 154, 166–67, 170; and urban space, 81–82, 138, 148. *See also* whiteness
racism, 10, 14, 90, 203n6; Ahmed on fear and, 83; *Caché* and, 81, 89; racial profiling, 73, 89, 181; Taubira and, 184; *Tomboy* and, 154, 155, 157, 219n22
remembering: binary of forgetting and, 27–29, 34–35, 44, 130, 131, 139, 149, 156; Marcuse's theory of, 100–101. *See also* memory

re-membering: Barad on, 29, 172; concept of, 30, 172–73; process of, 34–35; queer potential of, 173, 175–176
Renan, Ernest, 28–29
repressive hypothesis, 123, 212n72
Resnais, Alain: career, 40; cinematic style, 39–40, 41, 46, 51–52, 53–54, 59, 67, 68; experience with censorship, 52; modernist mise en abyme, 49–53; *Muriel*, 31–32, 39–62; *Night and Fog*, 198n12
rightlessness: Arendt on, 73–74
Rodríguez, Juana María, 124–25
Rohy, Valerie, 226n4
Rosello, Mireille, 5
Ross, Kristin, 44
Rothberg, Michael, 27, 81, 142
Rubin, Gayle, 97–98

Said, Edward, 5, 12, 57–58, 211n66
Sainson, Katia, 189n2
Sartre, Jean-Paul, 41–42, 105, 107, 197n7, 207n23
Scott, Joan, 20
Sebbar, Leïla: eschewing identitarian categories, 130, 213n9; *The Seine Was Red*, 33–34, 75, 127–49
Sedgwick, Eve Kosofky, 7, 8
Sedira, Zineb, 215n26
The Seine Was Red (*La Seine était rouge*) (Sebbar), 33–34, 75, 127–49, 223n57; countermemory, 131, 132; historical palimpsests, 129, 140, 141, 142–45, 148–49; memorialization, 139, 140, 144, 145–48; representations of violence, 141, 144, 145; role of women, 136–37; World War II, 34, 138–42, 144–46

Selao, Ching, 162
Sénac, Jean, 1–4, 5, 19, 20, 189n5
Sex, France, and Arab Men (Shepard), 21–22, 194n67
sexuality: contrasted with sex, 97, 122; Deleuze and Guattari's understanding of, 117; Foucault's study of, 97, 99, 118–22; language of sexual deviancy, 206n3; in queer theory, 7; regulation of, 20; and revolution, 33, 98, 101, 103, 107, 109, 111, 121, 123, 194n67; Rubin on politics and, 97–98; sadistic sexuality, 48; Sénac's, 2–4; subjectivity and, 99, 117–20; *Tomboy* and, 152, 153, 163, 168, 174–75
Shepard, Todd: 20, 21, 22, 28, 191n30, 194n67, 197–98n7, 200n36, 206n3
Shildrick, Margrit, 18, 78, 117–18
Showalter, Elaine, 42
silence: *Eden, Eden, Eden* and, 109, 114, 125; *The Seine Was Red* and 135, 149; violence of, 157–58
Silverman, Max, 134, 204n18
Simo Djom, Maurice, 163
Sontag, Susan, 40
spectrality, 16, 26, 129, 159
statelessness, 72–75, 86
state power: interpellation and, 168; Muñoz on, 161
Stoler, Ann Laura, 28, 211n66
Stora, Benjamin, 27, 195n91, 219n21
Sturken, Marita, 128
subjectification: disidentification and, 169–75; Foucault on links between sexuality and, 121–22; process of, 22, 98, 119
subjectivity: Aly on the formation of, 25–26; decolonization and, 98, 186; deconstruction of, 102–3, 104, 117–18, 187; *Eden, Eden, Eden* and, 99, 103, 104, 106, 109, 112, 114, 115, 117–18, 124, 125, 126, 207n16; Foucault on sex, sexuality, and, 22–23, 97, 119–22; fractured, 62, 69; hauntology and, 26, 30, 32, 59–60; Marcuse's concept of radical, 99–103, 124–25; queer theory and, 22–23; *Tomboy* and, 162, 163, 164, 168–70; transgender, 181
surveillance: *Caché* and, 32, 76, 77, 79, 80–81, 93; *Muriel* and, 54–55
Swamy, Vinay, 20, 184–85
symbolic capital, 80, 82, 84, 88
symbolic violence, 69, 75, 92, 124; Bourdieu on, 80; *Caché* and, 32, 80–88, 93

Taubira, Christiane: *Loi Taubira* (Taubira Law), 182; racist anxieties and marriage equality, 182–85
temporality, 18–19, 26–30; *Eden, Eden, Eden* and, 33, 116–17, 123, 124–26; Marcuse's view of, 101–2, 123; *The Seine Was Red* and, 128–29, 130, 148. *See also* futurity
terrorism: attacks on Charlie Hebdo, 14, 32, 72, 90–93; War on Terror, 13, 192n33
third space, 16, 148, 171, 175–77. *See also* hybridity; in-betweenness
Tiffin, Helen, 23
The Tightrope Walker (Genet), 63
time, 19–20; hauntology of, 26; nonsequential forms of, 27, 129; reconceptualizations of, 29, 123, 134, 148, 172, 187
de Tocqueville, Alexis, 81

Tomb for 500,000 Soldiers (Guyotat), 104, 109, 120, 121, 207n17
Tomboy (*Garçon manqué*) (Bouraoui), 15, 34-35, 151-77; Algeria and identity, 165-67; decentering modernist subjectivity, 153, 159; gender and nationality, 15, 153, 154, 156, 158-59, 164, 167, 170, 171; masculinity, 34, 152, 153, 155, 156, 158-61, 162, 166, 167, 170, 174, 175, 176, 177; memory and embodiment, 34-35, 152, 156, 159, 162, 164, 176, 177, 179; naming and becoming, 167-69, 175, 176; OAS (Secret Armed Organization), 173-74; place-names, 158, 221n45; resistance to classification, 161, 163
torture: Abu Ghraib, 86, 92; Alleg's testimony of, 11, 197n7, 207n23; French-Algerian War and, 4, 11, 13, 14, 41, 48, 86, 144, 197n5, 199n21; Lazreg on euphemisms of, 47; in *The Little Soldier* (Godard), 200n28, 207n23; masculinity and, 41-42, 46-47, 60-62, 197n7, 206n3; scene in *Muriel*, 31, 40, 41-42, 48-49, 50, 51-53, 55, 59-62; water as instrument of, 222n46
transfiliation: Provencher on, 135, 148. *See also* intergenerationality
transgender, 162, 180, 181-82, 192n33
trauma: of the French-Algerian War, 5, 47, 69, 152; inherited, 133, 159, 173-74; intergenerational transmission of, 29-30; masculinity and, 34, 156; memory and, 27, 28
Trinh T. Minh-ha, 155

universalism: in the French Republic, 11, 20
utopia: *Eden, Eden, Eden* and, 109, 124; Marcuse's sexual utopianism, 101-2, 123, 124-25, 186

Vassallo, Helen, 162
violence: colonial, 11, 12, 32, 41, 46, 71-72, 74, 75, 92, 93, 98, 100, 125, 129, 132; masculinity and, 21, 32, 42-43, 58, 62; *Muriel* and, 41, 51-52, 53-54; *The Wound* and, 64, 65, 67, 68, 69. See also *Eden, Eden, Eden*; symbolic violence

Waller, Marguerite, 57-58
Warner, Michael, 8
Weheliye, Alexander, 211n66
whiteness: Ahmed on regimes of, 82; *Caché* and, 77, 81-82, 84-85, 93; critiques of queer studies' approach to, 8, 190n17; Frenchness as a project of, 85; masculinity and, 20, 22, 31, 77, 93, 107, 114, 136; metaphoric significance, 165, 172; Puwar on white bodies as somatic norms, 84
Wilson, Emma, 54, 199n22
World War II: Cayrol on, 198n12; in France's memory landscape, 138-42; and the French-Algerian War, 12, 27-30, 44-46, 106, 121, 138-42, 144-47; *The Seine Was Red* and, 34, 138-42, 144-46
The Wound (*Des hommes*) (Mauvignier), 31-32, 42, 62-70
The Wretched of the Earth (Fanon), 19
writing: as activism and resistance, 130, 163, 164; for Guyotat, 104, 108-9

Young, Robert J. C., 15, 16, 25, 192n3

In the Expanding Frontiers series

Undesirable Practices: Women, Children, and the Politics of the Body in Northern Ghana, 1930–1972
by Jessica Cammaert

Intersectionality: Origins, Contestations, Horizons
by Anna Carastathis

Abuses of the Erotic: Militarizing Sexuality in the Post—Cold War United States
by Josh Cerretti

Queering Kansas City Jazz: Gender, Performance, and the History of a Scene
by Amber R. Clifford-Napoleone

Postcolonial Hauntologies: African Women's Discourses of the Female Body
by Ayo A. Coly

Terrorizing Gender: Transgender Visibility and the Surveillance Practices of the U.S. Security State
by Mia Fischer

Romance with Voluptuousness: Caribbean Women and Thick Bodies in the United States
by Kamille Gentles-Peart

Salvific Manhood: James Baldwin's Novelization of Male Intimacy
by Ernest L. Gibson III

Nepantla Squared: Transgender Mestiz@ Histories in Times of Global Shift
by Linda Heidenreich

Wrapped in the Flag of Israel: Mizraḥi Single Mothers and Bureaucratic Torture
by Smadar Lavie

Queer Embodiment: Monstrosity, Medical Violence, and Intersex Experience
by Hilary Malatino

Staging Family: Domestic Deceptions of Mid-Nineteenth-Century American Actresses
by Nan Mullenneaux

Hybrid Anxieties: Queering the French-Algerian War and Its Postcolonial Legacies
C. L. Quinan

Place and Postcolonial Ecofeminism: Pakistani Women's Literary and Cinematic Fictions
by Shazia Rahman

Gothic Queer Culture: Marginalized Communities and the Ghosts of Insidious Trauma
by Laura Westengard

To order or obtain more information on these or other University of Nebraska Press titles, visit nebraskapress.unl.edu.

www.ingramcontent.com/pod-product-compliance
Lightning Source LLC
Chambersburg PA
CBHW022004220426
43663CB00007B/949